Good Vermonters

The Pierces of North Shrewsbury

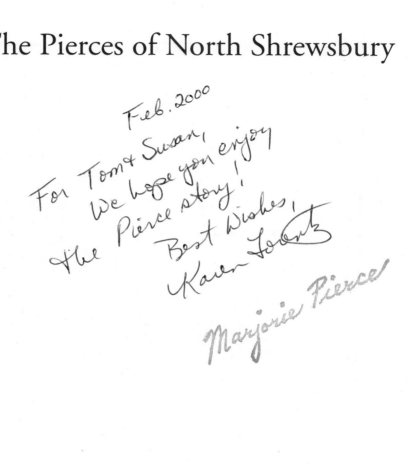

Feb. 2000

For Tom & Susan,
We hope you enjoy
the Pierce story!
Best Wishes,
Karen Lorentz

Marjorie Pierce

The Pierce Family, Circa 1929

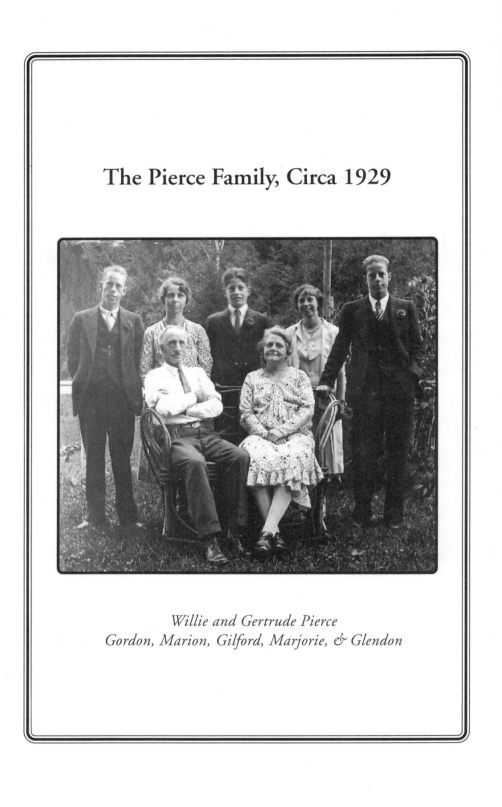

Willie and Gertrude Pierce
Gordon, Marion, Gilford, Marjorie, & Glendon

Good Vermonters

The Pierces
of North Shrewsbury

by Karen D. Lorentz

Mountain Publishing, Inc.
Shrewsbury, Vermont

Also by Karen D. Lorentz

Killington, A Story of Mountains and Men, Mountain Publishing, 1990

Okemo, All Come Home, Mountain Publishing, 1996

A Vermont Parent's Prevention Resource, A Guide to Raising Healthy, Drug-Free Children, PreventionWorks, 1995

Vermont Voices, An Anthology (Editor), League of Vermont Writers, 1991

ISBN:0-9625369-9-7

Cover Design by Larry J. Patin Jr.

Printed at Daamen Printing, West Rutland, Vermont

*In the spirit of Marjorie Pierce
and the Pierce family,
this book is dedicated
to two very special educators,
Michael and Mary Ellen Harlow.*

*As outstanding teachers
of English and Music, respectively,
they have made a difference in the lives
of many Vermont students,
our three sons included.*

*It is with sincere appreciation that this
story is dedicated to you.*

Acknowledgments

I am most grateful to Miss Marjorie Pierce for sharing the story of her long and interesting life and that of her family. It was a joy to witness her love of history, community, and family in the many hours we spent together in interviews and in review of hundreds of photographs of Pierce relatives and early Shrewsbury. Marjorie is a treasure and a wonderful resource for anyone who wants to understand the story of rural Vermont in the twentieth century. *Merci beaucoup.*

A special note of appreciation is extended to author Howard Coffin who took the time from his own busy schedule to pen the Foreword. A seventh-generation Vermonter and historian, Howard's friendship with the Pierces confirms that they really were good Vermonters and "friends to their fellow human beings."

I am indebted to several readers of the manuscript. Poet and teacher Joan Aleshire made many helpful suggestions with content and format and even solved the title dilemma. Her careful reading and thoughtful comments helped me to round out the Shrewsbury history and to learn more about Marjorie's "mischievous" side. Shrewsbury historians Anne "Nancy" Spencer and Dawn Hance, contributor to and author respectively of the book *Shrewsbury, Vermont: Our Town As It Was,* also painstakingly proofread and provided much historical information. They were wonderful resources who supplied important material previously unknown to me. Joan, Nancy, and Dawn always lent a willing ear and gave an encouraging word. Thank you all.

I also wish to acknowledge Dr. Janet Gerba for her wise counsel regarding the order of the book's early chapters and Jason Lorentz, who helped shape them. There are numerous others who assisted in various and invaluable ways—supplying missing information, a photo, a story, or a memory. To all, thank you. You have done a kindness in helping to preserve the story of this special Vermont family. Credit is also due to photographers whose images enhance the Pierce story.

Finally, I wish to acknowledge my husband John for his many hours of reading and critiquing the numerous drafts. To him and our son Jim, I promise things will get back to normal. I appreciate your patience and support during these long months of "finishing the book."

Contents

Photo Credits

The photographs used to illustrate the story of the Pierces were loaned by several people. Unfortunately, most of the photos in Marjorie's vast collection are unmarked, and it is therefore impossible to know who took them. We do know that many of the photos of the family and farm were taken by her Uncle Ned Pierce, who often made them up into postcards.

The photographers or contributors of pictures who are known are listed here by chapter and page. Thank you to all.

Chapter 9
> page 127 The Associated Press
> 132 Karen Lorentz
> 135 Grace Brigham

Chapter 10
> page 140 Snelling Family, Wilson Family, Karen Lorentz
> 144 Karen Lorentz
> 147 Mitchell Family

Chapter 11
> page 148-157 (the late) Russell Holliger

Chapter 12
> page 167 Castleton State College
> 168 John Heitzke
> 171 Lily French
> 173, 180 Grace Brigham (Marjorie teaching)

Chapter 14
> page 200 Eldred French (playground)
> 200 Richard Wiedmann (historical society museum)

Chapter 15
> page 223, 228, 231 Wilson Family
> 234 Karen Lorentz (store)

Other
> front cover, page xi, 240 Karen Lorentz

Foreword
by
Howard Coffin

The back porch on the old house bounced as people kept time to a fiddler, banjo picker, and guitarist playing reels, the music of old Vermont. It was the first day of May, 1999 and at her home in North Shrewsbury, surrounded by friends and neighbors, Marjorie Pierce celebrated her 96th birthday. The sky was blue, the air warm, the first spring flowers out, as it seemed the whole world had joined in the occasion. After extinguishing the candles on one of her cakes with a single whoosh, the celebrant was asked to make a wish. "Four more years," she responded. Marjorie Pierce had not been well through the winter. But with the arrival of spring, she had rallied to throw out the caregivers. The last of the Pierces had her eyes firmly set on the new century.

Marjorie Pierce by that May Day, 1999, had seen most of the last century of the second millennium. Born in 1903, she had lived most of the so-called American Century. Really a product of the nineteenth century, she had been a very active participant in, and keen observer of, the most dynamic 100-year span in the history of mankind. She had been forth into the world and made a contribution, particularly as a teacher, but had chosen nearly half her lifetime ago to come back to the mountain place that was home. Born in horse and buggy days, she well understood the space age. Raised hearing her grandfather sing the songs of the Civil War in which he had fought, she was deeply touched by the televised images of the refugees of Yugoslavia, walking weeping out of what the historian Barbara Tuchman once called "our worst century yet."

I met Marjorie Pierce one summer day in 1966 when I stopped by chance, at Pierce's Store in Northam. Glendon Pierce was behind the counter, and he introduced me to his sister Marjorie. I soon met brother Gordon and sister Marion.

Even at that time, by the mid-sixties, it was apparent that farming Vermont, the Vermont I had grown up in, was fast dying. Thus a place such as

Pierce's Store, where old Vermont authentically survived, caught my eye as a treasure. I returned time and again and after moving to North Shrewsbury (first renting a house from Jim Jeffords), I stopped at the store most days. Indeed, a morning visit to sit by the woodstove with Glendon and a few of the neighbors, such as Henry Fee, Olive Haley, Bennie Carrara, became part of my routine.

The Pierces became my friends. Glendon and I walked the hills, often searching out cellar holes where he would tell me of the people who had lived there, either from his experience or from memories passed down by his parents or grandparents. I joined Glendon and Gordon each fall cutting firewood up in the shadow of Jockey Hill. After the first, light snow touched the new-fallen leaves, we burned great piles of brush in the high fields they kept so carefully cleared. With Marion Pierce I often talked of her adopted city, Philadelphia, particularly of her beloved Philadelphia Orchestra. She knew its musicians name by name.

Marjorie Pierce, a fellow nighthawk, and I on countless evenings (especially deep in winter) talked into the wee hours. She is a wealth of information on long-ago days in Shrewsbury when the lumber mills thrived, young people learned in one-room schools, and men from the farms came after supper to the store to get caught up on things. We talked of her ancestor who died at Mount Independence in the Revolution, of her grandfather going West, of her brother Gilford who went down with his bomber "Vermont Lady" in World War II. We spoke of her sailing to Europe on the Normandie, her studies in France, of her teaching days in Vermont and Massachusetts. We talked of war and peace, of politics and pastures gone back to woods, of books and writers, of men and women long gone who had wrung a living out of the hill farms along the Coolidge Range. We got involved in stopping a ski development from pushing over the ridge into Shrewsbury from Killington Basin. She got me writing letters in support of Amnesty International. From her vantage point nearly 2,000 feet up in the Green Mountains, she always kept a world perspective. She still does.

It has struck me down the years that most people who visited Pierce's Store in its later years probably came away taking some satisfaction in having met some "quaint Vermonters" in a pretty little setting. WRONG. The Pierces of Northam were intelligent, kind, complex, informed, humorous, and involved individuals who chose to continue the way of life that produced them, not through some blissful happenstance, but through careful choices and difficult decisions made. Theirs became lives lived in the main for the benefit of others. They really did live in a house by the side of the road and were friends to their fellow human beings.

After Marion and Gordon died, Marjorie and Glendon ran the store for several years more before deciding to close it for "practical reasons." The last day Pierce's Store was open, I heard Glendon turn the whole thing around by thanking all the people his family had so ably served for so many years. In the hush of the crowded store, its scores on scores of years come down to minutes, he said, "Thanks for the memories." He managed to make of it an occasion filled with much happiness. Still, it was one of the saddest days of my life.

Marjorie is the last of the Pierces. She goes on always deeply interested in the past, but living every day very much in the present, always excited about tomorrow. From time to time I take myself to Northam where we sit up late, get caught up, and talk much of history. Somewhere past midnight she shows me to "one of the boy's rooms" for the night. As I settle down in that wonderful Vermont place, lulled to sleep by the ticking of the many clocks Glendon built or maintained, I never fail to feel an aura of peace and love. There is always the chance that, in dreams, I will wake into a bright mountain morning and make my way out through the woodshed to the store, where Glendon already has a fire roaring in the woodstove. Soon Marjorie will be in to ask if I slept well, and then Gordon and Marion with arrive, as other people of the town come in to start their days the way they always did, at Pierce's Store.

Marjorie, enjoying music and friends on her 96th birthday.

Glendon, Marjorie, Marion, and Gordon,
with Spaulding relatives from the West
July 1978.

Introduction

The "Good Vermonter"

The farmer in blue overalls with fifty cows waiting to be milked, that proverbial agrarian image of a Vermonter, no longer reflects today's Vermonter. An eclectic mix of natives, transplants, summer people, college students, and even telecommuters, modern Vermonters now work in travel, tourism, service, and manufacturing industries in numbers far greater than those employed on hill or valley farms. Vermonters by birth or choice, some can trace their roots to ancestors who settled the state's 256 towns and cities in the 1700s; others to immigrants who came during the 1800s when the stone and railroad industries boomed, and still others to the 1900s when many came in search of a better way of life. In more recent times, newcomers have often arrived seeking to escape urban lifestyles or to pursue retirement amidst peaceful and beautiful surroundings.

Each group has brought its culture and customs, and renders the question of what makes a person a Vermonter anything but easy. It is not simply a matter of the state of one's birth or one's occupation. A mix of values, traditions, traits, and behaviors come into play. Some old-timers will tell you that "puppies born in the oven don't make them kittens," while others will say that newcomers who adopt local ways and participate in the community have become Vermonters "by virtue of assimilation."

What makes a person a "Vermonter," though, is significant because Vermont remains a unique and distinctive state due to her people and their values. Vermont remains largely rural and beautiful because some people choose to keep it that way. They resist rampant development and seek community and quality of life while struggling to balance the preservation of the natural environment with the need to make a living.

Although no longer farmers, many Vermonters carry on the values and ideals that sprang from agrarian times. This includes the many newcomers who wish to preserve the "Vermont way of life" so as to avoid what they have left behind. The Yankee traits of resourcefulness, independence, industry, frugality, and perseverance were necessary during Vermont's formative years and remain so today.

To resist modern times and the appeal of the easier dollar takes the same tenacity, ingenuity and contrariety that enabled the earliest Vermonters to survive. Yet, ironically, it is sometimes the old Vermonter who wishes for progress. Tired of impassable roads in mud season, it was the native who often wanted to see dirt roads paved while today the new Vermonter seeks to keep speed down by preserving them. Wishing for a better way of life for their children, it was often the old Vermonter who gave up the family farm or chose to educate his children for other pursuits, while the new Vermonter cries out for legislation to preserve open lands and the dying farms.

Such admirable and contrary traits have set Vermonters apart from other New Englanders, both in the past and the present. These traits have been identified by such venerable observers of Vermont people and customs as writer Harold F. Wilson. He noted that, "Many a hillside farmer clung tenaciously to his homestead. There were many reasons—affection for familiar surroundings, independence of spirit, love of the hills, some sense of freedom that far hill vistas give, elbowroom, a home from which a man can neither be starved nor frozen as long as a crop will grow and wood burn."

Dartmouth historian Lewis D. Stilwell, author of *Migration from Vermont*, explained that it was their character that enabled Vermonters to deal with the challenge of a difficult environment. "They were a climbing and creative stock who delighted in obstacles, felt certain of their purposes, and proceeded to make over by means bold and dubious whatever environment they might encounter."

Writer Burgess Johnson summed up the independent and stubborn spirit when he depicted Vermonters as: "Just a lot of lovable but pig-headed individuals divided up into townships widely scattered on mountainsides and in valleys who will not let even their chosen officials command them or their chosen leaders lead them."

This contrary, nonconformist side was shrewdly described by Jael Kent. "There is only one quality that could be called 'typical' of the Vermonters I know. That is their extraordinarily irritating way of not conforming to any type. Each of them is an original. Born on the same hills, fed on the same beans, educated in the same schools, they have just one common denominator; they are all rare birds."

While such descriptions elicit appreciative chuckles, the stereotypical image of the obstinate, contrary, difficult Vermonter was somewhat debunked by author Charles Edward Crane, who wrote: "The climate and soil may make the Vermonter hard-shelled, but only rarely is he a snapping turtle at heart. His character is more like the chambered nautilus, with recesses of beauty not always easily seen but nevertheless there."

College professor and author Storrs Lee best summed up these traits when he noted two types of Vermonters: the resident who exhibited Yankee traits and the person who through capriciousness or genius aspires to some cause or ideal, be it a practical invention or quirky dream.

> Anyone can be a Vermonter—anyone who subscribes to a doctrine of frugality, self-reliance, and humility, who takes up residence in the hills and pays his poll tax—but to be a good Vermonter, native or immigrant, he has to have an eccentricity; somewhere in his background there is a gentle madness, a persistent fanaticism, an honest idiosyncrasy.

To be a "good Vermonter" Lee indicates there needs to be a special kind of striving, whether it springs from madness, obsession, or idiosyncrasy. The "good Vermonter" exhibits a single mindedness of purpose or passion, whether born from an ideal or an eccentricity. For Wilson "Snowflake" Bentley, it was the scientific study of snow crystals; for Stephen Douglas the Lincoln-Douglas debates; for Samuel Morey the invention of the first steam engine; and for ski pioneer Preston Leete Smith, the vision of better skiing.

While we know of the more famous persons who pursued their dreams, we are often unaware of the people who in quiet areas like Shrewsbury followed their passions and in doing so also made a contribution and a difference in twentieth-century Vermont. Displaying the contrary traits of the good Vermonter, they, too, have contributed in meaningful ways to the preservation of Vermont as a unique state.

That is the reason for this book: to celebrate one family of seemingly simple folk who, through their own "passions," have helped to make Vermont a special place. The Pierces were never famous people, but by striving to lead useful and upright lives they made a difference in the lives of others and in their community and state.

The stereotypical portrayal of the farmer 'living off the land' or the quaint storekeeper smiling kindly are simply caricatures that belie the deeper strivings of the Vermont soul. These early Vermonters who clung to rocky slopes were neither stupid nor indifferent. They were frugal, tenacious, and ambitious, and they actively sought success as well as a better way of life for themselves and their children. Willie and Gertrude Pierce were from this generation, and thus they instilled the values of hard work, frugality, resourcefulness, and helpfulness in their offspring.

Following the example of their parents, the Pierce siblings also changed with the times. They were not reclusive but were involved in ways that made sense to each of them. Their ways were not the way of a speeded-up world, conspicuous consumption, or the me-generation; rather, they were based on rich, deep-seated Yankee values that allowed them to be connected to their neighbors and community. They were products of another era but they were of this one. As such, they made valuable contributions, bridging times and places for new generations and imparting a legacy that helps Vermont retain its rural values of environment, tradition, and community.

The story of Marjorie and her family is a simple story on the one hand, but one of deep meaning on the other: of family pride and the importance of connections and contributions; of the significance of traditional values in a changing world; and of embracing change in deliberate and careful ways so that the best of the old are retained and passed on to new generations. This is the lasting legacy of the twentieth-century Pierce family.

I hope you enjoy getting to know them and learning more about Vermont and "good Vermonters."

Karen D. Lorentz
November 8, 1999

Early Northam with farms, church, school, blacksmith's house on left and blacksmith shop, Northam Store, and Henry Fee's barn and home on right side of photo.

Chapter One

A Sense of Time and Place

When Marjorie Pierce was born in 1903, Vermont was still an agrarian state where the horse and buggy provided transportation and dairy farming, logging, and cheese making were the heart of a rural economy. Some towns boasted a successful stone (granite, marble, slate), machine-tool, or textile industry or a thriving tourism trade, but they were among the exceptions. Most rural areas were still predominantly agrarian, boasting largely self-sufficient economies where loggers, sawyers, farmers, tanners, blacksmiths, harness makers, storekeepers, innkeepers, cheese makers, coopers, and carpenters depended upon one another for supplies, trade, and livelihoods.

Life in rural Vermont in 1903 was still the lifestyle of the nineteenth century. People lived in homes heated by woodstoves and generally had many children. Children walked to a local "district school," where one teacher taught all eight grades in a spartan, one-room schoolhouse. Few pupils ever went beyond the eighth grade. Farm families provided most of their own food and made and repaired their own clothing. Women were busy with domestic duties: cooking, raising children, making butter, and helping with farm chores. The "refrigerator" was a shed filled with blocks of lake or pond ice and insulated with sawdust, or it was a cold cellar under the house. The "washing machine" was a contraption of wooden stands, boiler, wringer, and tubs. At night, people finished their chores by the light of kerosene lanterns and went to bed early.

Most rural towns had several inns or taverns, for the convenience of travelers and local patrons. The village stores traded or sold the day-to-day supplies a family needed, from livestock feed to miracle-eczema cures. General stores were often the site of a rural post office as well as a place to hear the local news or play a game of checkers.

People had daily contact with their own extended families and depended upon their neighbors for socializing and occasional assistance. The church, grange, and school provided social outlets, but entertainment was infrequent and meant traveling through the night to a barn dance or a kitchen social that could last until three in the morning. "Home entertainment" consisted of quiet games, storytelling, and family-made music. A father or mother might strum on an instrument or play a parlor organ while singing old folk songs with family or neighbors.

The land was largely cleared and rural Vermont was particularly striking for its pastoral beauty, high mountains, sparkling rivers, clear lakes, verdant forests, lush valleys, snug villages, and patchwork of farms and stone walls. It was a time of seemingly idyllic simplicity and sturdy self-

Early view of North Shrewsbury, "Northam." Shrewsbury Peak to upper left; Northam Village below center peak with church. View is from Carrara farm.

sufficiency. Life had a slower pace behind a horsedrawn wagon and quieter sound with only animals, wind or rain, and children to break the silence.

But in 1903, life for the inhabitants of Vermont's beautiful hill towns wasn't, and indeed, never had been a rustic paradise. Farming at high elevations had been a constant struggle since the time of the first settlers; upland soils were thinner than those in the valleys, the weather more unpredictable and far colder, and the growing season often shorter. A poor crop season could mean not having enough to eat during the winter nor sufficient trade for needed supplies. Winters were several months of gray, somber days and deep snows that brought loneliness, isolation and not infrequently danger and death. Outbreaks of disease threatened even the healthiest young souls. Coupled with a declining and difficult economy, these hardships caused many early Vermonters to give up the struggle and migrate south and west to warmer climes and better farmland. No sooner had an intrepid settler made their new home in the rural towns than the fluctuating fortunes of the fledgling economy caused their children and even their own contemporaries to emigrate in the 1800s. The new "native born" Vermonters both loved their state and fled it.

Amidst this backdrop of beauty and hardship, rural simplicity and struggle, Marjorie Pierce's ancestors carved out a life in the northern hamlet of the mountain town of Shrewsbury. Knowing the time and place in which they lived is helpful to understanding the character and values passed on to her grandparents, parents, and to Marjorie and her siblings.

The Challenge of Early Vermont

When Vermont was being settled from 1761-1800, it presented exciting potential to New Englanders from New Hampshire, Connecticut and Massachusetts. They had left family farms that could no longer support them and were young and ambitious "Yankees." Some mined the potential of an untapped state and built their homes and prospered. Logging, woodworking industries, sheep raising, cheese making, and subsistence farming became the staple of the early Vermont economy circa 1800-1850, and if a farmer owned a good piece of land, he could do quite well. Logging and lumbering thrived as the land was cleared for settlement and homes were built. The introduction in 1810 of Merino sheep, which were well suited to Vermont's climate, led to hillsides being grazed by over two million sheep by 1820. Cows' milk was used to make butter and cheese prior to 1850, with nine-million pounds of cheese produced in 1849 alone. Between logging and pasturing, the Vermont landscape was 80 percent clear of trees and forests by 1880.

But the economic prosperity of the first half of the century was short-lived. The boom in sheep raising came to a halt in the 1840s when the wool industry lost its protective tariff and stiff competition from western U.S. and Australian wools took its toll. With a slump in the demand for wool and a prize ram selling for $600, Vermont farmers began to sell off their best sheep to men building up their flocks in the Mid-West, Texas, and California. The best bred horses were also exported with a Morgan colt fetching $1,000 or more.

As sheep raising and wool production fell off in Vermont, their bright promise to sustain a rural economy disintegrated. The raising of beef cattle and farm crops also declined as thin soils were worn out by poor agricultural methods and overgrazing by sheep. In addition, extensive clear-cutting and logging caused widespread erosion. Fish began to disappear as erosion runoff muddied the rivers, and wildlife became less abundant due to unrestricted hunting and trapping practices. By the mid-1800s, the Green Mountains of Vermont had seen their natural resources largely used up and offered little for people to live upon, noted historian Lewis Stilwell in *Migration from Vermont* (pages 151-154).

By 1860 Vermont had lost much of the "economic potentiality seen in 1776," he stated, noting the people "had mined the state rather than cultivated it." Pasturage of cows or sheep required large amounts of acreage but few farmhands so a farm could rarely support more than one or two families. Furthermore, children could be expected to labor on the family farm until the age of twenty-one. Under the law, their parents were only required to feed, clothe, and shelter them—no payment was necessary. By the age of fourteen, most children earned their keep, and their parents profited from their free labor. But only one or two offspring could inherit a family farm since it generally wasn't a big enough operation to support the five to fifteen siblings in the family.

The homestead most often went to the oldest or favorite child, and the rest had to move on. Without having been paid by their parents, these young adult children were often unable to purchase the large amount of land (which was expensive at $6 to $8 per acre) necessary for a successful farm. Farmers with large amounts of fertile acreage could raise beef cattle, dairy cows, sheep, swine, and horses and also produce corn, wheat, potatoes, oats, hay and maple sugar; they could be quite successful, and indeed there was prosperity for some. But not for everyone; for the smaller farmers, especially those on marginal land, there was little to stay for and being young and ambitious, they often chose to leave.

Education was another factor that influenced the young and native born to leave. Higher education often gave children "contacts with finer living and broader fields for success."[1] In many ways, the more educated a person became, the more "unfit for life in Vermont. Puritan enthusiasm for higher learning furnished the self-destruct button of the Puritan communities ... education drained them of some of their best blood."[2] The farming life represented monotony and hard work. Corporal punishment was legal and acceptable. Without a bankruptcy law on the books, Vermont still threw debtors in prison. This was hardly the climate for a well-educated or ambitious soul who desired more from life than to risk a livelihood on a hardscrabble hill farm.

Adding to the agricultural difficulties was the failure of manufacturing to offer the abundant job opportunities and better pay offered in places south of Vermont. Vermont was too far from markets and raw materials (except for those of wood, wool, and stone) and could not compete with other states that were manufacturing everyday necessities—from clothing to furniture, hardware to shoes—and shipping it less expensively and more quickly. A lack of easy transportation put much of the state's early manufacturing at a disadvantage. Even after the railroads crisscrossed the state in the mid-1800s, rail shipping was more expensive for Vermont factories than for those in Massachusetts

[1] Lewis D. Stilwell, *Migration from Vermont. (Montpelier, VT:* Vermont Historical Society, 1948), p. 237
[2] *Ibid.*

or Connecticut. As a result, Vermont manufacturing did not flourish as it did elsewhere in the 1800s and early 1900s. But just as there were exceptions in farming, several towns did do well. Estey Organ and the printing trade took hold in Brattleboro, while scale manufacturing flourished in Rutland and St. Johnsbury. The granite industry prospered in Barre, marble production in Proctor, textile manufacturing in Ludlow, and woodworking in Burlington. Enhancing such success, the quality of Vermont products was generally recognized as superior. Unfortunately, the majority of the state's rural towns did not possess such an industry.

Also exacerbating the general economic hardship in the majority of towns were losses of human life from farm accidents, childbirth, and disease. Rural existence could be hard, but it was particularly cruel when children, parents, and entire families succumbed to illnesses which the country doctor was powerless to treat. Prayer and a good constitution were among the best means for surviving the scourges of consumption, typhoid, meningitis, and scarlet fever. But epidemics could wipe out even the hail and hearty.

With the hardships of agrarian life heightened by the lack of other opportunities, migration fever took hold. "Going West" represented excitement in some otherwise difficult or dull lives as Vermont's surplus of small farming families began to leave. "Ohio fever" and "California fever" were the rallying cries of an exuberant evangelism for migration to better opportunities. As people learned of those opportunities elsewhere, the Great Exodus began, and Vermont endured a significant and prolonged out migration of its native-born population. By 1850, some 145,000 native Vermonters had fled the state, and by 1860, that number had increased to 175,000. [3] This increased the state's economic woes, which in turn intensified the exodus; by 1880, Vermont had lost 54 percent of her native-born population to emigration. From 1850 to 1900, two out of every five Vermonters gave up the struggle and headed for "greener pastures."

Additionally, 34,238 Vermonters volunteered to fight in the Civil War in 1861 and 5,224 were killed in battle; those who did return spread the word about places where the climate was less harsh, the terrain less rugged, and the land more fertile. It has been estimated that less than

[3] *Ibid., p. 216*

half of those who left to serve returned to become permanent residents. The railroads and Erie Canal provided an easy and cheap escape route to the beckoning country of the West and Mid-West, where the federal government was promoting homesteading at $1.25 per unimproved acre!

Mountain towns—Vermont has twenty towns with an elevation of 1550 feet or more—were among the most severely affected rural areas. They had always presented a harsh environment and constant challenge to their inhabitants, but the reversal of Vermont's economic growth was particularly cruel because their residents had depended on those occupations that provided subsistence living: sheep raising, farming, logging, hunting, and trapping. Towns which saw peak habitation by the mid-1800s began to dwindle in numbers until they reached historic lows one-hundred years later. As Vermont's total population grew slowly from 314,120 in 1850 to 377,747 in 1950, Windham dropped from a population of 1,000 to 150; Marlboro from 1296 to 311; Halifax from 1500 to 343; Stratton from 212 to 72; Searsburg from 1,431 to 84; Sherburne from 578 to 266; Glastenbury from 48 to 1; and Shrewsbury from 1,289 to 464.

While these upland settlements prospered early on and then faced significant declines in population, several towns that were located at or near the base of a major mountain fared much better. Wilmington, Manchester, Brandon, Stowe, Morrisville, and Woodstock were among the "spa" towns that were able to attract a good travel trade in the 1800s and established themselves as "summer meccas." They prospered during this hundred-year period when so many rural areas languished for lack of economic opportunity. Major cities like Rutland, Burlington, Montpelier, and Barre also thrived, but over 200 out of 256 Vermont towns lost population from 1850 to 1950.

Some of Marjorie's ancestors managed to adapt to these changing times; but like other residents of Shrewsbury, some departed for better opportunities elsewhere. Those who remained were quite successful. On the Aldrich side, many were farmers and one great-uncle owned and operated several cheese factories and a country store. On the Pierce side, all would move to other towns or out West, but the Edwin Pierce family would return and eventually prosper, making them one of the few families to remain in Shrewsbury for over two hundred years.

An Overview of Shrewsbury 1780-1950

With high elevation (average altitude 1,640 feet, but ranging from 994 feet in Cuttingsville to 3,737 feet at Shrewsbury Peak), rolling meadows, steep hillsides, and a harsh climate, Shrewsbury was one of the mountain towns whose settlers depended upon subsistence farming. The town was chartered in 1761 but was organized in 1781, at which time there were enough families to form a town government (as was mandated by the law of 1781). The town grew quickly with families hoping to find a hospitable place in which to farm and raise their children. With its first influx of settlers in the 1770s and 1780s, Shrewsbury had 72 families with 383 people by 1790. It grew to 748 residents by the turn of the century and reached a peak population of 1,289 people in 1830.

But with its bony soil and cold climate in the upland sections of town, Shrewsbury was also one of the many towns to suffer from the loss of the sheep industry and began losing population in the mid-1800s. Affected by the state's economic downturn and the ensuing exodus, the town's population experienced a long, slow decline to 540 residents by 1900. A second exodus during the first half of the twentieth century echoed the "out-migration" of the nineteenth century. From 1850 to 1900, Vermont had a net population gain of 31,521; but from 1900 to 1950 it was only 34,126—a far cry from what was happening elsewhere in this nation. During this same time period, Shrewsbury's population fell to 464 by 1950.

Although many of the small farms were given up as the young fled the mountainous community for the promise of more prosperous lives in the West or in cities in Vermont and New England, the railroad, which came through the town and state in 1849-1851, also helped to stem this trend. It brought newcomers into Vermont and Shrewsbury, and it provided transportation of dairy products (cheese, butter, and milk) to the New York and Boston markets. As refrigerated railcars came along, Vermonters began to export greater quantities of milk.

Prior to rail transportation, milk was produced mainly for local consumption and for making butter and cheese at home on the farm. With new markets, large-scale butter and cheese making moved to local

The Northam Cheese Factory of Wilson Aldrich had an apartment in back.

"cheese factories," which exported great amounts by freight train. With a railroad station in the Cuttingsville section of Shrewsbury, farmers could continue to supply the local cheese factories and ship their excess milk to growing cities in the East.

By 1890, milk production reached 200 gallons for each inhabitant in Vermont, and dairy farming supplanted sheep raising as a viable business. Dairy farming made it possible for Shrewsbury to sustain an agrarian economy during the late 1800s and into the early 1900s, and it also slowed the rate of decline in the town's population. Shrewsbury boasted many dairy farms, a number of large lumber mills and cheese factories, several one-room grade schools, and a few blacksmith shops, inns, and country stores amidst a setting of rural beauty at the turn of the century.

The Industrial Revolution of the nineteenth century, on the other hand, was making its way to New England towns and cities, bringing economic opportunity and major change in the early 1900s. Vermont's rural towns suffered their second period of exodus as young people sought out such opportunities, especially during the 1920s and 1930s. Increasing mechanization made it possible to produce shoes, clothing, furniture, and other items more cheaply in factories. Such goods could be easily shipped to major New England towns thanks to rail transportation and the advent of trucking.

The automobile, which could be seen in most rural areas by 1920, made traveling to the larger towns easier and enhanced the lure of shopping in the new stores. Nearby Rutland offered an exciting array of shops and less expensive products than could be had in Shrewsbury, so this meant less business for the local producers of goods as well as less business for the country store. The local blacksmith, cobbler, tanner, harness maker, and woodworkers began to go out of business. Additionally, the lumber mills closed down by the 1930s as they had nearly stripped the forests. As local farmers began to get more money by shipping their milk directly to Boston and New York, the town's cheese factories began to close. The Northam Cheese Factory, owned by Marjorie's Great-uncle Wilson Aldrich, was the last one in Shrewsbury to cease business in the mid-1940s.

Mechanization and emigration, along with natural decreases in population from deaths due to illness and old age, spurred further declines in rural populations. By 1950, Shrewsbury reached its nadir of just 464 residents. The post-war baby boom that greatly increased the country's population was largely absent in Vermont's hill towns.

A Vermont Way of Life

Due to the uncertainties of life span and survival, rural couples often had large families of five to ten or more children in the 1800s and early 1900s. If the little ones survived, they were expected to help with farm chores from a young age. They were important to the household, and school sessions were scheduled around the cycle of planting and harvesting, sugaring and haying, so that children could help on the farm.

Most rural homes lacked indoor plumbing and central heat in 1903. The woodstove provided heat for warmth and cooking, and the kerosene lantern provided light for home and barn. Wood heat and kerosene lamps were also responsible for many fires that spread out of control as bucket brigades were often powerless to save a home or barn, especially in the dead of winter.

But if rural life was not easy, if farming was difficult and homes lacked the amenities or safety we take for granted today, life on the farm also instilled the values of hard work, resourcefulness, frugality, and helpfulness, and in the process built character and pride and often an indomitable spirit and will.

Families could raise their own food, fix things that broke, bake bread, and make their own clothes. When some members of the community could not do this much for themselves, the problem of poverty was addressed on a local rather than state or federal level. From 1870 to 1903, Shrewsbury supported a Poor Farm, a 184-acre farm (14 cows) where the less fortunate lived and worked to-

Roy Whitney & Carrie Pierce walking to Northam from Pierce Farm.

ward their keep. After it was sold, townspeople appointed an "overseer of the poor" who doled out town moneys to indigent families.

Vermont was unusual in that its Constitution (adopted prior to statehood by the Republic of Vermont in 1777) provided for the public education and welfare of its inhabitants, an indication of the industrious and practical nature of its people who held lofty ideals and cared about the betterment of the entire community. That concern extended to the prohibition of slavery and the establishment of universal manhood suffrage, two features not found in colonial state constitutions of that time.

The ideals of learning for all and neighbor helping neighbor were only part of the emphasis on community life in early Shrewsbury. The church, school, and grange were respected institutions that provided sources of activity and fellowship as well as education and spiritual enlightenment. The general store was no less important. As a place of trade that provided every manner of necessity for survival in a settled section of a rural town, the country store was a symbol of a self-sufficient community, often the site of a local post office, and always a place for meeting and socializing. For towns like Shrewsbury, the country store became a community hub, and the small store at Northam was to play a significant role in the life of the community for 128 years. As its owner and operator for seventy-five of those years, the Pierce family became a special part of this rural hamlet.

View of the village of Northam from Northam Church, left; blacksmith home of Perrin J. and Minnie Whitney and across road is the blacksmith shop. Beyond to the right is the peaked roof of Pierce's Store. Out of view is the Northam School to right rear of church.

Edwin Pierce   *Damaris Colburn Aldrich Pierce*

Chapter Two

The Pierces of Shrewsbury
1780-1903

*My grandfather was about twenty-two years old, and there
he was crouching behind a stone wall. The enemy was charg-
ing. When the firing ceased, he looked down and saw his
best friend Billy Cairns had a bullet in his forehead. He was
dead.*

I said to him, "Why Grandpa, Weren't you afraid?"
He said, "Yes, I was Marjorie."
I asked, "Grandpa, why didn't you run?"
"I wanted to but I was too proud," he answered.

As Marjorie told of this conversation with her grandfather,
Civil War veteran Edwin Pierce who fought in the repulse
of Pickett's Charge during the Battle of Gettysburg, it was
clear that growing up with her grandparents living next door was a
major influence in her life. Not only did she hear the many stories they
passed on, but she learned firsthand about exciting times in the history
of our country. There were tales of her own ancestors who had fought
in this country's wars starting with the Revolutionary War and stories
of how they settled in Shrewsbury and then migrated West. Through
their adventures, Marjorie learned about history in a personal and interesting way that she would later employ in her own animated storytelling.

It's a truism that grandparents often hold a special place in the hearts
of their grandchildren, but in Marjorie's case the influence of grandparents extended into other aspects of her life. From them she acquired a
sense of family history, who they were and what the family roots were.

Direct Pierce Family Line on Willie E. Pierce Side

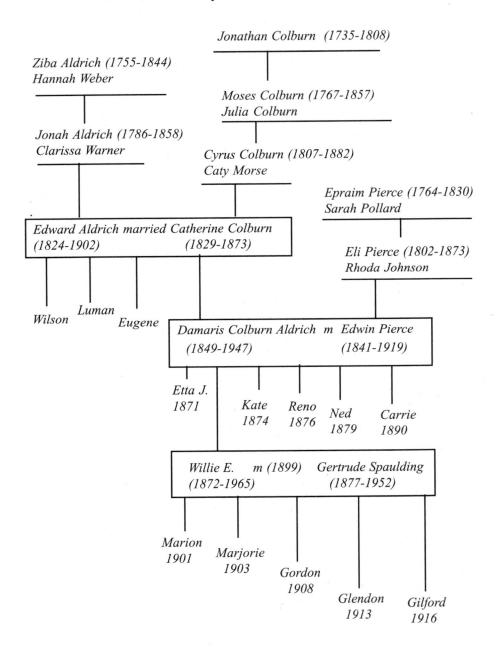

Jonathan Colburn (1735-1808)

Ziba Aldrich (1755-1844)
Hannah Weber

Moses Colburn (1767-1857)
Julia Colburn

Jonah Aldrich (1786-1858)
Clarissa Warner

Cyrus Colburn (1807-1882)
Caty Morse

Epraim Pierce (1764-1830)
Sarah Pollard

Edward Aldrich married Catherine Colburn
(1824-1902)   (1829-1873)

Eli Pierce (1802-1873)
Rhoda Johnson

Luman
Wilson   Eugene

Damaris Colburn Aldrich m Edwin Pierce
(1849-1947)   (1841-1919)

Etta J.
1871
            Kate   Reno
            1874   1876   Ned   Carrie
                              1879   1890

Willie E.   m (1899)   Gertrude Spaulding
(1872-1965)   (1877-1952)

Marion
1901   Marjorie
          1903
                    Gordon
                    1908
                              Glendon   Gilford
                              1913   1916

She also learned to tell a good story and developed a desire to travel and explore faraway places. She learned practical things, too, like the domestic role of women and a calm acceptance of household duties from Damaris, the excitement and horror of war from Edwin, and the importance of the grange, church, and farm in community life.

Perhaps most influential would be the Yankee traits passed on to her own father and mother, and through them to herself and her siblings. No wonder, then, that Marjorie could still recite the names and dates of her many relatives. With the help of her written notes made at various times over the years, she related the following history of the Pierce family.

Damaris Colburn Aldrich (1849-1947) was born the year of the Goldrush. She grew up in North Shrewsbury on the road to Eastham at what is now the Herb Farm, then owned by her parents Edward Aldrich (1824-1902) and Catherine Colburn Aldrich (1829-1873).

Catherine's father was Cyrus Colburn and his father was Moses Colburn (1767-1857), another of Shrewsbury's earliest settlers who was in residence by 1800 on a parcel below the store and now a cellar hole. Moses' father Jonathan was a Revolutionary War soldier who was born in Massachusetts in 1735 and died in Shrewsbury in 1808, and that is how I am a member of the Daughters of the American Revolution.

Cyrus married Caty Morse and her father was Esquire Morse, and that's how I may be connected to Samuel F. B. Morse [inventor of the Morse Code]. My grandmother displayed a picture of the Morse Monument, and now I have it hanging in my kitchen.

Esquire Morse and Jacob Guild came to Shrewsbury as early settlers and settled on the Old Plymouth Road, where two sawmills and District Schoolhouse #15 were once located. The children sat in Shrewsbury and the teacher sat in Plymouth, because it was a union school that straddled the town line. There's just an old lilac bush and wilderness there now, but there once were quite a few houses near that road. One of the Guilds was eventually owner of the store here.

My Great-grandfather Edward Aldrich (Damaris's father) was the son of Jonah Aldrich who was the son of Ziba Aldrich, a Revolutionary War soldier. Ziba was born 1755 in Massachusetts, married in 1775 in Richmond, New Hampshire, and brought his family to Shrewsbury in 1780. They were the fourth family to settle in town. [They first settled near the Mill River, but Ziba reportedly thought the dampness aggravated his rheumatism so he sold that property in 1796 and a year later bought 350 acres on the road to Eastham in the vicinity of the present-day Herb Farm, where he built his cabin on a knoll behind the present red barn.] His son Jonah built his house nearby; and Jonah's son Edward (1824-1902) had the present Herb Farm farmhouse built for him in 1860 by Moses Lefevre, who built some of the Greek Revival homes in the area.

On my father's father's side, my Great-great-grandfather Ephraim Pierce (1764-1830) was from Walpole, New Hampshire. He bought 100 acres in 1788 near the northern end of Road 14—now called the Bennington Camp Road—in North Shrewsbury, where he built a house. In 1799, Ephraim married Sarah Pollard (1778-1857) from Plymouth, and they had five children.

When Ephraim and Sarah Pierce lived on Road 14, they were not the only settlers to clear their land and try to farm there [this is very difficult, rocky, high-elevation terrain without much topsoil]. To their north, Henry C. Wright cleared a farm and built a sawmill. The Thomas Stewart

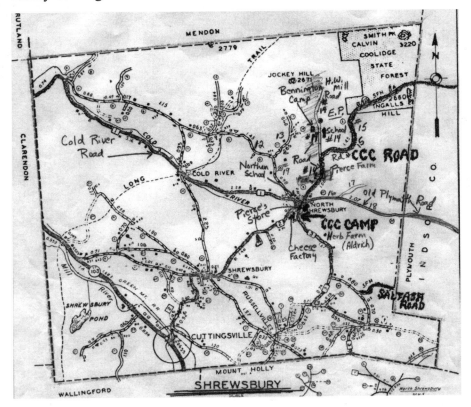

was cleared on the west side of the road, where the Bennington Camp is now. Other farms included the Thomas O'Connor place and the Elwin Headle farm. Eventually, Ephraim and Sarah started another farm when they moved down the road a way, perhaps because the land was better there. Just below this place, south of it and on the east side of the road was the schoolhouse, which was known as School District #14.

This settlement was two miles from the village of Northam and up a long steep mountain road to get to it, so the families supported their own schoolhouse here for many years—as was the custom in the town which had fifteen such "district" schools at this time when its population was still over 1200. The schoolhouse was built in 1849 and had nineteen scholars in 1850. Ephraim's grandson Edwin taught here for a few terms. (Teachers for these early one-room schools would live with one of the families and seldom had more than a grade-school education themselves.) This area of farms was abandoned in the early 1900s, and none of Ephraim's children ever lived here as adults.

As Marjorie continued, she occasionally embellished the story of her family's beginnings by adding interesting tidbits or pertinent facts from history:

Ephraim's father may have been Ebenezer who was shot by a New Hampshire Tory; his wife Sarah smoked a pipe!

Their son Eli married Rhoda Johnson, whose parents had a farm at the top of Road 14 [later known as the Mandigo Farm], which wasn't too far from Eli's childhood home. Eli and Rhoda settled on Upper Cold River Road, where Eli was a farmer and cooper. They had nine children, including twin sons Edwin and Eli.

Edwin (1841-1919) married Damaris Colburn Aldrich in 1870 and continued the Shrewsbury Pierce line that includes my father Willie and ends with me. His twin Eli (1841-1915), who also fought in the Civil War, married Eldora Lamb and moved to nearby Plymouth, where they lived and raised five children.

Eli and Eldora had a daughter Aurora (1868-1956) who lived in Plymouth and was President Calvin Coolidge's housekeeper for many years. I visited her every summer. She was a very staid and proper New England spinster who was very thrifty. She was the boss of the Coolidge household! We once had relatives in Plymouth, including first cousins, but there are none left there now.

18

Sarah Aiken Spaulding   *Joseph Kennedy Spaulding*

My mother, Gertrude Spaulding Pierce was born in 1877 in West Bridgewater, Vermont, to Joseph Kennedy Spaulding (a child of Mary and Obadiah Spaulding who were from Massachusetts) and Sarah Aiken Spaulding, who was born in 1840 in New Hampshire.

My grandfather Joseph Spaulding owned and operated a grocery store, which is probably where my mother got her interest in country stores. She was eager to see my father purchase the Northam Store in 1918, and she often worked in the store since he would be busy farming.

Joseph Kennedy (1694-1768)

Capt. James Aiken
m Jennie Waugh

Matthew Kennedy (1741-1776)
m Jean Gilchrist

Mr. Amy
Buswells

J a m e s Aiken married Mary Kennedy

Obadiah and Mary Spaulding

Hannah Buswell   m. Benjamin Aiken

Sarah Buswell Aiken married Joseph Spaulding

Gertrude	Carlos	Hattie	Grace	Clyde	Charlie	Carrie
m	m	m	m	m	m	m
Willie Pierce	Kate Pierce	Clarence Coates	Bert Hill	Jennie Martin	Nora Bridge	Herbert Johnson

Marion Marjorie Gordon Glendon Gilford

J. K. Spaulding with grandchildren Hazel and Herbert Johnson at his West Bridgewater Store, circa 1902. Post Office was on right in store.

Sarah's father Benjamin burned to death in 1881 while trying to get horses out of a barn fire. His parents were James (born 1774) and Mary Kennedy Aiken. Mary's father was Matthew Kennedy, born 1741 and died 1776. He was my Great-great-great-grandfather and his father Joseph was one of the original settlers of Goffstown, New Hampshire.

Matthew was in the Revolutionary War. He was one of 10,000 soldiers Washington sent to Mount Independence to stop the advance of the British down Lake Champlain. [They succeeded and bought about a year's time; when the British returned a year later, they were forced to surrender at Saratoga.] I have a copy of the sad letter he sent to his brother Robert Kennedy in New Hampshire, asking him to come and get him. He wrote, "I have been in a low state of health for some time. I earnestly entreat you not to delay in coming for me. There is hardly any sustenance to be had for man or horse between this place and (Fort) Number Four so I advise you to bring provender."

He died before help reached him and was buried at Mount Independence along with about 1,000 soldiers. A comrade wrote an affidavit saying, "He was the first man I ever helped to bury without a coffin."

Mount Independence is now an historic site. I gave them a copy of the letter [for their educational displays at the Visitor's Center]. The original was given to the University of Vermont by my Uncle Clyde Spaulding.

James' father was Captain James, who married Jenny Waugh, whose family came from Scotland. On Sarah's mother's side, there were the Buswell and Amy families. Mr. Amy was killed by Indians around 1725.

So on my mother's side, we are Scotch and Irish and on my father's side, English and maybe Dutch. You see the Pierces first were in England and then Holland before emigrating to the United States. I don't know how long they were in Holland, but I imagine it was for some time or I don't think my grandfather would have mentioned it to me.

As Marjorie related some of the details of her ancestry, the hardness of early life often slipped in along with some of the attributes that she admired in these people. It was surprising to learn, however, that she has outlived all her first cousins and that her remaining closest relations in 1999 are their children, two of whom, Midge and Pete Spaulding (Clyde's grandson), live in Springfield, Massachusetts. "The rest are children of cousins once-or-twice-removed, who live in scattered places as far away as California. I used to see them occasionally or correspond with them, but I don't see much of them now. The last visit from an Aldrich occurred some years ago—they have their own lives," Marjorie observed, noting that many live so far away due the Westward migration of the 1800s.

As she lapsed into the story of her grandparents Edwin and Damaris, Marjorie grew animated and clearly enjoyed reliving their adventures.

Edwin and Damaris Pierce, my grandparents, married on January 19, 1870, and had six children: Etta Juliette, born in 1871, who died at age ten on April 6, 1881 from scarlet fever; Willie Edwin born 1872; Kate Beatrice, 1874; Reno Arthur, 1876; Ned Eugene, 1879; and Carrie Essie, 1890. All married and moved away except Aunt Carrie, who remained single and lived with her parents and then moved to Rutland with them in 1918. My father Willie married and carried on the Shrewsbury Pierce family line.

The brothers and sisters, Marjorie's aunts and uncles, lived well into their eighties with her father living to almost ninety-three and his sister

Kate to 101. The family's longevity, which Marjorie attributes to "being in the genes," was repeated with her own siblings, except for Gilford who was killed in the war, living into their eighties and Marjorie a sharp ninety-six at the time this book was printed.

Edwin and Damaris first lived at his father's farm, the Eli Pierce farm, on the Upper Cold River Road. Eli died in 1873, and in March 1875 Edwin and Damaris migrated with their three small children to Nevada, where Edwin's favorite sister Sarah Ann had moved with her husband Jeremiah Jaquith. These were the years of "migration fever," and Marjorie speculated that "they went West after Eli died because they may have sold the farm and had the means to make this trip and start a more challenging life."

Having heard many tales of that journey from her grandparents and father, Marjorie wrote this description while Willie was still alive:

> They left in winter while snow was on the ground and were surprised on reaching Reno, Nevada to find the gardens up. Enroute to Reno, Edwin and Damaris had the care of three small children (Etta, Willie, and Kate) on the long train ride. This was probably hard on Damaris, because they had poor meals and none too much to eat. The Tom Thumb Theater Troupe was on the train, and they offered to take care of the children so Edwin and Damaris could get off the train at Cheyenne, Wyoming, and get a good meal. Damaris appreciated that kindness so much that she never forgot it.
>
> In Reno, Edwin bought a little house with picket fence on a corner lot—Corner of 4th and Sierra Streets. The home of his sister was nearby. In Edwin's yard were young fruit trees and a handsome yellow rosebush. Edwin was unfortunate in going into business with Jaquith who proved unreliable. Edwin worked in the harness shop or store and ended up losing his money and so returned East. At the shop they sold harnesses and saddles to cowboys who were rough fellows and more or less outlaws.
>
> Living in the West, Willie played "lasso" and Etta had a nice doll. Willie remembers their house and that of his aunt and also going down to a sort of settlement where his father worked in the harness store. He remembers a cow and meeting Indians, who would keep to the sidewalk three or four abreast, forcing Damaris to step aside for them when they approached. Then they would turn and laugh.

Sometimes the Indians would come through the gate and press their faces against the windows to watch the family eat. Damaris, a timid woman and not accustomed to the West, kept a kettle of hot water on the stove in case they became bolder.

Sarah Ann's husband Jeremiah Jaquith was a handsome man but fussy about his food. When he wouldn't eat what Sarah cooked, Sarah would take it over to Damaris who was glad to have the extra food to feed her family. The Jaquiths eventually moved to Centerville, California, and had three children.

My father told me about a Chinese laundry in Reno where Chinamen would sprinkle their clothes by holding water in their mouth and squirting it out through their teeth. He remembered his mother's brother Luman visiting them and seeing a prairie fire during their return trip to Vermont. Great-uncle Luman Aldrich traveled a lot; he would make a fortune, then lose it. He was a speculator in property and gold and silver mines.

Other stories Marjorie heard from her grandparents included the times that her grandfather witnessed some western-style lawlessness and her grandmother's sad story about Etta. These narratives always impressed her, both as a young girl listening to them and as an older woman who repeated them for others.

Down in the business section and more thickly settled part of Reno, a clerk came out on the sidewalk and was opening a crate with a hatchet. A drunken Indian came along and insulted or annoyed him in some way and the man split his head open with the hatchet. Then several Indians arrived and carried him off and nothing was ever done about it.

Another time a man was standing in the doorway of a horse barn. Two men got into an argument, pulled out their revolvers, and started shooting at each other. Edwin knew one of these men. By accident the innocent man in the doorway was shot and killed. "Guns were the law in those days," my grandfather used to tell me.

Damaris liked it in Reno and would have stayed if Edwin had found another job, but her folks hounded her to return East. She told me that Etta, sorry to leave Reno, threw her doll into the Truckee River. This bothered Damaris for many years.

Later, after Etta became sick with scarlet fever and died, Damaris was often haunted by the thought that she might have lived had the family stayed in Reno.

When they returned to North Shrewsbury in January 1877, the Edwin Pierce family rented a house near the Northam Church. "The baby

Edwin driving cows to pasture, circa 1900.

who was born in Nevada was about six months old and hadn't been named yet, so a neighbor suggested Reno after where he was born, and that's how Willie's brother came to that unusual name," Marjorie related.

While living near the church, young "Willie would often run away to the close-by blacksmith shop, rap on the door, and ask to be let in to watch the blacksmith, Newell Green, work. Men of the community liked to congregate there, talk, and play cards," Marjorie noted. Willie would also run away to visit the Red School, where George Whitney and Willie D. Aldrich were pupils and which his mother Damaris had attended as a child. It subsequently burned down in late 1877 and was replaced by another one-room schoolhouse on the same site, which school Willie began to attend in September of 1878.

In January 1878, Willie's father Edwin bought a farm about a half mile from the Northam School on the lower section of Road 14 where it begins to rise sharply up the mountain and moved his family there. Land records show that the farm consisted of about fifty acres and that the parcel had changed hands many times and formerly had an older home there years before. Marjorie added:

> The home Edwin purchased was a large one built by Rodney P. Burditt for Lyman Aldrich around 1860. It had been the home of Lyman's son Jasper before Roswell Wright bought it in 1872 and later sold it to Edwin for $3,000. Shrewsbury's last blacksmith Perrin J. Whitney told them that a Whitney woman was said to be buried in the meadow behind the house by a shelving rock. It was a story that so frightened Willie's sister Carrie, that she refused to play there.

Willie grew up on his father's farm and went to school at the Northam School District #7. It was the same one-room school where we [Marjorie and her siblings] went through the eighth grade.

Although she didn't know much about the early education of her other relatives, Marjorie did recall that her Grandfather Edwin Pierce had attended the Black River Academy in Ludlow, where President Calvin Coolidge, Senator Mortimer Proctor, and Vermont Attorney General John Garibaldi Sargent (later appointed U.S. Attorney General by Coolidge) received their secondary educations. Marjorie thought that her father Willie went to Northam for eight grades and then to Albany, New York, for further schooling. "That is where his brothers Ned and Reno went to Albany Business College," and since "they all had the same beautiful handwriting," she deduced that "Willie probably went there, too." Written records of his working life begin at the age of eighteen so it is likely that he got some further education after grade school. (He may also have worked at the W.E. Aldrich Store in Lake Placid during this time.)

In his early years, Willie helped his father on the farm. Around age eighteen (1890), he worked two winters at the Russell Saw Mill [later the Bissell Mill] located two miles up on Road #15 [between the later-built Northam Picnic Area and Stone House] on property John Russell bought in 1845. At age nineteen, Willie also began to learn cheese making with his Uncle Eugene Aldrich, who was a cheese maker at the Northam Cheese Factory which was owned by Wilson E. Aldrich (who owned or operated cheese factories in Cuttingsville, East Wallingford, Belmont, Plymouth, Reading, and elsewhere).

For his first year's work there, Willie received $12 a month plus room and board. Thereafter, he made cheese in West Bridgewater for about five years and then about 1897 went to work for H.P. Hood and Sons in Lynn, Massachusetts. In 1898 he was employed for a summer in the grocery store of W. E. Aldrich in Lake Placid, New York, This was his Uncle Wilson's store, an indication that the cheese factory owner and operator was quite an entrepreneur.

Willie returned to Vermont and again obtained a cheese making position in West Bridgewater, where Gertrude Alice Spaulding lived in the house across the road from her father's store. The cheese factory was very close by and notes in Willie's diary indicate that he had become acquainted with her by 1894 and that they were going to dances together.

Notes from Diary of Willie E. Pierce

Willie E. Pierce, 1894

1892

Jan.	4 - 8	Went to school.
	18, 19	to school.
Feb.	15	Drew logs.
	21	Drew logs.
Mar.	17	Went to dance at grand--pa's [Edward Aldrich].
Apr.	6	Dance at Geo. Whitney's.
	26	Uncle Will's [Wilson Aldrich] factory started today. Gene & I made cheese.
May	3, 4	Made cheese.
	9	Made cheese at W. Bridgewater.
Aug.	29	Had picture of W. Bridgewater factory taken.
Nov.	30	Came to Shrewsbury for good. Walked from Plymouth.

1894

Jan.	1	Mrs. Colburn had fits
	5	Party and dance at Orlo Frost's until 3 A.M.
	8	Took Gertrude and Grace to dance Bridgewater Corners Kate went with Carlos.
	10	Donation at Dr. Moore's.
	17	59 couples at Cuttingsville dance until 2 A.M.
	20	Dan & I went to a horse trot on Spring Lake & had dinner at D.K. Butterfields.
	26	15 to 20 couples at dance at Geo. Plumleys until 4 A.M. Dan & I came home in 30 minutes.

Feb.	1	Father & I bought a Rochester lamp for kitchen.
	13	Hired by Jen Madden to make cheese at West Bridgewater at $40 per month.
		P.J. Whitney shoes horse.
Apr.	13	Reno & I went to Rutland to have our pictures taken.
	26	Went to Uncle Warren's in E. Wallingford.
	28	Gene's folks [Eugene and Mary Aldrich] moved to Plymouth.
	30	Went to Frank Holden's after oats [Heath farm]
May	7	Started making cheese at West Bridgewater.

1895

May	18	Mrs. Poore died today.
Apr.	9	Warm. Went down to Rutland to hear Cold River murder trial. Stayed all night. Lots went from here.
		Big thunder storm in evening.
May	6	Gertrude started teaching at Daley Hollow
	7	Began making cheese at W.B.
June	27	Eaton Lord and Ernest Wright came over to see me.
Oct.	26	Finished making cheese.
	30	Commenced boarding at J.K. Spaulding's.
Nov.	5	Mrs. Madden started for Iowa.
	18	Gert 18 yrs. today. I gave her a gold pen.
	25	Herbert Johnson & I got out lumber for a crokonole board.

Glendon displays Willie's croquenole board, photo circa 1980s.

Spaulding Family, L to R: Grace, Clyde, Gertrude. Charlie, son Ralph, Joseph, Sarah, Herbert Johnson, daughter Hazel. Nora (Charlie's wife), Carlos, Hattie, her husband Clarence Coates, and Carrie, wife of Herbert Johnson.

Willie and Gertrude were married on May 10, 1899, in Rutland by the Reverend C.H. Scholefield, pastor of the Christian Church of North Shrewsbury. Willie's sister Kate married Gertrude's brother Carlos Spaulding, so the family enjoyed close friendships throughout their lives. Gertrude's sister Hattie married a Canadian, Clarence L. Coates, with whom "Willie engaged in general carpentry work for several years. They built houses, did the interior finishing of the church at Plymouth Notch opposite the Calvin Coolidge Homestead, and got out scythe sticks one winter. For this last job, they were paid $160 in gold," Marjorie recounted in a biographical sketch of Willie which she wrote in 1964.

It is likely that they did this work during the winters as Willie was also farming with his father for $30 a month and had built an addition to his father's house. His parents lived in the "new apartment side" while Willie's family lived in the older section. Willie eventually took over the entire operation of the farm, at first renting it from Edwin and then building it up to sixty-five animals and purchasing it outright. From 1908 to 1913, Willie also cut Christmas trees with George Whitney, shipping out some seventy-five carloads by train during those years.

Willie and Gertrude Pierce were married on May 10, 1899.

It was while Willie and Gertrude were living at the farm that their five children were born. On September 9, 1901, Gertrude Marion (called Marion) arrived, and on May 1, 1903, her sister Marjorie Anna came into the world. They were actually born in West Bridgewater at the home of their maternal grandparents because in those days women often went to be with their mothers who could take care of them during and after childbirth. On February 20, 1908, Gordon Willie was born, followed by Glendon Spaulding on September 15, 1913, and Gilford Edwin on January 21, 1916. "They were all born in Shrewsbury because by this time my mother was experienced," Marjorie said, expressing the wish that she, too, could have been born in Shrewsbury.

Chapter Three

Growing Up on a Vermont Farm
1903-1917

Marjorie was to live on her family's farm in Northam for the first fourteen years of her life. One of her earliest memories of growing up there is the fright she suffered as a toddler in the barn.

> There was a wooden wall to keep the cows in. We named each of the cows and the names were written on the wall. There was a step down to the pig pen.
> I had been in the barn looking at the piglets when I leaned too far over and toppled in. I was lying on my back screaming and couldn't get up. The big mama pigs were nuzzling at me, and I was screaming bloody murder. I must have been three years old, and I was so scared. The hired man Harold Plumley, who was probably sixteen or seventeen, hurried down and rescued me. He was my hero!

Laughing and shuddering as she recalled this scene, Marjorie added, "Those mama pigs made a big impression on me." A much fonder childhood memory was of playing with Marion.

> We got along well. We had arguments but we got along very well most of the time. There were other children in Northam, but they were far away so we played with each other.

30

Marion, Marjorie, and Gertrude Pierce in West Bridgewater.

As we grew older, Cousin Constance who lived in New Jersey would come to visit our grandparents with her family. She was Uncle Reno's only child. She had nice clothes and white shoes. We had old gingham dresses or commonplace clothes. Her mother wore a lovely white skirt and shirtwaist with a lace collar. Mother and Grandmother wore long house dresses

Constance was bossy! We'd go to my mother and say, "We don't want to do so and so," and Mother would say, "Constance is our guest and you have to do what she wants."

We grew up playing with very simple things, having few toys. When we played in the house, we would play paper dolls. The mail-order catalogue came maybe twice a year. Some pages had colored pictures of children, men, and women. We cut them out. Marion had hers, and I had mine. I'd take mine behind the Morris chair and we'd talk.

Marion and I were content to play with our dolls in the sitting room. Our sitting room was like a family room today. It led into Grandma's parlor which was more formal, like a living room. The parlor had an organ, carpet, lovely pink chimney lamp, a love seat, a green velvet Morris chair, and a rocking chair by the stove, which had green isinglass in the door.

Our games were Dominoes and later, Authors. We had cards with authors on them. And we had our own storybooks.

Marion and I played outdoors a lot in the fresh air. We had a favorite spot under the apple tree, which we called our 'house.' We gathered stones and made walls and rooms. We would play house and use sticks and stones to represent family. Mother would be the cook. The only food we made was mud pies. We would go to the frog pond and get mud. We made a lot of mud pies. There was a cute poem about mud pies.

Tell me, little housewives,
Playing in the sun;
How many minutes
'Till the cooking's done?

Henry builds the oven,
Lucy rolls the crust,
Clara buys the flour,
All of golden dust.

Pat it here and pat it there;
What a dainty size!
Bake it on a shingle,
Nice mud pies!

Don't you hear the bluebird
High up in the air?
"Good morning, little ones;
Are you busy there?"

Pretty Mr. Squirrel
Bounces down the rail,
Takes a seat and watches,
Curls his bushy tail.

Twirl it so and mark it so,
Cooking very wise;
All the plums are pebbles
Rich mud pies!

One time someone told us if we dug a hole far enough, we would get to China. So Marion and I got tools and dug for days. We dug and dug, and then we gave up. We didn't have all the toys children have today. We had to make our own games and use our imaginations. Sometimes we would ask our mother to tell us stories or sing to us. We loved to listen to her. Mother always sang when she did her work in the kitchen, and she whistled, too.

The Pierce home had a large kitchen with a step down to an adjacent woodshed, which had a stairway to the attic. "Over in the farther corner of the woodshed there was a little room painted yellow-orange with a two-holer and a little window that looked out on the back meadows. It was clean and nice looking. It was sheltered and warmer than a barn would be," Marjorie recalled.

The kitchen was a busy and special place where the laundry, cooking, and other chores like taking care of the milk and making butter

Marion and Marjorie on the big rock on the Pierce farm.

were done. In one corner of the kitchen was the dish cupboard with drawers underneath. There was a window and sink along the back wall and off to the back a separate pantry. The kitchen had a hardwood floor, a large table, and a wood cookstove for cooking and heat. One of Marjorie's fondest memories is of sitting with her older sister Marion on the woodbox.

When mother mopped the floor, Marion and I would have to sit on the large woodbox behind the wood cookstove. The woodbox was painted a cream color with red trim and had a red wooden top.

To entertain us, mother would sing or recite nursery rhymes or poetry to us. The first rhymes we learned were One, Two Buckle My Shoe, Humpty Dumpty, and Jack and Jill.

Our favorite song was called Cabbage and Meat. I also liked Fair Charlotte [also known as Frozen Charlotte] because it was so thrilling and was supposed to be a true story! My grandmother said that she knew a woman who knew a woman who was in the hall when Charles carried in Charlotte's frozen body. Charlotte was vain and froze to death because she refused to put blankets around her when they went to a dance in freezing weather fifteen miles away from their home. Charlotte lived on a mountainside and the dance was supposed to have happened in nearby Ludlow, so that was a very exciting story to us!

These songs told stories. They were entertaining. Not having many toys to play with, we would plead with our mother to sing these songs to us. They would have a moral or lesson. We would sing in the evening, too.

She also recited poetry. Our favorite poems were The Ride of Jenny McNeil, Johnny Sands, The Three Little Kittens, The Two Kittens, and The Blackberry Girl.

To the left side of the kitchen, there was a door to a "sitting room" and off that a bedroom for her parents. Upstairs over the sitting room was a large bedroom with a big four-poster bed for Marion and Marjorie. "We had a featherbed, a puff filled with hen feathers—you had goose feathers if you were rich." The bed itself had metal mesh to hold the thin mattress and on top of it, the featherbed, "which was about four-inches thick and very warm," Marjorie recalled. In winter, they would use flannel sheets and homemade quilts as well. The house had ceiling registers (open grate work) so that heat from the woodstoves could rise through them to warm the rooms on the second floor.

There was another large open area on the second floor which Marjorie recalled was "maybe a part of a hall." It was there that Gordon and Glendon slept. Her parents room had "a double bed and a white painted iron half-bed with gold knobs, where Gilford, who was just a baby, slept." Since the girls were older and already in school when their brothers were born, Marjorie didn't recall playing with them much. She remembered that Gordon suffered a bout of pneumonia or consumption as a baby. "The doctor really didn't know how to treat him," she said of a time when the country doctor made house calls but lacked the modern antibiotics that render childhood illnesses less threatening today. "I remember my father carrying Gordon around in his arms until he was two-years old."

Since Marjorie's grandparents lived in the adjacent newer "apartment," Marjorie and Marion saw them often.

Marion, Percy, Gordon, and Marjorie Pierce, circa 1909 on the Pierce Farm. Note the ell on the left of the house, which is where Edwin and Damaris lived.

We were very close. We would beg Mother to be allowed to go visit Grandma, always having to get permission first so that we wouldn't be pests or bother her.

Percy Pierce with brook trout his dad Ned caught.

We would go through the sitting room and the hall to Grandmother's parlor and dining room, then to the kitchen. We'd go over to the sink and to the cupboard. In the lower drawer was a ball of red and blue yarn. We would ask permission to play with the ball. We loved to play with it because inside there was a bell that tinkled.

Grandmother was a spotless housekeeper. Her floor and her chairs were as white as snow. She would wash them so everything was always immaculate. She knit mittens for us every winter. We told her to make long wrists for us.

Uncle Ned, my father's brother, was a fisherman. He would come to visit and go up the Plymouth Road to Alder Meadow Brook and bring back a string of fish. Grandmother had an old-fashioned big brown bowl that he would dump his fish in. Then he'd clean the fish, and we would have trout for supper.

I have a vivid memory of a visit to the apartment in April 1912. My father was sitting in a wicker chair reading the paper. I said "What is that?" I saw a picture of a ship and heads bobbing in water. It was the Titanic!

We knew very little of the outside world in those days. There was no radio or television. Our world was home, school, church, and grandparents and visits with aunts and uncles in the summers. Those visits were interesting but occasionally pesky when Constance came.

We had kerosene lamps, not candles, and we went to bed earlier. We lived day-to-day. It was a quieter time. Mother and father worked hard, but I think they were happy and had fulfilling lives. Women were busy with children and domestic duties.

36

Edwin in his garden on the farm, circa 1903.

Mother had five children, and she was busy with sewing, doing the laundry, and cooking. She had to get three meals a day, and when we went to school, she prepared us for school and gave us lunch to take.

She took care of the milk. We had fifteen to twenty-five cows at the farm. They brought the milk into the house in big cans. We had milk pans about twelve inches in diameter and six inches high; she would fill the pans and put the pans on the pantry shelf and the cream would rise. A day or so later, she would take down the pans and skim off the cream for butter and some for the table.

We would use the cream to make butter with a big wooden-barrel churn. Mother and father churned. I can see my father now, turning the handle. Some milk got fed to the pigs, and some went into jars for the family. The surplus was left in the big pails. The milk not used for the home was taken to the Northam Cheese Factory and sold for money. We got our cheese from the factory. In later years, the milk was put into a separator. We had a machine called the DeLaval Separator.

In the pantry, there was a barrel of flour and a barrel of sugar. They bought by the barrel. Down in the cellar, we had a barrel of apples and a big box of potatoes. (Later, when we lived at the store, there was a barrel of vinegar.) There was an apple orchard below the house, and we also picked raspberries in summer and strawberries. My mother made mincemeat so we had mincemeat pies and pumpkin and squash pies, too. We had chickens and hens and my mother would put the eggs in a special liquid called "water glass" and place the container of eggs on the stairs to the basement away from the heat. Hens didn't lay eggs in winter then, but the eggs could be used all year. [Marjorie produced a newspaper clipping which explained that "water glass silicate" was a traditional preservative used for keeping eggs fresh for one to three years!]

Mother sewed and she did embroidery work, but she didn't have much time for that. In the morning, she would get breakfast, bake bread, take care of the milk, do the dishes, peel potatoes and get ready for the next meal or do the baking and get the children off to school.

On some days she did a big washing. We had a contraption that was kept in the shed to do laundry. It was four pieces of wood and five-feet high. You put a wash tub on each side and in the middle was the wringer. One side was wash, the middle was wring, and the other side rinse. The whites had to be washed and then put through the blueing—that made them look whiter.

We had to get the wash boiler out of the shed and heat the water in it on the stove. We had to boil the white clothes with Fels Naptha soap. Then you lifted the boiled clothes with a long wooden forked stick and put them in the wash water, then through the wringer which put them out in the rinse water. And wring again, and then they were hung on double lines on the porch, or in summer we put them out back on the grass. Sometimes mother ironed. Grandmother even ironed her stockings!

My mother sang to occupy herself when doing these chores. She had a lot of responsibility for the home and farm chores. She had a beautiful voice, and I think she sang to help pass the time. Once, when we lived at the store, I heard her tell Avis Poore, a neighbor who lived in the little cottage next to us that, "When you're singing, you can't think." She used to whistle, too.

Marjorie didn't recall having assigned chores, but she and Marion helped her mother by, "setting the table, wiping the dishes, helping with the laundry, or sweeping the floor." She also remembered, "making our beds, feeding the chickens and hens, collecting eggs, and doing odd little things, like piling up the sap buckets after they had been washed."

Her father took care of the milking, feeding and care of the cows, chickens, hens, pigs, and horses, and the planting and harvesting of potatoes and corn, while her grandfather was in charge of the vegetable garden. In 1908, as previously noted, Willie had bought the Tom Stewart Farm and the Headle Farm on old Road 14. He had twenty or more cows, so to feed them, he hayed the meadows at those two farms, which were a mile up the mountain. In those days, farmers often did not have enough feed to keep their cows producing milk in winter, so cows usually dried up or produced very little milk then (a reason that men worked in the cheese factories from spring to fall but not in winter). After their

Willie, Marion, and Constance taking milk to cheese factory, circa 1904.

Willie on the load with Fred Maccabbee hired to help on Edwin Pierce farm. Horses are Jack and Dennis, the work horses.

Gertrude and Willie gather sap on Edwin Pierce farm, early 1900s.

hay supplies ran out, farmers fed their cows whatever they had, often pumpkins and root vegetables which would keep in their unheated barns during the long winters. They also bred the cows to calve in the spring so there would be grass for them to eat then and they could get a good start. The "all-purpose" cow of that day produced far less milk than today's specially fed animals and this helps to explain why Willie both bought the additional land to use as hayfields and why he wanted to grow the size of his herd.

Edwin helped with the haying and as children, Marjorie recalled "liking to go with them to play and to ride back on the hay wagon." She also recalled "gathering pails of cranberries, which we found on a meadow near the old Thomas Stewart Farm in the fall." Willie also collected sap and made maple syrup in season, using both the sugarbush at the farm and one on Road 14.

When there was fresh snow on the road—the side roads were rolled last and seldom in time for the girls to get to school—Willie would often hitch Otto and Togo (named after a Japanese general) to one of the two sleighs he owned and take the girls to school. "They were Morgan colts and had special light harnesses. Mother would bundle us up in leggings and wrap newspaper around our bodies for warmth; it made good insulation for the cold ride," Marjorie stated.

But when Willie was too busy with milking or some other chore, the walk could be an arduous task for the two little girls who were on the petite side. So in the worst weather, when deep snows lay on the ground, "Mother would wait for Royce Mandigo, who was maybe four-years older, to come down off the mountain. When she saw him coming, she would shoo us out the door so we could walk in his tracks for the half-mile trip to school." Marjorie related this with a laugh and genuine de-

District School # 7 or Northam School

light at having had their own personal and ingenious "snowplow" lead the way.

Northam School, as the District #7 school became known, was a one-room schoolhouse with a four-holer (outhouse) out back. "There was a two-holer boys' side and two-holer girls' side. Each had a door, and Glendon always said, "You didn't have to be too smart to know which was which,' " Marjorie recalled of an oft-told Pierce story.

The classroom contained a variety of ages and up to eight grades, although some years there might not be every grade represented.

After a salute to the flag and a reading from the Bible, the teacher would tap the little bell on her desk; the first grade would come up and sit in the front seat, and she would explain things to them for maybe ten minutes. Or she would have them recite or question them on a lesson they had. Then she would ring the bell again, and grade two would come forward and have a lesson. And so on.

She had a blackboard on the wall used for spelling and arithmetic lessons. The first day each child was given books and a pencil.

"Come and play. Away." I learned to read by recognizing the word "come" as a unit.

There were two coat rooms, one for girls and one for boys. Each had an entrance to the outside—that's how we got into school. The boys' coat room had a door to the woodshed, too. In the main classroom, there was a big square stove with stove pipe. The boys would feed it. The blacksmith Perrin J. Whitney who lived nearby was paid $5 a year to build the fire so the room was warm when children got there. It was always an honor to get to sit near the teacher because that was where the heat from the woodstove was in winter. Boys who did something wrong had to sit on a chunk of wood by the stove, instead of standing in the corner.

At recess we could go out and play in the yard. It was dirt, not grass. We played Hide and Seek and Prisoner's Base, the game we liked the most. You played this by digging a line with your heel and choosing captains and teams for each side. You tried to put your foot across the line without being touched. You would dare someone to capture you. If they touched you, you had to go to their side.

In winter, the sixth and seventh graders would bring sleds to school. The older boys would ask you to ride on the sled. They would draw you back and forth, back and forth—it was kind of like dancing. You would worry you'd not be asked or if the right boy, one you liked, would ask you.

We didn't have homework, but we had splendid teachers.

Recalling her grade school teachers, Marjorie noted that Roy Whitney, the blacksmith's son, was the only male teacher she ever had at Northam. "Lena Wood, a beautiful and very charming woman was one of my favorite teachers. Amy Burditt, a descendant of the mill family, was another. When I was ten or twelve years old, Amy invited Marion and me to her home in North Springfield one weekend. We took the train from Cuttingsville, my first train ride, to Gassetts where Amy's father met us with his horse and buggy."

As she told this story in 1998, one of the many connected thoughts that so often flash through her brain like a modern computer chip sending out signals suddenly struck. Marjorie was out of her chair and back in a wink with her first report cards. She read them aloud and enjoyed a good

Report of Marjorie Pierce

For 10 Weeks Beginning Sept. 7, 1909

Ending Nov. 1909

1 Grade No. Shrewsbury School

				Average
Reading	E	E	E	
Arithmetic	E	E	E	
Geography				
Grammar and Language				
History				
Physiology				
Spelling	a	a	E	
Penmanship	a	a	a	
Music				
Drawing				
Average	a+	a+	a	
Effort				
Half days absent				
Tardy				
Dismissed				
Deportment	a	a	B	

Lena E. Wood, Teacher

Classmates at Northam School, circa 1909. L to R, front row: Royce Mandigo, Harold Stillwell, Marjorie, Armina Petrazlia, Marion, Frankie Cook, Dolly Seery, Carrie Harrison. Back row: Ross Seery, Frank Plumley, Erwin Stillwell, Roy Stillwell, teacher Lena Woods, Verna Aldrich, Daisie Whitney, and Seery (?) girl.

Rolling the roads with team of horses, circa 1920.

chuckle at her grade in deportment, allowing that she must have been a little unruly or a bit talkative on occasion.

Another favorite memory was visiting the blacksmith's wife, Minnie Sanderson Whitney. "Minnie would let Marion and me come in and play with the toys and eat lunch there. She had lots of toys and was very good to children. She was a good church woman who kept the Northam Church going. Her daughter Daisie became a teacher but died in her twenties. Roy married Marion Thomas, daughter of Middlebury College President John Thomas, and moved to Delaware where he taught school."

During their early years, Marjorie and Marion visited their relatives in West Bridgewater for a week or two every summer. "We would stay with Aunts Hattie, Carrie, or Grace, my mother's sisters. They made dresses for us and gave us books," Marjorie recalled of the attention they received from their aunts who also gave her her first book, *Little Prudence's Cousin Grace.*

Willie would drive them over in the sleigh, buggy, or wagon, using Otto and Togo. When he was too busy, Gertrude would take them. They would travel past the Burditt Mill, Union School, and houses on the old Plymouth Road (old Roads 16 and 18) to Plymouth Union and from there along a dirt road to West Bridgewater. The trip was probably close to ten miles one way and covered some rough terrain that followed the Great Roaring Brook, crossing it several times, as it passed over the main ridge of the Green Mountains. The elevation of their home was about 1,900-feet above sea level, and the route they took climbed to 2,400 feet before dipping down to 1,300 feet on the Plymouth side. When she took the girls alone, Gertrude drove May, the Morgan mare.

The family also visited their Bridgewater relations at Christmas or Thanksgiving, often making the twenty-mile round trip in just one day. "A stone would be heated up, wrapped in cloth, and put in the bottom of the sleigh to put our feet on. It was called a freestone. We also had a buffalo robe for cold weather and lighter lap robes—light, sand-colored squares to put over the lap to keep from getting dusty in dry warmer weather. As we got older though, we went less often. In high school, we were busy with other pursuits," Marjorie explained.

Another of Marjorie's special memories of her "growing-up years" was of going to Sunday School and church, which she and Marion did "quite faithfully." In later years, her mother played the organ at Northam Church and occasionally helped sweep it out and dust but "with her duties and five children, she was often too tired to go in her younger years," Marjorie recalled, adding that her parents went "more for the sake of the family."

My parents weren't extremely religious, but they were respectful.

Lizzie Plumley was my first Sunday School teacher. I learned a lot from her. We had Bible stories and I remember leaflets for Sunday School lessons. There would be a story of Jonah and the Whale and then questions and empty lines to write on. We would have discussions of the lesson. I got my knowledge of the Bible from those lessons. I am so grateful to her.

Father had a surrey with red fringe on top. We would get all dressed up, and he would drive us to church for Easter in style! That was very special. He loved his Morgan horses and wanted them to pull a surrey—he couldn't bear to see them drag an old wagon! Those Morgan colts were his pride and joy, and that's why he had light harnesses for them.

Christmas at Northam Church was a special time, too.

Willie and nephew Percy with Marion, Marjorie and Damaris going to church on Easter in the surrey drawn by Togo and Otto.

As she recalled these stories from her childhood, Marjorie enjoyed her keen memories of a time when the Northam community came together for Christmas Eve. Then, pausing a moment, she left the room and came back with a copy of her Christmas story, written at age seventy-nine on her Smith Corona portable typewriter.

A Recollection of Christmas in Northam

People sometimes ask me how Christmas used to be celebrated when I was a child living on the Edwin Pierce farm in North Shrewsbury that is now [in 1982] owned by Joe Orlich. My father and grandfather operated the farm together and lived in the big farmhouse that was built for two families. The big barns are gone now and the southern section of the house, where grandpa and grandma lived, has been torn down. The tall mountain ash tree with its red berries, and grandma's syringa bush have long since disappeared.

Holidays were big events. About three weeks before Christmas, the Northam school teacher, aided by local church volunteers, planned the program of recitation, songs, short skits or plays, and the school children and Sunday School members were assigned their special parts. In addition, the adults in the church choir held frequent rehearsals of the Christmas carols they would sing. I especially recall that Harry Russell would play his violin, "Ete" Lord would be an enthusiastic choir member, along with Warner Aldrich and Wallace Philbrick, and that Verna Aldrich and Daisie Whitney (the "two belles of Northam") usually sang a duet. The strains of carols like "Joy to the World" rang throughout the church.

When barely able to print, I remember composing a letter to Santa Claus and nailing it on the front wall of the house. It was gone the next morning.

In those days, neighbors did not have Christmas trees or receive gifts in their homes. All we had at home was our stocking, a long, black one that we left on the Morris chair in the living room. The next morning we hurried to find what Santa Claus had left us. A nice orange was always tucked in the toe. You must realize that fresh fruit was a luxury up here in the country, although we did have about two barrels of apples in the cellar every winter—maybe russets or pound sweets. Besides the orange in the stocking, my sister and I would find some unwrapped Christmas candy, a few nuts, and one special gift. The ones I remember best were a small brass clock and a rose colored celluloid bracelet (plastic had not yet been invented).

Before school closed for the holidays, the Northam teacher sometimes allowed her pupils to draw names for a gift exchange, a most exciting project. I can't remember a single thing I ever gave for this important event, but I still have two that I received. One is a small green and gold vase with the words "Souvenir of Rutland, Vt." The other is a brown and blue cream pitcher shaped like a deer so the cream poured out through his mouth. Each was probably purchased at Woolworth's for ten cents. The teacher also gave a small remembrance to each one, maybe a handkerchief or a red pencil. The one I still treasure is a picture of my fifth grade teacher, Amy Burditt. Amy now lives in North Springfield and I visit her every summer.

The real Christmas was celebrated in the Northam Church, decorated for the occasion with a huge fir tree that reached to the ceiling. How it glistened with its colored balls, tinsel, real candles, and strings of popcorn and colored paper rings!

Long before the holiday, the women of Northam had made small, draw-string bags out of different colored netting, and filled them with nuts and ribbon candy. These, too, were hung on the tree and each child received one. By 8 p.m. the church was filled with families who arrived on foot or by horse and sleigh from Cold River, Eastham, and Northam. Cuttingsville and Shrewsbury Center must have had separate festivities,

Christian Church of North Shrewsbury, circa early 1900s.

since Northam had its own minister and the parsonage was near the present home of Con and Eva Cyr.

As the people arrived, they brought their family gifts which were mostly unwrapped and either hung on the tree or piled under it. The children sat with their teacher in the front seats, ready to take part in the program, while the choir members surrounded the pump organ to the left of the platform. How wide-eyed we were as we gazed at the gleaming tree and all the toys, storybooks, dolls, mittens, and sleds almost within reach!

One year an aunt in New Hampshire sent my mother two huge capes, maybe discarded Eastern Star regalia, lined with red velvet. Mother had Mrs. Paul Carter, a fine seamstress who lived across the road from the Wilmouth Hill Bridge, make my sister Marion and me each a velvet dress that we proudly wore more than one Christmas Eve in Northam.

Long before that, when I was too young to take part in the Christmas program, I would sit farther back with my grandmother, Damaris Aldrich Pierce. My mother was probably in the choir and my father standing in back with the men, the church being so crowded. A big woodstove gave off plenty of heat with its long stovepipe rising up toward the ceiling and then extending the entire length of the room before it exited the building.

Grandma was a small, slight person who dressed in black, wearing a long black skirt, black coat, gloves, shoes, and a small black hat. After her mother's early death at age forty-four, her father had married a much younger woman and had two sons, Ernest and Warner Aldrich. Uncle Ernest lived to celebrate his seventy-sixth wedding anniversary. Uncle Warner worked on the farm and later became the Northam cheese maker, living with his mother in the apartment at the rear of the cheese factory.

But to get back to my story about Christmas at the Northam Church. I sat close to grandma, amazed at all the excitement of being in a large crowd, staring at the dazzling tree, and surrounded by the talking and laughter before the start of the program that finally came to a close with everyone singing, "Silent Night."

Suddenly, there was a loud ringing of sleigh bells outside the door, cries of "Whoa, Whoa" and the frightening stamping of feet on the porch. Then the door opened wide and Santa rushed in, shouting, "Ho, Ho, Ho; what a night, and this heavy bag to carry!" Maybe not his exact words, but something of the sort. He hurried down the aisle to give out the presents, calling each adult or child by name.

I was really scared and upset, and began to cry and cling to grandma. Not knowing what to do, or how to calm me, she reassured me, saying, "Don't be afraid Marjorie, he's just Uncle Warner!"

As this story shows, Marjorie was ever the teacher and ever the historian with a sense of humor and connectedness to her home and her world. She also became a collector and saver of anything having to do with family history. Still stored in the top washstand drawer of each sibling's bedroom in 1999 are assorted clippings and keepsakes, including report cards and other records. Among Marion's things is this recollection of her childhood as written for a college English class (in an extraordinarily neat longhand on lined paper), dated October 18, 1921. Here, in her words as written and punctuated—many omissions of commas were duly noted by the teacher—is the assignment for which she received an "A" and the comment, "Very well done and attractive."

The Autobiography of Marion Pierce

After twenty years of life, I pause for a time to review the past. One's future is a plain, white canvas, stretching far away into eternity, but the past is a painting of glorious colors. Some are bright and gay, reflecting happiness. Here and there are sombre tones, representing the deeper, more serious experiences.

I was born in West Bridgewater, Vt., September 9, 1901. It was the home town of my mother, Gertrude Spaulding Pierce. My father, Willie E. Pierce was a native of Shrewsbury, Vt., a little town across the mountains in Rutland County. It is in Shrewsbury that most of my life has been spent. My father was a farmer and carried on his father's farm.

My childhood was very happy. For many years my only playmate was a sister, Marjorie. A farm was an ideal place for two little girls to enjoy themselves. Under an old gnarled apple tree we had our playhouse. I see again the cupboards of dishes, the cookbook and the old frog pond, where we made mud pies and carefully pinched the crusts for the custards, as we had seen mother do.

Mother taught me the alphabet and a little spelling before I entered school. I remember sitting in the kitchen and trying to write words on a piece of paper. She told me that soon I'd be going to school for a long,

Marjorie and Marion in costumes.

long time. There would be eight years in rural school. The thought of the enormous task before me filled me with grief and dread.

Nevertheless, the fall that I was six years old, I entered school. I remember the first day quite well. As the schoolhouse was a half mile from home, I was to carry my dinner. To my great delight, I was to take it in grandmother's little yellow, tin pail, that I had always admired. So I trudged down the road that first day, yellow pail in one hand, new pencil grasped tightly in the other. Like most little boys and girls I liked school and at the end of the first year I entered the third grade. All of my elementary education was received in this school—not the little red schoolhouse that writers tell about, but a bright yellow schoolhouse with brown trimmings.

In winter the snow was deep, and the drifts were high. The wind was sharp and cold. How it whistled around that old schoolhouse! Yet day after day Marjorie and I plodded through the snow carrying dinner pails and books and sometimes a hot potato in our red mittened hands to keep us warm. Noons we gathered around the little box stove to eat our dinners. Lucky the one to secure the "teacher's chair." We laughed and joked as children will. Then out of doors we rushed, grabbed our sleds and scampered away to the long hill for a few good coasts, before the bell summoned us to work.

How gladly we welcomed the coming of spring! That meant vacation was near. How stuffy the school room seemed! Then one memorable June day teacher said we might have one afternoon session of school out of doors. So seated around on the grass, we studied and recited our lessons. It was a day long remembered.

When I was about nine years old, I became interested in books. The first book that I read for my own pleasure was "Little Susie's Cousin Horace." I liked it. I read that book again and again. I could quote parts of it from memory. Then came the desire to read other books. I did so. I read more and more. I read everything interesting that I could get hold of. Thus was established a habit which is mine to-day. Books are my friends. Give me a good book and I am content.

A wagon house or tool shed stood near my home and there I used to go with my book and read and read. Then the idea came to me of writing a book. Of course I could write a book! So seated on an old box with a piece of wrapping paper and a pencil on my knees, I waited for inspiration. I wrote a few lines, describing in the longest, hardest words I knew an old castle in England. But here I stopped. The story did not come. I grew tired. Perhaps I wasn't meant for an author. Dropping my writing materials, I hastened to join my brothers and sister in their games. Thus ended my dream of fame as a story writer.

When I was twelve years old, I became addicted to writing poetry. I remember gazing soulfully out of the schoolhouse window (on November 1, 1912) and expressing in poetic language my most fanciful thoughts. I used this slight ability to make rhymes in teasing my sister and the hired girl.

Rev. Hurlburt

Colors have ever held charms for me. Even to-day the mention of certain words, names of people, places, etc. brings colors to my mind. To me New York is a bright yellow; New Orleans, orange; London, gray. I like to draw pictures and at one time became very interested in sketching likenesses of people. Sometimes I succeeded. More often I did not. It is with shame that I mention the fact that for several Sundays, I studied the minister's profile instead of listening to the sermons. The result was a sketch of our pastor which people recognized at once to my delight.

Meantime my school work was going on regularly.

Most of my teachers in the rural school were young women with ideals. One is now a teacher in the Philippines. Another has been a successful instructor in the state of Washington. My last teacher in this school graduated with honors from Mt. Holyoke this June and is now a student at the University of Chicago. These women inspired me with a desire for greater things. At last I completed the work in the Shrewsbury Public School. Our town has graduation exercises and I was the one to give the valedictory. What a big thing it was then! How trifling it appears now!

Marion's story continues with her account of high school and will be picked up in Chapter Five, where we will hear from Marjorie about going to school in nearby Rutland for a secondary education. It was to be yet another unusual occurrence that set the Pierce children apart—most rural Vermont children simply did not have the opportunity to go beyond the eight grades, which was considered a basic, public-school education at that time. But Gertrude and Willie were ambitious and desired further learning for all their children. So to make that possible, they bought the country store at Northam. The move to the store was a significant change for the family; it likewise became an important event for the community, with family members operating the country store at the crossroads for the next seventy-five years.

Haying time at the (former) Tom Stewart farm, which Willie purchased circa 1908, on old Road 14 (now site of the Bennington Camp). L to R, front row: Damaris, Marjorie, and cousins Arthur and Percy Pierce, sons of Calista and Ned Pierce. Back row: Edwin, Maude (wife of Reno), her daughter Constance, Marion, Carrie, Calista (Ned's wife), and Willie Pierce.

At Pierce house, 1919, L to R,: Gilford, Gordon, Glendon, dog Teddy. Maude Pierce, Marion, and Carlos O. Spaulding.

The home and Northam Store, circa 1918, before Willie made changes.

Chapter Four

The Country Store
at Northam

On April 24, 1918, when Marjorie was a week shy of fifteen and just finishing her first year at Rutland High School, her father purchased the general store at Northam along with its adjoining house, the barn across the way, and several acres of surrounding land for $2,000. The store had been in the extended Aldrich family for several generations so Jasper Aldrich had been pleased to sell to his Great-great-nephew Willie. Willie had long been a store customer, first buying penny candy as a young boy and later purchasing supplies for the farm. It was not a big store, although it had been enlarged once, but it was a busy one.

Here, women in long swishing skirts, often with several children in tow, purchased necessities, shared the latest news, and brought in items such as eggs or butter for trade. Cash was a scarce commodity so some families bartered for their goods or paid their tab when their crops were sold or when the mills paid the men. Children eagerly made their selections of candy from the glass case, handing over precious pennies to the storekeeper. For those lacking a sweet tooth, the pickle barrel offered a briny treat.

Farmers often stopped in after delivering their milk to the nearby cheese factory. They purchased one-hundred-pound bags of animal feed and other supplies. When they had time, they gathered around the pot-

Northam Store of Eaton E. Lord and site of Post Office, circa 1900. Perrin J. Whitney is standing by wagon wheel. E.E. Lord is behind him. Roy Whitney, young boy to left of bicycle. Willie D. Aldrich is man in cap standing on porch behind him.

History of the Store at Northam

Nathaniel Jones Aldrich was the first owner of the general store at Northam and probably operated it from 1865 to 1876. He may have started it earlier, but in 1847 when he was only twenty-seven years old, he bought a sawmill and later added a grist mill, both of which he operated with a partner. *Walton's Register*, a precursor to the *Vermont Yearbook* and an early directory of businesses and statistics for Vermont towns, lists an N.J. Aldrich Store for the first time in 1865, so, considering his other interests, this is most likely the year store operations began at this particular location in Northam. The house and store were built as separate buildings but were later joined by a series of connecting sheds.

In 1876, Aldrich sold to his first-cousin-once-removed Willard Guild, who operated the store until selling to his first-cousin Luther Lord in 1897. Lord ran it for just three years, passing it on to his son Eaton Lord in 1900. Eaton operated the store until 1911, when he sold to his first-cousin-once-removed Jasper Aldrich.

Aldrich owned it until 1918, but for the last few years his son Willie D. actually ran it. Willie E. Pierce purchased the store from Jasper, who was his great-great uncle. After Willie's death, Marjorie and Glendon operated the business for two years. Marjorie became the official owner in 1967 and operated Willie E. Pierce Groceries with assistance from her brothers. Pierce's Store, as it was generically known, was one of the oldest and longest-continuing family-owned general stores in Vermont when Marjorie, at the age of ninety, closed it in 1993.

bellied stove, lit their pipes, and swapped stories or played a game of checkers on a board placed on top of a wooden barrel.

Traditionally, the Vermont village store was the social and commercial center of a community, the one indispensable unit of a self-sufficient agrarian economy. As the market place and information center, it was the place where connections with neighbors and the world were made. Many a storekeeper dispensed advice along with the latest news, and many a business transaction was made over a discussion of crops and the weather.

Geographically large towns like Shrewsbury often had two or more stores, with each usually located at a crossroads. Some stores were located in larger villages that included an assortment of businesses and shops and large inns that catered to locals and travelers. When Willie became the owner of the store at Northam, where the main roads from Cuttingsville and Rutland converged with those from the southeastern and northernmost sections of town, there was just the blacksmith shop, a one-room schoolhouse, a country church, a cheese factory, and a few homes in the small village. But many people who worked in the mills and on the farms within a two-to-three-mile radius did most of their trade here, so business was good.

In recalling life at the store in the early days, certain details like how much her mother enjoyed working in the store and the pranks her brothers played on customers stood out in Marjorie's memory. She described a store scene vastly different from anything found in supermarkets today. That experience, as Marjorie remembers it, is depicted here in vignette form to convey what it was like to work or shop in a small country store during that era.

A Scene from Willie E. Pierce Groceries, Circa 1918

A wiry and thin man, Willie always dressed with a tie and greeted customers with a warm smile. It was his first season in the store business and deliveries to homes out by the mills along with his own farming kept him busy, so Gertrude often worked in the store, too. She loved to tend to the customers and was pleased that their oldest child Marion could watch two-year-old Gilford in the house.

On this pleasant, early summer day, Marjorie, her second born, was out in the backroom rummaging for the salt pork and salmon that Willie had sent her after. Gertrude knew that Marjorie disliked putting her arm into the big barrels of cold brine where they kept the salmon and pork. Gertrude had also disliked that chore when she had helped in her father's store.

Gordon and Glendon were nowhere to be seen, but Gertrude knew where they were by the sounds of hushed giggles and the sudden looks of consternation on the men gathered around Willie's croquenole board. The boys' favorite game was to hide in a nearby barrel with holes in it and poke the men with a stick when no one was looking. At least that was less harmful than the time they hooked up a battery to the front doorknob so Uncle Warner got a shock when he came in.

Glendon was only five, but already he was quite a prankster. Just last evening when old John Quinlan came in with a pail of nice eggs to swap, Glendon had secretly replaced his eggs with tiny bantam eggs. "By Jehovah!" John had exclaimed when he discovered the deed, causing Glendon to squeal with delight over his mischief. And today Glendon had put a tack on the chair that Mrs. Farmer had almost sat on—luckily Gertrude had diverted her.

Gertrude loved working behind the heavy brass cash register. It had been painted silver and was new looking even though it was eighteen-years old. The big pot-bellied stove stood impressively toward the back of the room. It was proving practical for taking the chill off the cold June mornings they'd been having. The store was neat and clean, just like her father's had been. As she rang up a sale, the loud cha-chang of the register filled the room.

Barrels of flour and sugar, bags of salt, several rows of dry goods, the new "canned" goods, hardware, patent medicines, and an array of practical items from footwear to clothing and farm tools filled the store. Willie had stacked the high shelves with yellow pads for the horse collars. He knew what good farmers required to take proper care of their animals.

Even though he was just ten-years old, Gordon had done a wonderful job lining the canned goods on the shelves behind the candy counter. With an eye for detail and a sharp mind, he could already help clerk and even add figures in his head for the penny-candy sales. Gertrude surveyed the room with pride and delight as she handed Harry Russell change for his purchase of a half-pound of chocolates.

Glendon Pierce

Measuring out flour and sugar for the blacksmith's wife, Gertrude observed that the barrels of flour, sugar, and crackers were almost empty, a good sign. Just yesterday they had sold two pairs of boots, ten sacks of grain, a buggy-whip, and three pounds of salt pork in addition to the usual small orders. It had been bold of her to encourage Willie to buy out old Jasper, but Gertrude wanted to send all their children to high school so they would need more than a farming income.

Whistling a tune her father had taught her, Gertrude turned her attention to a small child who was standing on tiptoe on the overturned box at the candy counter. He was pointing to the chocolate teddy bears. They had been Marjorie's favorite candy when she was his age. When Jasper owned the store, he liked to make sure Marjorie got a bear with a penny tucked in its marshmallow center. She had been his favorite because she reminded him of his own little girl who died at an early age.

Just then Marjorie came in with the salmon and pork and gave it to Willie to weigh. Mrs. Whitney said they were "just the right size," and Marjorie smiled as she returned to the storeroom for the canning jars. Just fifteen years old, she was already an industrious worker and straight "A" student like her older sister Marion.

After ringing up the sale, Willie went out to pump the kerosene for Quincy Wheeler and Richard Mandigo. Richard said that they'd had

Gordon as Black Hawk

snow on the mountain that morning. Gertrude was glad the kerosene tank was outside; other stores had it inside, where it always dripped from the can onto the floor. She preferred the aroma of the store without the kerosene smell mixed in—it was so much nicer and the pine floor stayed so much cleaner.

It had been an especially busy day at the kerosene pump because tonight the men would come to the store after dinner to play cards or croquenole and talk about their crops. It would be dark when they left, and they would need their lanterns to make their way home. Willie would be there with them, but Gertrude would be in the house, playing the organ and teaching Marion and Marjorie a duet for the church service on Sunday. Daisy Whitney and Verna Aldrich had sung at the grange supper last week, and Marjorie had been after Gertrude all week to teach her and Marion a new song. Marjorie noticed things like that, but Marion was more mild mannered. Still, she had a nice sisterly influence on Marjorie and that had helped Marjorie adjust to living in Rutland the past school year. That pleased Gertrude, too.

The wooden-works clock struck four. Time for Gertrude to go to the house and put the supper on. She instructed Marjorie to stay and help Willie until closing time and called to Gordon and Glendon to accompany her. It wouldn't do to have them poke Reverend Hurlburt when he came in for his salt pork!

Marjorie laughed as she enjoyed her memories of how "Glendon was quite the jokester" and had often engaged his older brother Gordon in some mischief in the store. "He continued to do that throughout his life," she added with a smile, noting he "got it from my father's side of the family." She also delighted in telling about all the items that her father once sold and how "he would go out back to his storeroom and wheel the heavy sacks of grain out onto the store platform in front. The sale of grain was really the big income producer," she noted of his early years in the store business.

In recalling the move from the farm to the store, Marjorie described it as, "a time of excitement as we went from room to room, exploring the new place where we each had our own bedroom." What happened at the family farm also stands out in her memory.

Edwin, Damaris, and their daughter Carrie moved to Rutland. Edwin died a year later in 1919 and Damaris lived to be almost ninety-eight.

My father rented the farm to George and Florence Clark, and they let the farm run down and the horses grow thin. George would carry milk to Northam Cheese Factory and stop at the store on the way home. My father felt very sad to see the condition of the old gray horses that used to work so faithfully for him, so he would wheel out a one-hundred-pound sack of grain onto the store platform and give it to George, admonishing him to "Take this grain and feed it to old Jack and Dennis!"

As soon as he could find a buyer, my father sold the farm, which angered George. He sold it in September to Charles Lawrence.

Later, Charlie Lawrence was killed with a cant hook by a man named Kennison who was standing on a load of logs down by the mill in Pitts Hollow—also called Humble Hollow by Harry Russell. It was self-defense, as Lawrence was drunk and angered by some kind of fracas his son Fred had in Rutland the night before. Lawrence started to climb up on the load, threatening to kill the man who warned him to come no nearer or he would strike him. Lawrence died a few hours later. Then his son Fred got the farm.

When Charlie's estate was settled, my father was an appraiser for the probate court. The relatives thought Charlie had money hidden away. Willie helped search through the sugarhouse and wagon shed, but no money was found.

Since then the farm property changed owners several times, some of the acreage was sold off, the barns were torn down, and the ell was taken off the house. As the farm reverted to a residence, the meadows and gardens grew over and trees were left to the wild. [The restoration of the house in the 1990s by its new owners, the Orlichs, pleased Marjorie immensely.]

With help from Gertrude and their children, Willie operated the store and continued to do "quite a bit of farming for many years," Marjorie added.

He kept horses and six to eight head of cattle, cut hay, planted potatoes, and carried milk to the cheese factory. He used the meadows he owned on the Bennington Camp Road, the Cold River Road, and the Upper Cold River Road for pasturing or haying. He kept his cows on the lower level of the barn across from the house and the horses on the upper level.

My father also made several repairs to the house. He added a large back porch, insulated the house, and built a dormer window. He tore down the old Thomas Stewart house and the dilapidated Northam blacksmith shop, which he had bought for $75, and used the lumber to repair his shed and barn and to build a two-car garage. He replaced the floor of the front porch, which connected the house to the store, with a cement surface. In 1942, the government geological survey put a bench marker in the cement by the store. It gives the elevation of the property as 1,758 feet above sea level.

Willie's barn and carriage shed opposite the house. The family had corn roasts on bank beyond the barn.

Hardworking and frugal, Willie was talented at making things stretch. Although soft spoken, he was affable and active in civic affairs during these years. He had already served as a Representative to the Legislature in 1912 and soon became a town selectman. Willie was also very practical and not against adapting to change when it made life a little easier. Thus, he bought a Republic truck around 1920. He also hooked up a gasoline-powered electric generator in the store in the 1930s to have electricity there before the power line came to Northam, Marjorie related.

The friendly and industrious natures of Gertrude and Willie made the store a successful venture and a community resource. Later, in the 1940s, they would begin to see a steady decline in business due to the changing nature of the town (the loss of the mills, farms, cheese factories, and other small businesses) and the attraction of larger stores in Rutland. But Willie, practical as ever, was fond of saying that there was nothing to do about change except "learn to live with it," and tending store remained a source of satisfaction for as long as they lived.

Although she was destined to one day own W. E. Pierce Groceries, Marjorie didn't spend a great deal of time working there in her teenage years. As she was already in high school in Rutland, she recalled that she probably helped out the summers after her freshman and sophomore years and when home on weekends or for vacations (as did her siblings). But it would be 1958 before she "had any regular hours as a store clerk."

Uncle Reno Pierce, Glendon, Gordon, Gilford, 1927.

The store front after Willie remodeled it, but before his sign went up. He added the gasoline pump around 1923.

62

Marjorie, top left and right college age; left at camp clowning around.

Waitresses shelling peas at Eagle Camp. Marion is second from left with big smile, and Marjorie far right.

Chapter Five

From Northam to the University
1917 - 1925

Marjorie remembered her parents as providing good role models for their children during their growing-up years. Their example reinforced within her and her siblings "the need to work hard and do well."

Father paid for twenty years of room and board to put his five children through high school. It wasn't easy for him. He was very industrious.

My mother wanted to see us go further. She was a school teacher before she married my father, so she taught us the alphabet and nursery rhymes at a very young age. Then my mother worked in both the house and store and sold milk to a neighbor for seven cents a quart to help put us through school. She was ambitious.

So starting with Marion, all five Pierce siblings went to school in Rutland for grades nine through twelve. Interestingly, the three oldest, Marion, Marjorie, and Gordon, all earned the distinction of being named the valedictorians of their respective high school classes. "Education beyond high school became each child's responsibility," Marjorie added, noting that "we not only had to study hard but also work to be able to afford college."

64

Her parents also inspired an attitude of service to others; Gertrude through her activity with the church and by serving on the local school board for many years and Willie through positions as a selectman, overseer of the poor, and state representative. Both parents also extended a warm welcome to patrons at the store and to newcomers. They showed folks that they were happy to see them and have them as customers and as neighbors. It was a trait that was to become a Pierce family trademark.

Willie and Gertrude never made "a big deal" out of any of this, however; they simply followed and practiced the Puritan work ethic which carried with it a strong sense of duty and responsibility. Their example led to ingrained traits of industry, thrift, helpfulness, friendliness, and resourcefulness in their children. It also led to a love of learning and the desire to do well in school so as to "please our sacrificing parents."

Career planning was not a term in use in 1919 or 1921 when Marion and Marjorie graduated from high school, but with guidance from people who recognized their intelligence and industriousness, they set out to develop their gifts with a university education. This was somewhat unconventional for men or women during this era, but for both Marion and Marjorie, a "quiet ambition" was stirring within.

182 South Main Street, Rutland. Home of Clyde Spaulding.

It was during their teenage years that Marjorie and Marion both made the transition to living away from home. They spent weeks at a time living with relatives in Rutland so they could attend high school there. (In those days, most rural towns did not have their own secondary schools, so boarding in a town that did was necessary where the distance was great or inconvenient.) During these separations from their parents and brothers, the young sisters learned to be on their own. Because Marion was two years older than Marjorie, she "knew the ropes. This softened the shock of going away" and made Marjorie's transition somewhat easier, although she recalled "being filled with some trepidation, too."

I entered Rutland High School ten miles away on a dirt road barely passable in winter and spring "mud time." It was often lonely, being home only once in three or four weeks, and I recall one period of eight weeks before returning to my family. I walked a mile to school the first year, up a long hill on South Main Street. It was called Gouger Hill. The school was where the fire station is today, near the park.

My first year Marion and I lived with my mother's youngest brother, Uncle Clyde Spaulding, across from the Fairgrounds, where the McDonald's is today. He was secretary of Howe Scale Works and worked there for forty-two years.

The next year Marion and I lived on Morse Place, which was only a few blocks away from the school. We boarded with a family who were related to Willard Guild of Shrewsbury. My third year, I lived with Uncle Carlos, who had moved to a big house on the corner of Woodstock Avenue and East Street. My last year, my uncle had purchased the house with the peaked tower by the Dana School, and I lived there.

My father would pick us up in the two-seat wagon or the sleigh and take us home for a weekend or a school vacation. There were many times he would get stuck in mud season down by alcohol springs, a place where men stopped to get water for their liquor.

By my senior year, he had a Republic truck and would often stop at Eddy Ice on the way home to get a big four-foot block of ice which he would fasten to the front bumper.

Marjorie has fond memories of several of her high school teachers.

Grandma Meldon, the French teacher, dressed in black clothing with black beads and black shoes. The school was called the Meldon School after Grandma Meldon, because she was held in such high esteem. Miss Ruth Temple, the Latin teacher, was a very tall, regal woman who was college caliber. Mr. Harold O'Brien, a stern man, who was also an athletic coach, was my math teacher.

Lots of the pupils were afraid of him or stood in great awe of him. I was in awe of being in his class. He enjoyed teaching and took a lot of pleasure in having a small class of good scholars. I remember how he conducted math class.

He would say, "Miss Pierce, you will go to the board. Miss Pierce, you will make a triangle. Miss Pierce, you will make measurements and explain the solution to today's problem."

One time, I just stood there, semi-scared.

He said, "Why don't you start?"

I faltered, then began: "The square of the hypotenuse is equal to the square of . . ." and then hesitated as he boomed, "Say it with flowers!"

Say it with flowers was frequent advice in newspaper ads of a prominent Rutland florist of that time. So he was making a kind of joke, but no one dared laugh. He appeared domineering and aloof, but at heart he was not. He was probably chuckling to himself.

For English classes we had Helen Harlow and her sister Genevra. Both were nice, mild-mannered, and refined ladies.

Teachers always wore long skirts or dresses down to the ankles. They were very proper and formal, and more distant than when I was teaching or today.

It was during these years that Marjorie was beginning to seek out and enjoy the larger world. Living in Rutland had spurred her inter-

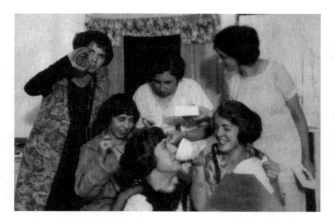

Marjorie and high school girlfriends in Rutland.

est in new places, and her own outgoing and vivacious nature allowed her to make friends easily. She attended the Universalist Church there with her new friends and joined its active youth group, thus enlarging her social circle. Her enthusiasm for new experiences and adventures also led her to take a job working at a summer camp on Lake Champlain.

One of my high school girlfriends, Dorothy Perry, invited me to wait on tables with her at her grandparents' camp, telling me to write to her grandfather and ask for a job. Eagle Camp catered to families, and guests ate family style at long tables in a rustic log dining hall. Young girls were hired as waitresses for the three meals and also had some kitchen duties for food preparation and clean-up.

Eagle Camp was located in South Hero on a nice cove and had cottages for older campers who wanted more comfort, but most of the camp had tents with comfortable cots, two to a tent.

The motto of the camp was "Style is Dead, Comfort is King." It was one of the owner's rules to dress informally. Staff wore bloomers, middy blouses, and tennis shoes, nothing fancy. If guests arrived dressed in formal clothes, they were shown the sign with the motto, and Grandpa Perry would tell them "Comfort is King!"

The Perry family were very nice to me, and I ended up calling them Grandpa and Grandma Perry, Aunt Alma and Uncle John, as if they were my own relatives. They were connected to the Shrewsbury Russells, too.

Marjorie spent three pleasant summers working there during 1920, 1921, and 1922. She saved many photographs from this era and could still recall names and stories about the friends she made there. She also remembered making "seventy dollars one summer and spending ten dollars on a pretty coat," while saving the rest for college. [Later, during war time in 1945 when staffing was hard to come by, Marjorie received a frantic call from the owner's "granddaughter asking me to help out again." At age forty-two, she returned as head waitress and enjoyed her time there as much as she had in her younger years.]

During her college years, Marjorie also worked as a waitress at a large hotel on Loon Lake in New York with a Shrewsbury friend Katherine Hinkly. "It was different from Eagle Camp. It was a more formal place where more well-to-do people summered. It probably paid more, and I wanted to live in a college dormitory so maybe that was why I switched. I don't think I liked it as well, though."

68

Marjorie with hat, Alice Perry Fuller head of camp 5th top row, sister Rose Perry Fuller to her left, Grandpa Perry to right and Robert Drury, camp supervisor and in charge of men, to his right. Marion is third from right middle row.

Marjorie,Barney McGoogle, camp.

The UVM Years

Having enjoyed high school, Marjorie began to think about her future. She knew she wanted to learn more and see new places, but she also realized that her family had limited means and that she herself would be expected to pay for any further schooling. Marion had put off going to the University of Vermont where she had received a scholarship for a year's tuition because money for room and board was a problem. So Marjorie was well aware of the difficulty of making plans, yet very desirous of doing something. Fortunately, someone recognized her talent and ambition and steered her in the direction of a good college education.

When I got to be a senior, I began to wonder about my future. I decided to go to Rutland Business College, which was owned by L.J.

Eggleston, who was distantly connected to Shrewsbury. He was a brilliant man who had married a Shrewsbury girl.

One day Principal Abbott of Rutland High School called me into his office. He asked me what I intended to do after graduation. I told him my thoughts, but he said I should go to college, not business school.

I told him I had no money. He said, "I'm going to help you." As class valedictorian, I received $100 to be used toward tuition. He also arranged that I should live with a professor and earn my room and board.

Marjorie, 1921

With Mr. Abbott's support, her savings from her summer work, the scholarship, and some small financial help from her parents, Marjorie was able to enroll at the University of Vermont (UVM) that following fall. In a letter she wrote to "Little Seymour" Bassett on the occasion of his seventy-fifth birthday in 1988, she recalled this time as follows:

In 1921 North Shrewsbury and Burlington were two different worlds. I was just a country girl, from a small town and very unsophisticated, a far cry from other college freshmen. Determined to warrant the support of my sacrificing parents and my Rutland High School principal, I began this new career with both anxiety and anticipation.

It was fall 1921 when, at age eighteen, I settled in the cozy, third floor bedroom at the home of Professor and Mrs. Bassett at 295 Prospect Street and was introduced to their three children, Raymond, Catherine, and Seymour. They must have been good and well-trained youngsters, for I can recall no untoward behavior or dissension ever occurring.

I was involved with survival in a strange environment, new and exacting housework duties, adjusting to the new family, and especially to the long hours of study required to maintain a creditable standing in my classes at UVM.

Of course, the children were in school and upon returning home might play outdoors while I would be in the kitchen or studying in my room. I had no real responsibility for them other than to house-sit and see that they went to bed on time the rare evenings when their parents went out on social occasions.

Although an employee of sorts, I always sat at the table with the family after serving the meal. Seymour sat beside his mother so she could help him with his food. Often, she would help clear the table and carry the dishes through the pantry and into the kitchen.

Professor Bassett, a Greek professor at the university, was a quiet man who seemed to me somewhat eccentric. I stood in awe of him and his unusual daily routine and diet. For breakfast, I prepared his hot oatmeal, fruit, and dark bran toast. He always had a supply of brown, crumbly squares baked with various grains.

Mrs. Bassett kept an enormous jar of mayonnaise in the pantry. She made it with eggs and a certain oil and it would last for days on end. Only Professor Bassett could use it!

Professor Bassett rarely remained downstairs for any length of time. During a brief morning period, he might sit in the living room to read the newspaper while I dust mopped around his feet. After dinner he would remain downstairs whenever men gathered for a meeting at his home or if visitors like Professors Prindle or Myrick arrived. Otherwise, he would retire to his workshop and studio on the third floor until very late at night, usually shouting goodnight to me as he descended the stairs.

An undoubted head of the family, Professor Bassett made sure to give me explicit orders as to the exact words I should use when going to the front door or answering the phone. This type of discipline has often proved helpful to me in later years.

I believe he took a real interest in my welfare and scholastic progress. If we both had classes the same hour, he liked to have me walk the fifteen-minute distance to the campus with him, while engaging in "elevated conversation."

When my Latin professor persisted in asking me out, I did finally attend a symphony concert with him. Shortly after, Professor Bassett commented to me, "Marjorie, you don't have to go out with Lester if you don't wish to."

Mrs. Bassett was not only a person of charm, but also a capable and kindly home manager. In a letter dated March 14, 1922, I found the following comment: "The Boy Scout Troop is going to have a Pie Walk.

Instead of walking for the cake, they will walk for the pie. Mrs. Bassett is going to make a pie for them."

Her white hair contrasted with her almost black eyebrows and ice cream complexion. She scorned make-up, but when going out for an evening, would bathe her face with very hot water followed by dashes of cold spray that gave her cheeks a rosy-pink glow. Mrs. Bassett's graceful ease and warm personality gained for her the respect and admiration of all with whom she came in contact.

By the end of my sophomore year at UVM, I felt the need to mingle more with my classmates and have the experience of living in a dormitory. After obtaining a needed loan from the Wilbur Fund, thanks to President Guy Bailey, I was able to spend my last two years with good friends at Campus House.

*Marjorie practicing
the sword dance at UVM.*

There was a certain reluctance in leaving the Bassett family and their now-familiar home surroundings. It was there that I grew and learned lessons that have served me well in later years. For their kindness and support I shall always feel grateful.

Marjorie's first impression of UVM was that, "It was very large. It was far smaller than it is today, but to me, coming from a small town, it seemed enormous!" She also recalled that she "entered the dormitory after two years out of a feeling that I should have closer contact with college life." The loan helped make this possible, but she also augmented this assistance by washing and ironing for the House Mother, Miss Cummings. Her Uncle Ned Pierce, who had worked his way up to president of the Elias Lyman Coal Company, and his wife lived nearby on North Prospect Street, so she had dinner at their home on occasion and also did housework for them to earn extra money.

The classes she took included French, English, math, and education courses. Her most specific memory of this time was written down some years later when she wrote a five-page essay entitled, "A Few Recollections of a Teacher."

> My favorite teacher was Professor Arthur Myrick, head of the French Department. The subject was easy for me since I had received excellent training in both conversation and fundamentals from my outstanding high school teacher Miss Meldon. Influenced by Professor Myrick's stories of life in Paris and the Alpine city of Grenoble, I resolved to study there also some day. It was largely due to his recommendations and those of Professor Douglas, under whom I did practice teaching in Burlington, that I obtained my first job in Bethel and paid off my college debts.

Marjorie couldn't remember the exact cost of her four years of college, but a university researcher reported that from 1921 to 1923 tuition was $175 a year and $225 for each of the next two years. All high-school valedictorians graduating from a college-preparatory program of studies received a $100 Honor Scholarship to be used toward the first year's tuition; room and board was $320 a year; fees probably ran under $50 for four years; and textbook costs, $8 to $25 a year. So her college tab probably came to $1500 plus personal expenses.

What Marjorie most vividly remembers was her desire to live at Campus House. She told this story as if it were yesterday.

> Marion didn't go right to college after high school. She became a teacher at Northam and had both Glendon and Gordon as her pupils. She earned $15 a week and taught for two years which made her rich!
> So you see, because she had savings, Marion could afford to live in a college dormitory all four years, but I had to work for my room and board in the home of a college professor.

It's a note of sibling rivalry that Marjorie told good naturedly, chuckling at the notion that Marion was "rich," and realizing how it had bothered her and that she had been a little envious. [Marion had probably earned around $1000, which together with her Honor Scholarship, parental help, and summer earnings probably paid for her four years without the necessity of loans, thus making her truly "rich."] In telling such stories, Marjorie often noted the contrast in their personalities and characters. It is an observation that shows up well in this continuation of Marion's story.

Marion's Autobiography Part II

In the fall my parents gave me the opportunity of attending the Rutland High School. I was lonesome at first, but gradually became accustomed to the new life. I took the classical course and found the new subjects very fascinating. My high school days were uneventful—just the life of an ordinary high school student. I made few close friends, yet I liked all the girls and had no enemies. Two of my high school teachers, whom I greatly respect and ad-

Marion 1919

mire, have had no little influence on my life. Finally June 1919 came, bringing my high school days to a close. I happened to be valedictorian and so received an Honor Scholarship from the University of Vermont.

I wished very much to enter college that fall, but, because of my health and for financial reasons, my parents did not advise it.

Although I had not teacher's training, I was offered a school in my home town—the very school that I had attended for eight years. I accepted the offer and thus began a career as a rural school teacher. Here to-fore I had thought of a teacher as a paragon of knowledge whose education was practically completed and whose life was one of ease. I soon found out my mistake. How much I had forgotten about history, geography, physiology and numerous other subjects taught in a rural school!

The first year there were thirteen pupils. The grades ranged from first to eighth; the pupils, from tiny tots and active youngsters to boys and girls in the overgrown, awkward stage of life. I found I had to work and study as hard as ever; that, in fact, I must know the subject I was trying to teach.

Then the problem of discipline! What teacher doesn't have it? The fact that I was in my home town, in my home school, schoolmate of some of my pupils and intimately acquainted with each one certainly had its

Northam School, where Marion and Gordon taught.

advantages and disadvantages. Of course I was called "Marion." That was to be expected. I did not mind. The little people did not prove difficult, in spite of the fact that one was a lively brother of mine. The large boys and girls worried me the most. But isn't it true in most country schools? One boy laughed easily. One big girl twisted, squirmed and sulked every time her test mark was low. Another large boy had the reputation of being a regular "cut-up."

My days were days of worry. My nights were horrible nightmares of an uproarious school room. Morning, noon, and night I practiced stern and terrible looks, which I might perhaps deem necessary to use. I am thankful, beyond measure, that my fears were in vain. I have never used corporal punishment to correct a child. In my experience the honor system answers in most cases. Naughtiness on the part of a pupil did not make me angry, but it did hurt me deeply. If boys and girls have plenty of interesting work, they will find no time for mischief. I tried to keep constantly in mind the old saying, "Keep them busy, or they will keep you busy." In this way my problem of discipline was solved.

So for two years I worked and planned in the little old schoolhouse, which I had attended as a pupil. I have written of the vexations of school life for a teacher, but these are not uppermost in my memory. I see, as if it were but yesterday, the red geraniums in the window, the sun flooding into the room, the rows of bright faces before me. What a happy time! How much it has meant and still means to me and how grateful I am for the privilege of that experience!

This spring I had a decision to make. Should I teach in this school a third year or should I continue my studies? Duty seemed to point to the last. And wisely, I hope, I chose to enter U.V.M. with my sister.

I have no definite plans for the future. One can only trust. But may my life be useful to my fellowmen, and, as some one has said, "may this world be a little better, because I have lived."

Prophetically, the teacher had commented in the left margin, "I am sure of it."

After their successful UVM years in the literary-scientific course of study, Marion graduated magna cum laude and Marjorie graduated cum laude; both were elected to Phi Beta Kappa and earned Ph.B. degrees [a bachelor of philosophy degree] in 1925. Having found her direction by now, Marion went on to further studies in social work and counseling at Smith College before going to work in this field in Philadelphia. Marjorie had also discovered a calling and went on to a career that spanned thirty-two years in teaching, further study, and wide travel.

These were pursuits to which the learned young women were ideally suited, but for the first time since leaving the confines of a small rural community, they were going their separate ways. Following their hearts' inclinations, they set out in different directions. Industrious and independent, they were eager to enter the larger world and use their skills to earn a living.

Marjorie, left Marion, right at home in Northam circa 1929.

Mademoiselle Pierce in the classroom in Attleboro, 1949.

Top L to R: Miss Sharp, Marjorie, Helen Whipple, Mrs. Snow, Mrs. Allen Middle row: Mrs. Tirrill, Gladys Whipple. Bottom: Mr. Prator, Prof. French, Miss Urban, Evelyn Fuller, Audrey Poeckert, Jane Reinaud, Miss Wilson, Miss Bradley, Madame Fombaron, Miss Anderson, Dr. Snow. Seated: Ruth Moody.

Chapter Six

A Life in Teaching & Travel
1925-1958

If Marjorie had known very little of the outside world while growing up in Northam during her grade-school years, she had begun to make up for that during her high school and college years. Had there been a high-school position open in the Rutland region when she finished college in 1925, she might have returned to live at home or in the area with relatives. Instead, she left home to pursue a teaching position in Bethel, Vermont and once again saw her world expand.

Her independence and love of learning also led her to travel out of the country, first to Montreal and then to France, so that she could become more proficient in French. She was finding herself drawn to teaching this language, and, as we have seen, she was being increasingly influenced by those whom she admired in the professional world.

A sense of adventure also figured into this desire for expanding horizons and exploring the world. The stories told by Edwin and Damaris—as well as by other relatives who traveled—had fueled her imagination from a young age. Perhaps one must live in a rural area like Shrewsbury to appreciate the "pioneering spirit" that comes from living close to the elements in a rugged mountain environment. Surely, those early trips over the Green Mountains had reinforced an adventurous soul nourished on firsthand stories of the Civil War and the Wild West.

As a young girl, Marjorie was neither a homebody nor timid. She tried skiing on the rudimentary wooden boards of the day (over behind the barn), but "never feeling comfortable on them," she preferred and stuck to snowshoeing and ice skating. Her love of the outdoors carried over to her adult teaching years and eventually to her penchant for travel. Another factor which fueled her growing ambition to see the world and learn more was her innate interest in and appreciation for world events, whether Lindbergh's first transatlantic flight, Amelia Earhart's missing plane, or the sinking of the Titanic. She was an inveterate clipper of newspaper stories about the major events of the day and saved hundreds of articles throughout her life. The world was a fascinating place to her and well worth learning about, so she took on extra jobs to be able to afford to travel and experience firsthand the places and history that so intrigued her.

From 1925 to 1940, Marjorie used seven of her summers to pursue a master's degree and several more for educational travel. This affinity for travel and study didn't change until 1950, when her mother's health began to fail and she returned home summers to help her family.

After college graduation, Marjorie found a position in Bethel, Vermont, where she taught French, Latin, and math at Whitcomb High School for three years. She recalled that her starting salary was "$1,100 and increased $100 each succeeding year." She was particularly pleased to have obtained this job because her Uncle Carlos lived in Bethel and gave her some additional part-time work.

> Carl [Carlos] Spaulding was my mother's brother and owned the Spaulding Press and the Bethel Theater. He gave me small jobs, and the extra money helped me to pay off my college loans faster. I worked in his printing office on occasion, doing jobs like folding Town Reports, which he printed for most of the surrounding communities.
>
> He hired a woman or his son Kenneth to play piano in the pit at the movie theater, playing along with the film's action as this was the day of the silent movie. I saw my first "talking" picture at this theater [probably in 1927].
>
> Once in awhile, he would give me a piece of clear glass, about 2.5 inches by 4 inches, and a flier advertising the next movie. I would take a

pen and colored inks and sketch the picture on the glass and write out the announcement: "Coming Next Tuesday and Wednesday, The Cobra!" or some such intriguing title that would be flashed on the screen at the end of the first movie. It was difficult work because the inks would run on the slick glass surface.

The Fisher residence in Bethel

While she enjoyed being near her relatives, Marjorie actually boarded with the Fishers, a kindly German family with three children, who lived at the top of a big hill overlooking the White River. "They lived in a fine brick house with a large front yard not too far from the school. I took my meals with them and was treated as a member of the family," she recalled fondly.

Altogether, it was a "most pleasant time" as she enjoyed both her surroundings and her pupils. In a remembrance, which she entitled "A Few Recollections of a Teacher," Marjorie wrote:

Life in Bethel was pleasant and not too demanding. The school numbered about one-hundred pupils. The principal, who also taught, and three teachers composed the faculty. There I taught French, Math, and Latin.

An art teacher came about twice a week. She nearly proved my undoing, for I was told to take her Mechanical Drawing classes during her absence of a month.

Having recourse to an artist's correspondence course, the small class of about six rather reluctantly drew circles, squares, cubes and parallel lines ad infinitum, along with the intricate (to me) drawing specified in the day's lesson book.

Not knowing how to correct the work they passed in, I decided that Clayton M. seemed capable and knew what he was doing. I then compared the other drawings to his, checking with red pencil any places that differed. Two red marks rated an 'A,' 3 or 4 a 'B,' and more, a 'C.' I dared not fail anyone and no questions were ever asked or protests made before the regular teacher's welcome return!

The only real scandal to upset the faculty and students was caused by a very pretty, well-mannered girl in my class who was noticeably pregnant, yet who persisted in attending school, sweetly smiling at everyone and dutifully preparing her lessons. Our principal was an affable man, reluctant to hurt anyone's feelings. As a result, neither he nor the school-board authorities did anything and the girl stayed on until Nature forced her to retire. Nevertheless, this situation became the talk of the town.

. . .

One stormy winter's night, I chaperoned the girls' strong and skillful basketball team to Rochester. Our boys' team took to the floor first. The girls played between the halves and drew as much interest and cheering in winning as did our boys who lost.

After the games, there was a gay party with refreshments and dancing on the gym floor. In spite of the cold and uncertain driving conditions, our old, seven-seater car lumbered through the drifts on the late return trip.

Upon reaching the stately brick home of the Fishers, I crept quietly up the stairs and turned on the light. There sat a bulgy looking man in the rocking chair by my window, with wide-brimmed hat pulled down over his eyes as if asleep. Amazed, but not really frightened as Mrs. Fisher had feared I would be, I left him there, and the next morning the family and I had a good laugh on the joke they had played on me.

One of Marjorie's contributions to the school was to found a Girls Outing Club, for which she organized sporting events and conducted meets, complete with ice skating and snowshoeing contests. She also ran some hikes in the fall, but it was the winter events she remembered most, adding that about fifteen to twenty girls participated in the club and its activities.

I always enjoyed snowshoeing in winter so I bought a pair of snowshoes from a man in Gaysville. He made them by hand and charged me less than ten dollars for them!

I thought my pupils might enjoy snowshoeing, too, so I asked a few to go out with me. Girls never had a chance to get out and be athletic. I

Outing club sports meet, Marjorie on right.

thought there should be more opportunities for them. We would go out once a week and take little trips on snowshoes.

During her third year in Bethel, Marjorie lived at the home of Frank and Edith Putnam where she had a "nice room with big windows." This home was on the other side of the river from the school, so Marjorie reached it by walking through a covered bridge and up a hill. It was while living there that the Great Flood of 1927 occurred. It began on November 2 when two different storms, one from the Gulf of Mexico and one from the Great Lakes, converged over Vermont and dumped torrential rains for three days. Because the ground was already saturated, many towns saw their rivers overflow and flood the streets, causing tremendous damage. Marjorie recalled the devastation with a sense of awe and tragic loss.

It was worse than anything I had seen in Vermont. I woke up one night to find Edith out walking, patrolling the street and watching the river rise. It was a very bad flood. We saw an entire house go down the river. All night there was the incessant sound of debris crashing along the swollen waters.

Morning brought an unbelievable scene of disaster. The covered bridge had been washed away; houses were undermined, toppled over, or washed away entirely; bridges were gone; and the railroad track was hanging suspended over the river like a loose rope swinging between two posts.

Work gangs put up a crude fence along one side of the drooping track. Men stood six to eight feet apart to give a hand to those of us who were obliged to cross the river to get to school. For many days, this fearful crossing took place, a distance perhaps of one-hundred feet along the swaying track with gaping empty spaces between the ties.

After the flood, we took a ride to Gaysville and saw that the entire river side of the town was gone. I believe it was the worst flood in Vermont's history. [Historians concur, noting both the numbers of towns affected and the extreme loss of life with fifty-five persons drowning.]

For her fourth year in teaching, Marjorie accepted a position in Montpelier, the state capitol, where the school was larger and the salary "more generous at $1600 a year!" She taught French and English and found her students "courteous, well behaved, and cooperative." She felt fortunate to share an apartment with another teacher, Polly Parker, who helped her adjust to the new school and new town. In her "Recollections," Marjorie wrote:

> Principal Kambour was efficient and popular. We all looked forward to mornings when there was an assembly, and especially when Mr. Kambour stepped to the front of the stage and sang, accompanied by the fine school pianist. Everyone's favorite was "Lord Jeffrey Amherst," his college song, which always resulted in prolonged applause. Mr. Kambour was a vigorous, thickset man who could really belt it out! The students loved that ballad. . . .
>
> In those days of 1928-1929, teachers were highly respected and never mingled socially with their pupils. Accordingly, I received a real surprise early in the school year at a dance presented by the Seniors.
>
> As chaperones, the faculty sat in a small balcony reached by a narrow stairway, while students and their guests occupied the main floor of the hall where an orchestra was playing.
>
> Soon a dauntless student ascended the stairs and asked me to dance. I hesitated, aware of the school's strict, though unwritten code of conduct, but Polly nodded, so I accepted and enjoyed a most pleasant evening for I loved to dance. This marked a start in pupil-teacher communication, something quite common today.

During the summers of 1926 and 1927 (the year Lindbergh crossed the ocean by plane), Marjorie and her college friend Doris Hall, who taught French in Massachusetts, attended McGill University's Ecole d'Ete in Montreal, where they took French classes and received a diploma of First Class at the Royal Victoria College. In 1928, they began discussing the idea of taking a year off from teaching "to enlarge our

The bridge Marjorie crossed when the covered bridge was swept away.

Wreckage of RR bridge near the station, Bethel, VT.

*Devastation of the
1927 Flood
in Bethel, VT*

*River St. looking from Miller house toward the bridge,
showing the Charles Lilley house gone.*

Doris Hall

French experience. I was asked to return to my Montpelier teaching position; I wasn't fired," Marjorie stressed with her usual impish delight, noting that, "What I really wanted to do was to travel and learn more."

Inspired by the professor who had studied abroad and regaled them with his stories and impressive knowledge of French culture, they decided to "follow in his footsteps." In June 1929, having paid off her college debt and with her life savings of over $1,000 in hand, Marjorie joined Doris and took a train to Burlington and then on to Montreal and Quebec, where they boarded a steamer bound for France. After landing, they took a train to Paris, arriving amidst the glory of summer and the excitement of study and seeing the world!

They took some summer courses at the University of Grenoble in the French Alps, as Professor Myrick had done, and then traveled before enrolling for the school year at the Sorbonne in Paris. Their stay was enlivened with side trips to England, Scotland, Holland, Belgium, Switzerland, Italy, Germany, the French Riviera, and Venice, one of Marjorie's favorite places.

Their adventures included being arrested for sitting in a train station waiting room without a ticket, a loitering clearly forbidden by the sign they had read. "The window hadn't opened yet," Marjorie noted in their defense. The local gendarme came along, and, since they had no tickets to show, he mistook them for "ladies of the night." Marjorie was hauled off to the local police station to give an accounting or be jailed, leaving a worried Doris sitting there with the luggage.

At the station, Marjorie cleverly faked being "etudiant American ne comprend pas," poor French for "I'm an American student and don't understand." She repeated this, throwing in a good, "Ne parlez Francais," (no speak French) until they finally let her go!

"Imagine ME being taken off to jail!" she was fond of exclaiming whenever she recounted this episode, enjoying the absolute ludicrousness of it and feigning mock horror at the indignity.

Messages on the postcards she sent to family, which were saved for posterity after being shared with friends, neighbors, schoolmates, and relatives [an important connection to the wider world in the era before radio and television], show that almost getting arrested wasn't the only excitement she was finding. Marjorie enjoyed walking around the towns everywhere they

Marjorie sailing on the Normandie

went and especially delighted in experiencing the culture and traditions of the places they visited. Taking in the Passion Play in Germany was one such highlight, while visiting Mount Vesuvius in Italy was another.

> It was after our final exams at the Sorbonne that I went to Italy and had a most unusual experience. I was on a group tour and was quite surprised that the people in the group were allowed to go up to the top of the volcano. I climbed to the very top of Mount Vesuvius, stood on the rim, and looked down into the center of the volcano. It was smoking!
>
> Now, how many people in Vermont or New England have done that?
>
> I was impressed that it was a dangerous thing to go up there because it could have erupted. It was amazing to look down into the abyss and actually see the mass of smoking lava. That was quite an experience!!

In recalling that episode, Marjorie conveyed both her gratitude for having had that opportunity and the significance of travel for her. She also noted that, "For my entire year abroad, including study and travel, I spent $1,300. That was quite a bargain."

Back in Vermont, Marjorie began to look for work. She had declined to sign another year's contract in Montpelier before she left, "because I had no wish to be tied down and felt some other type of work might appeal to me after spending a year abroad." Since it was the Depression and jobs were not easy to find, she registered with an agency in Boston.

It was June 1930 and I had come home to Vermont with no money. Having learned of a Boston Teachers' Agency that would help one find employment, I submitted my letter of qualifications. In a prompt reply, I was informed of several openings but was especially impressed by one listed in Massachusetts at Attleboro High School. I wrote to the school superintendent, who replied and invited me to meet with him in Boston. My parents went there with me for the appointment. Mr. Fales proved to be a pleasant but serious man. He offered me the position of French teacher at $1800 a year.

In September 1930, I went by train to Attleboro and made my way to his office to receive necessary instructions. He found me a rooming place in the home of Mrs. Chandler Brown, a widow with twins, Alden and Priscilla, who were in third grade. Their home was on Prospect Street near the school and the business district. I paid $3 a week for my room, ate lunch at school and took breakfast and dinner down street, often at Watson's Diner.

I stayed with Chan for twenty years; until about 1950, when she went to California. Priscilla was in my French class for three years and was always an exceptional student and great joy. We have kept in touch with each other for sixty-nine years, and she visits me every summer. She became a French teacher and now has children and grandchildren who have visited us.

During her visit to see Marjorie in July 1999, Priscilla Brown Grindle recalled Marjorie's living with her famiy as "very special."

My mother made sure that the teachers she accepted liked children— another teacher had a room with us, too. She also was very strict about their privacy and their rooms were off limits to us even in summer when they weren't there. When they were home and the doors to their rooms were closed, we were not to disturb them unless it was important. Then I would knock on her door, and Marjorie would allow me to come in. If she was very busy with school work, she would tell me and the visit would be brief. But she was always very nice to me and rarely refused me a visit. When I had sewing class in school and couldn't figure out a pattern, I could ask Marjorie for help. Marjorie was an excellent sewer, and she was very patient. She was good at so many things!

Did you know that she was valedictorian of her class and Phi Beta Kappa? She never told me this; I only learned it later in life. She had the opportunity to tell me, but she was always modest about her achievements.

Priscilla's mother, Effie Chandler "Chan" Brown, and her grand-mother, Abbie Saunders who came for extended stays, were both "very fond of Marjorie and were proud of her accomplishments," often telling the children that "Marjorie had studied abroad." As Priscilla recalled this, she agreed with Marjorie that Chan probably saw Marjorie as a good role model and influence. Priscilla summed up that influence, noting that Marjorie became her mentor.

I loved languages. I took four years of Latin and all three years of French with Marjorie, which was the most offered in our school at that time. The classroom was more formal during the years I went to school (I graduated in 1940), and we stood up to recite.

But times were starting to change and if a student didn't stand up when called upon, Marjorie would say, "Monsieur, levez-vous." She was a good disciplinarian. You didn't cut up in her class. She was always in control, but she smiled a lot and laughed a lot, thereby adding a levity to the class. She had a good sense of humor.

What was so special about Marjorie as a teacher was her method of teaching. She used a method of speaking French in class that was before its time. In those days, many teachers simply taught grammar and vocabulary. Not all French teachers used the oral method. But Marjorie taught us to speak the language and to hear it spoken correctly.

Not all French teachers could speak French in the 1930s! The audio-lingual method wasn't really developed until after World War II. (It was during the war years that the rudiments of the oral method were used to teach French quickly to service men. The Monterey Institute in California then developed this method after the war and speaking French in the classroom became accepted practice.) But long before this approach was developed, Marjorie was using it in her classroom, speaking to us in French from our first class and expecting us to speak in French, too.

Another thing Marjorie did was to incorporate lessons on French history, geography and culture into her classes. She developed handwritten, mimeographed handouts that she gave us. And she had large, beautiful posters of France all over the room. She was very thorough; she made French history and culture come alive. With her speaking method and her lessons in history and culture, she was very *avant garde*!

She was a superior language teacher and my enjoyment of Latin classes and the learning experience in Marjorie's classroom influenced me to become a French teacher. I went on to major in French at Wheaton College and taught school for awhile before I had children. Also, under Marjorie's influence, I went to Middlebury to study language between my Junior and Senior years of college and after graduation. I attended the summer program there for a total of ten years and earned two master's degrees, one in French and the other in Italian.

Like Marjorie, Priscilla would also go abroad, travel throughout Europe, study in France during the summers, and pursue a rewarding career as a language teacher. Enamored of both French and Italian, her favorite countries were to be France and Italy, where she eventually would live for two-and-a-half years with her own two children. Altogether, she would take sixteen trips abroad and spend thirty years in teaching French and Italian, including college and preparatory-school teaching and tutoring.

Beyond serving as "a wonderful mentor," Marjorie also became "a very special friend" with whom Priscilla stayed in touch by letter, telephone, and visits. After Priscilla married, her physician husband was transferred to California so she lived there until 1968. It was during one of her own summer-study trips that Marjorie visited the Grindles in San Diego. Later, when Priscilla lived and taught in upstate New York and then New Jersey, Marjorie would visit her there as well.

Priscilla also visited the Pierce home whenever traveling or living in the East. She brought her two children to visit the Pierces many times, noting it was a wonderful learning experience for them and that they had met all the Pierces except for Gertrude.

They were used to an ultramodern, California way of life in the suburbs so to experience the Pierce home and store was intriguing and special. Once when Marion was on duty in the store, they asked if they could tend store, and she let them take turns waiting on customers.

*Priscilla, Jane (other roomer)
Marjorie, Chan, Alden, 1937.*

*Priscilla and Marjorie,
who is wearing her fur
muskrat coat.*

*Marjorie at Carnac,
France 1935.*

Attleboro High School in MA.

Marjorie in the 1940s.

Well, when a customer gave his purchase to my son whose turn it wasn't, my daughter rudely snatched the box of crackers out of the surprised man's hands, exclaiming that it was her turn to ring up the purchase!

Marion explained to them that "the customers don't know whose turn it is" and that the children would have to be gracious and accept a customer out of turn so as not to be rude to them.

As Priscilla recalled this story, she enjoyed both the humor of the situation and Marion's rising to the challenge of dealing with such unruly behavior. Daughter Heather has since grown up and brought her own children to visit the Pierces several times, evidence of a tradition in which keeping in touch is valued. "Marjorie and I cherish our friendship, too," Priscilla added, noting that she admires Marjorie not only for all her accomplishments and achievements but for staying in touch with so many former students, who also became her friends over the years. "I'm sure I'm not the only student who became a French teacher due to Marjorie's influence," she added, an observation which Marjorie proudly confirmed.

Marjorie's remaining eight years in Attleboro were spent living at the home of another widow, a Mrs. Wilmarth, where she recalled paying about $7 a week for room and board. Marjorie particularly liked "living just south of Boston and taking Saturday shopping trips both into the city and to nearby Providence. The train made it very convenient to get around and I loved to go shopping," she recalled of the twenty-eight years she lived in Attleboro. She also recalled that because Attleboro was "the Jewelry City," it presented a rather unique situation for some of the teachers.

It was the home of Swank, Balfour, Simmons Chain, Knobby Kraft, Saart Silversmiths, and others. It often proved embarrassing to the teachers when pupils presented them with an expensive piece of jewelry, especially if that person happened to be receiving low grades.

On one occasion, Sandra R. scorned the usual type of gift and gave me an elephant, about three inches high, carved out of ivory. I added it to my table collection of animals that we had been using as a topic for French conversation.

Several days later, the girl stopped by after school and asked to take her elephant back, to which I readily assented. However, it was returned to me the very next morning when Mrs. R. found out what her daughter had done! I still have the carving on my bedroom shelf beside a miniature metal pot containing a lone tulip. That curio was a gift from a tall, lanky student, Martin B., given to me after we read Victor Hugo's novel *La Tulipe Noire.*

Her life as a teacher would be full of twists and turns, with an occasional tribulation or a good laugh encountered, as this excerpt from her "Recollections" shows.

On certain days, the pupils returned to their Home Room for a study period. I often wandered around the room, standing by the windows or in back of the class to check on their study habits or to answer questions. Looking down at the back of a girl's head, I was shocked to see dozens of lice crawling through her dark hair. Shortly after, I reported her to Mrs. Wendell, the Health Nurse.

The girl was absent a few days before resuming her studies. However, I soon learned that she had presented me with a few of her pets and then recalled that she had leaned over my shoulder the previous day when I was sitting at my desk and helping her with her homework.

Reluctantly, I went to my excellent and understanding hairdresser, Theresa, who gave me some effective treatments. The girl returned to school with a close haircut and of course had to bring an excuse for her absence from home, a necessity for anyone absent or tardy.

The excuse notes were delivered to the Home Room teacher who checked them and then sent them to the office. I have kept copies of some of these gems and will quote a few:

March 1941. Please excuse Laura for being absent for when she got up yesterday coldent go up or downstairs she has cramp in her lages.

October 1938. Miss Pierce, Due to the absent of Margaret G. on Oct. 18 she was sick. thank you.

September 1936. Dear Miss Pierce, Nancy lost her locker key so as her books were in her locker she stayed home and finally found it in her books of all places.

1945: Miss Pierce, Kindly excuse Roland of his absents for Wed. and Thur. He had a thriving toothache and at last had gone to the dentist to have it out.

Once, "real" history affected life in Mademoiselle Pierce's classroom:

It was during the 1930s and the pupils in my French II class were reciting their usual lessons. High windows occupied the entire western side of the classroom, with trees and shrubbery of Capron Park visible in the distance.

Suddenly, someone less attentive to studies noticed a strange cigar-shaped object moving up over the tree tops and drifting low along the horizon.

Contrary to all usual rules and regulations, the entire class was allowed to hasten towards the windows and watch in amazement as the German Zeppelin "Hindenburg" sailed slowly and majestically past our school and headed towards Boston, as we learned later. It seemed almost within arm's reach, its name clearly visible along its side, with windows clearly outlined. This was indeed an occasion to remember, not only for its historical significance, but for the teacher's relaxation of customary discipline in allowing the students to leave their seats during the class.

Such momentous occasions in the classroom were followed by many summers of exciting travel and study as well as other jobs and activities. During the summers of 1935 and 1936, Marjorie returned to France with Boston University's Classroom on Wheels. "Professor Charles French, assisted by Professor Lambert and Madame Fombaron, led the tours and gave lectures at the sites we visited. He'd lecture, we'd take notes, and then there would be an examination at the end of the tour," Marjorie recalled, adding that she was later able to apply credits from these studies (and from McGill) toward her Master's Degree.

She also wrote an enthusiastic article about her travel experience, which was published in the April 1937 issue of "The Modern Language Journal." She found her tour "so enjoyable" and she "received so much help and inspiration" that she wanted to let fellow teachers of French "in on the benefit of this particular summer session," she wrote in introductory remarks to the article, which is excerpted here.

To begin with, we had a "little corner of France afloat" for eight days on a French Line boat. We enjoyed the courteous attention of French-speaking stewards, an unexcelled French cuisine, opportunities for deck games, for dancing, or for basking in the sun, watching the ever-fascinating expanse of blue Atlantic. We quickly made the acquaintance of our congenial tour-companions, united already by a common bond of interest in France and things French, while our tongues soon became more adept at prolonged conversations, no longer limited to the traditional classroom vocabulary. Interesting lectures on French history, geography, art, and the like, given by our expert leaders, proved a most helpful preparation for the further enjoyment of our tour.

Voici enfin la France! At Havre a comfortable motorcar is waiting to speed us through the beautiful Norman countryside to Rouen, where we are destined to *descendre* at a picturesque hotel under the very shadow of the famous Grosse Horloge! We visit the cathedral with its imposing "butter tower." Do you know the story? Professor French is right beside you to explain, pointing out with his cane the details of this beautiful Gothic tower. Next we explore the old market-place and are shown the very spot where Joan of Arc was burned at the stake five-hundred years ago.

Thus the Classroom on Wheels travels through the cities and towns of France. We learn our geography in a way never to be forgotten. Details of history we learn on the actual spot. Here is a castle built by William the Conqueror, there the famous Bayeux Tapestry depicting the Norman Conquest of England, while yonder rose the formidable ruins of the fortress erected by Richard the Lion-Hearted in order to hold Normandy against the Capetian Kings.

Yes, we really are in Paris at last! Am I hurrying you? Did you wish to linger longer in Normandy? We spend ten wonderful days in the City of Light, living in a splendid hotel right off the Avenue de l'Opera! Imagine Bastille Day in Paris, with dancing in the streets until dawn! Picture if you can the beauties of Notre-Dame and the Sainte-Chapelle, the splendor of Versailles and Fontainebleau! You had better start now to plan and work so that you too may realize the wonderful dream which came true for me.

But our motorcar is waiting, and we are reminded that Mother Poulard's famous omelet can be had only at Mont St. Michel and not in Paris! Motoring through green Normandy, via Caen and Lisieux, we finally reach the remarkable Mont, the eighth wonder of the world—an architectural marvel of the Middle Ages, which will ever be an outstanding memory of our trip! We spent an entire week exploring the quaint, unspoiled towns and colorful fishing villages of Brittany, viewing ancient megalithic monuments erected by Druids, and meeting everywhere wizened old peasants dressed in curious costumes. . . .

Making our way southward via Nantes and the old fortified town of La Rochelle, steeped in its memories of Richelieu, we were pleasantly surprised to find in the environs of Niort an extraordinary network of canals, a real "Green Venice of the North." A visit to a porcelain factory in Limoges offered us an opportunity to observe another great French industry of absorbing interest, and to admire the work of the skilled artists who produce the beautiful French chinaware.

I had always longed to see the Massif Central. I had heard of its high plateaus, of the odd volcanic character of its deep valleys and fantastic grottoes. Outstanding in my memory is our sojourn in that marvelous town of Rocamadour, perched high on its rocky crag, and whose city gate is so ancient and narrow that our motorcar must remain outside! We are back in the Stone Age, visiting strange subterranean rivers, and caves filled with drawings made by prehistoric man. From Clermont-Ferrand, with its memories of Vercingetorix and Peter the Hermit, we made excursions to some of Auvergne's remarkable thermal resorts, and ascended the extinct volcanic cone of Puy de Dome, where Pascal tried out his theory of barometric pressure. . . . Do you recall the old song Sur le Pont d'Avignon? The ruined bridge is really there, for I saw it, and nearby the imposing turrets of the castle of the Popes. . . .

. . .

The Maison Carree at Nimes, the Pont du Gard, and the Roman arena at Arles were outstanding monuments of Gallo-Roman France on our way towards the Riviera playground. Who wouldn't thrill to the beauties of Cannes, Nice, and Monte Carlo? Imagine the joy of bathing in the blue Mediterranean, of strolling along the splendid palm-lined Promenade des Anglais at Nice, or of attending the White Carnival, that evening festival of unsurpassed fun and merriment! Then too, we see Monaco and visit the colorful gaming-rooms of Monte Carlo! The perfume factory at Grasse induces even the men to indulge in a few choice purchases.

As Marjorie's description continues—of the Route Napoleon to Grenoble, the glimpse of Chamonix and Mt. Blanc on the way, a week in Switzerland, and a visit to Alsace and its capital Strasbourg, where the "storks were less plentiful than before the war"—it becomes clear that just as the Classroom on Wheels made history and culture come alive for her, so too, this experience enabled her to bring France and the

Marjorie, third from left, at La Mer de Glace, Switzerland, 1935.

French language to life in her classroom. Encouraged by her study-tour experiences, Marjorie enrolled in the French graduate program at Middlebury College during the following four summers (1937-1940) and was awarded a Master's Degree in 1940.

What might have been further travel and study abroad was then interrupted by WW II. During the war years, Marjorie did after-school work at the Wolfenden Dye Company in Attleboro, where she packed skeins of yarn into cardboard boxes. In the summer of 1944, she worked at the Electric Products Division of a large company in Rutland, Vermont, where she inspected parts for war planes. She also was an Attleboro Defense and Air Raid Warden in 1943, hostess for Junior War Service Volunteers form 1942-1947, an organizer and sponsor of the Junior Red Cross, and on the War Ration Card Board.

Other activities during her Attleboro years included being on the Executive Board of the Attleboro's Teacher Association for three years, secretary of the Attleboro High School P.T.A., and ten years as secretary of the Woman's Club of the Attleboro Universalist Church. From 1944-1951, she worked after school and evenings at the Attleboro Post Office during the Christmas rush, making extra money. She often went ice skating after school in winter and continued to enjoy going to dances. Hers was a busy life; she thoroughly enjoyed her many activities and being an active part of the community in which she lived.

Marjorie had also become good friends with Professor French, whom she described as "a very intelligent man who used to visit my classes as a guest lecturer." In 1949, she and a friend, Evelyn Fuller, joined another group tour led by Professor French and went out West for the summer, traveling through California, the Pacific Northwest, and the Canadian Rockies. Marjorie saw Mt. Rainier, the Grand Canyon, and while in California visited Priscilla. The tour concluded with a trip into Canada, visiting Victoria and British Columbia, and a train ride across Canada to the Great Lakes before heading home.

Although she liked to travel, it was to be her last trip beyond the eastern United States. Her mother was ill and much had happened within her own family, so future summers would be spent back in Shrewsbury where she could be of assistance to her family.

Marjorie, Professor French, Evelyn Fuller, San Diego, 1949

Marjorie at Mt. Rainier National Park, 1949

Chapter Seven

The Pierce Family
1925-1958

During the years that Marjorie had moved away to teach and travel, her siblings were embarking on their own educations and careers as their parents continued to operate the store. As Marjorie noted, Willie continued to farm for many years but probably gave it up by the early 1940s as his sons left home for other jobs and the service. He eventually sold the barn to a Herbert Johnson, a visitor from New York who had long admired it. [He in turn sold it to an art teacher Wendy Belle from Boston, who converted it into a vacation home that she and her family enjoyed. Her children inherited the "barn" but rented it out in the 1980s and 1990s.]

Many changes were occurring in Shrewsbury and the world during this time, and Marjorie's family witnessed those changes as they affected the community and themselves and kept her informed of them through frequent letters. They also participated in a number of historic events, and of these, the CCC era and World War II were two that would profoundly and forever affect their lives.

Marion had gone on to study at Smith College after graduation from UVM and received an MSS certificate from the School of Social Work in 1926. After Smith, she moved to Philadelphia and got a job for the White-Williams Foundation as a counselor and lived at the Settlement House for many years. Eventually she got her own apartment in a row house and became head of the Division of Pupil Services for the Philadephia school system, with overall responsibilities for the guidance programs. She also enrolled in the University of Pennsylvania School of Social Work, earning a Master's Degree in 1947. She went on to teach classes in social work at the University of Pennsylvania for several summers.

"Working in Philadelphia during the Depression Era proved to be a time when social workers were put to the test. Poverty and joblessness were always problems in the large city, but Marion worked extra hard to deal with those issues as they affected children trying to go to school and survive," Marjorie recalled. Marion's life revolved around her dedication to the children of others. "She led a quiet but intense life, devoted to working with the less fortunate," Marjorie observed of the sister whom she often visited.

Gordon, who was five years younger than Marjorie, taught school at Northam for a year after he finished the eighth grade there. He received a document dated June 15, 1923, stating that he was "certified at Northam School for having completed the course of instruction for elementary schools" and was pronounced "eligible for free advanced instruction." Instead, he went on to Rutland High School (living with relatives of the Poore family who lived next to the Pierces in Northam) and graduated as valedictorian of his class in 1927. His valedictory address was entitled "Fingerprints" and outlined the inception and development of the practice of fingerprinting, citing its use in the detection of criminals and as a method of establishing the identity of persons in other instances. He ended his speech by expressing "sincere appreciation to our parents who have sacrificed so much in order that we might have a high school education" and thanking the faculty and school board for "assisting in our development. Whatever we are," he added, "may we always keep in mind that determination to do our best, cheerfully and unselfishly, in whatever field of service we shall choose. The future lies with us. Let us make it worthwhile."

Like his sisters before him, Gordon received an Honor Scholarship of $100 for tuition, which helped him go on to UVM. There he majored in economics and commerce and enrolled in the Reserve Officer's Training Corps (ROTC) from September 1927 to May 1929, at which time

Gordon gathering sap, 1942.

he was certified as a corporal in the organized reserves. After graduating in 1931, he spent a year working in Maryland, where he collaborated in an electric water-heater enterprise with Clarence Poore, father of the family he stayed with and owner of the Poore cottage in Northam. A country boy at heart, Gordon soon returned to Vermont, where he found seasonal employment in town, helping out various farmers with haying or sugaring and doing maintenance at Northam Cemetery.

He then learned cheese making from his Uncle Warner Aldrich at the Northam Cheese Factory and worked on the town roads. He loaded gravel in summer and shoveled snow in winter to open the roads wide enough to enable teams of horses to get through with wooden plows that made a two-wheel track. One year he worked at the Howe Scale Company in Rutland, doing office work for $8 or $9 a week. In 1934, he began working for his parents, doing farm work as well as bookkeeping, clerking, and maintenance at the store. "He improved the accounting system there," Marjorie related with pride.

In 1942, Gordon joined John C. Stewart and Son in Cuttingsville, where he was in charge of the service station until retiring in 1973. He boarded in Cuttingsville during the week, living first with Ora

Gordon and his car, 1943.

Gordon, aircraft spotter 1941.

Fiske and later with Clint and Lucille Fiske, because the roads were still so difficult to travel. On weekends, he would make the four-mile trip home and help tend store. By 1952, Gordon was living at home again and commuting in a truck he had bought. He also used a small motorcycle for the commute in good weather—often pulling boys on bicycles up town hill behind him.

During the war years, Gordon took a course in aircraft recognition and on August 10, 1943, was formally certified as a Recognition Observer for the First Fighter Command Ground Observer Corps of the Army Air Force. This was a group of trained personnel who were charged with scanning the skies for enemy aircraft that might attack the U.S.A. "He wanted to serve his country," Marjorie related, adding that a disability from a knee problem and his age (thirty-five) kept him from "active" duty.

Vermont was on the U.S. bombing target list of places the enemy might strike because of the machine-tool industry in Springfield (twenty miles from Shrewsbury as the crow flies). The machine tools and parts made there were known throughout the world. During World War II, four Springfield plants produced more than five percent of the nation's machine tools and were considered so indispensable to the manufacture of everything from tanks to atomic bombs that Springfield was ranked seventh in importance as a U.S. bombing target! The high hills of Shrewsbury provided ideal places for faithful observers like Gordon to observe the skies for enemy aircraft.

While still in high school, Glendon served as a Page in the Vermont House of Representatives in 1926-1927, having to return in the late fall for a special session called to appropriate funds to cover Vermont's extensive flood damage (the state refused federal aid, proudly floating its own rebuilding bonds). Glendon graduated from Rutland High in 1931 and then studied two years at the Drexel Institute in Philadelphia, living with Marion while there. From August 1 to November 12, 1934, he was a construction laborer at the CCC Camp at North Shrewsbury. Subsequently, he was employed from 1934-1938 by the Town of Shrewsbury and the State of Vermont, doing road work under Road Commissioners Ernest Aldrich, George Smith, and Edgar Ridlon. He also took courses in diesel engines at the Albany

Herbert Johnson, Glendon, and Marjorie at Montpelier.

Diesel Institute (New York), graduating in 1938. In 1939 he began driving a Tarvia truck for the Barrett Company, a division of Allied Chemical and Dye, and worked throughout the state in road resurfacing until February 1941.

Marjorie wrote this account of Glendon's military service after he returned home and when it was still fresh in his mind:

In 1941, Glendon was drafted to serve in World War II. From Fort Devens, he was sent to Fort Knox for basic training, graduating from the Armored Force School, then assigned to the 4th, Armored Division at Pine Camp, New York. In October 1942, he was commissioned 2nd Lieutenant from the Ordnance Officers Candidate School in Aberdeen, Maryland. From there he was sent to the Presidio in San Francisco, then to the 3432nd Ordnance (MAM) company in Seattle,

Minnie, Marjorie, and Marion visiting Glendon in Baltimore, 1942.

doing duty both there and at Fort Lewis, Washington. For a time he was in charge of the Fort Lewis Automotive Parts Depot. He graduated from the Northwest Sector automotive Maintenance School and left Seattle March 1944 for the European Theater of Operations, embarking from Newport News, Virginia.

He saw service in Oran and Algiers, North Africa (where he made First Lieutenant March 31, 1944), Sicily, mainland Italy, and subsequently took part in the invasion of southern France, advancing with the 7th Army under General Patch from St. Tropez through Aix, Avignon, Lyon, Besancon, Vesoul, Epinal, Thaon, Charmes, Nancy and Sarrguemines.

Glendon was proud to serve his country.

Upon leaving Kaiserslautern, Germany, the company crossed the Rhine near Worms; then on April 14, 1945 he was transferred out of the 3432nd Ordnance and assigned to Headquarters 337 Ordnance Battalion as Battalion Supply Officer, advancing to Stuttgart, Ulm, Augsburg, Landsburg (site of a concentration camp) and to Herrschung on Ammer See. Glendon was at Herrschung when the war ended on May 8, 1945.

Upon arriving at Epinal, France, trucks and jeeps were parked on the outskirts of the city. Glendon and Captain George Brown went to a church to see the priest who allowed the company to be quartered in the building overnight. All night the hammering of the artillery boomed like a severe thunderstorm so that the church walls shook, but the men were so weary they slept.

The next morning all except Glendon and Brown returned to the trucks. Brown sought the priest to see that he received payment, while Glendon stayed outside talking as best as he could in French with several children gathered round him. When they rejoined their group and trucks, an officer exclaimed, "Where have you been? We feared you were dead."

Returning to the church, they found it in ruins, having probably been hit by a shell. Women were running about crying and screaming; bodies, including those of children, were lying in the street. They never learned what happened to the priest.

Glendon returned home in 1945 and was formally discharged in February 1946. He went back to work in road resurfacing, where he was in charge of a crew that traveled within Vermont and continued to live at home except for being away on work-related jobs.

Gilford graduated from Rutland High School in 1933 and became a clerk at Pierce's Store. On January 19, 1934, he enrolled, at age eighteen, as a member of the Civilian Conservation Corps at North Shrewsbury Camp 2193. There, he joined the 1219th Company, which had begun working in North Shrewsbury on November 20, 1933, when they built the CCC Camp. Work crews improved the road up the mountain (old Road 14) and the road to the old mills (old Road 15), and from there they cleared and built a new road to Plymouth. They were met at the Plymouth boundary by a CCC group based in Plymouth, which group built the road up from the Plymouth Union Road, now called Route 100. They also built the Northam Picnic Area and associated camp sites. This construction took place during 1934 and 1935.

"It was the custom of the CCC to hire a few men who were familiar with the area and country life to teach the recruits. Those experienced men from Shrewsbury who were stationed at the Northam Camp included: Ralph Plumley, Richard Buckey, Charles Graham, Howard Lavalley, Clyde Ross, and Gilford Pierce," Marjorie typed in her research notes on this period. As this company was from New York and January 1934 was reported to be "the

Gilford with plow rigged to fit a town tractor, 1930s.

104

Gilford, Florence, Minnie and Glendon

Marion and Glendon

Gilford, park caretaker, 1936.

Building the CCC Road. Gilford on left.

Northam Picnic Area. Pavilion building (log structure) and well(upper left).

coldest in Vermont in seventy years," it must have been quite a shock for city boys to find themselves in mountainous, snowy North Shrewsbury that first winter!

In addition to his duty in Northam, Gilford served at Fort Ethan Allen with Company 165 for ten days in July 1935. On August 3, 1935, he was transferred to the 166th Company at Peru, Vermont, while the 1219th company went on to Panama, New York. (A Massachusetts Company of 208 men replaced them at Northam and completed the projects that they had started.) On August 23, 1935, Gilford was sent to the 131st Company at Lyndonville, Vermont, where he was a truck driver until being honorably discharged on September 29, 1935.

The CCC-built Northam Picnic Area had begun to be used in the summer of 1934 and was a beautiful state park with a log shelter picnic pavilion, individual picnic sites with tables and fireplaces, a spring for drinking water, several tent sites with platforms and fireplaces, and a caretaker's quarters. One of Gilford's record sheets shows that he was a caretaker of the Northam Picnic Area in 1936. On August 11, 1936, he reported that: 54 people registered in May, 639 in June, 1162 in July and a "total of 2420 to date." They were from 24 states and Mexico, England and Canada, he wrote. He also listed sales of 137 fuel tickets for $13.70 and 8 camping tickets for $4. His comments included: "Place seems to be liked by nearly everyone. Good many people seem interested in swimming in this hot weather and ask if there is a pool near-by. Case where man sleeps in car. ???"

After his CCC and caretaker experiences, Gilford entered the New York State College of Forestry at Syracuse University and graduated with a Bachelor of Science degree on June 3, 1940. He then worked for the Vermont Forestry Department surveying state forest boundaries. A relative remembered that while he was working in northern Vermont, he lived with a family and became very close to their son. The youngster went to the barn to see a new calf one day and was gored by an anxious cow and died. It was a tragic accident that deeply affected Gilford, she recalled.

On January 7, 1941, Gilford went to enlist in the Army Air Force but induction papers that survive in a scrapbook kept by his (late) wife Florence show he was rejected as "IV- F: disqualified for military service because of defective and missing teeth." This was signed by the local

106

board member George N. Harman with notes on this page indicating: "left upper teeth 1st and 4th supplied by plate." The examining physician W.R. Harkness wrote, "Physical fitness impaired by reason of not having the minimum requirement of six masticating and six incisor teeth." He also checked a IV-F status.

A year later Gilford received authorization to report to Maxwell Field, Alabama on June 22, 1942. It is probable that he either had his teeth further fixed or requirements were relaxed or both. The United States had passed the Selective Service Act of 1940 to mobilize U.S. military forces and had declared war on the Axis powers in December 1941. Additionally, there was mounting concern regarding Hitler's occupation of western Europe as well as worry about military preparedness in our own country.

Home on a thirty-six-day leave, Aviation Cadet Gilford E. Pierce married Florence Smith, whom he had dated while in college, on July 19, 1942. Florence, a little over two years his senior at age twenty-nine, was a local elementary school teacher and a fifth-generation member of the Shrewsbury (Nehemiah) Smith family. After a short honeymoon in

Florence and Gilford Pierce were married by the Reverend Olaf C. Johnson at the Northam Church and were attended by Shrewsbury friends Ralph and Marjorie Plumley (right and left respectively). Ralph was Gilford's best friend when growing up in Shrewsbury and the two attended high school together.

the apartment at the Northam Cheese Factory, Gilford received training in Alabama, Florida, South Carolina, and Georgia. Although his letters to Florence indicate that aviation training was tough and he sometimes feared he would "wash out," he graduated from the AAF Advanced Flying School at Moody Field in April 1943 with his silver wings and Second Lieutenant commission. Further training as a pilot of a B-17 with the 799 Bombardment Squadron followed in Louisiana, Texas, and Ohio. Florence had several visits with Gilford during these years, but her last was in Ohio in October 1943 just prior to his being sent to the AAF Bomber Command Station in England as part of the 8th Airforce.

Gilford became the pilot of a B-17 Bomber, which he named "Vermont Lady." He and his crew of nine

Army Air Force Pilot Gilford Pierce

flew thirteen missions to targets in Norway, Germany, and France. They survived four air encounters where they took considerable flak and one time returned to base with large holes in their Flying Fortress, as the B-17 was universally known. On January 1, 1944, Gilford was promoted to First Lieutenant.

Gilford wrote frequently to Florence and she to him (as did his family). His letter to her dated January 4, 1944, complained of not receiving a card from her in five days because of the mail being slow. He asked her to excuse him for complaining, ending his last communication to her with:

> I am a little tired, without sleep, a very small trifle on edge, and so, just a little "owly." I never want to be "owly" with you ever again, as I guess I'll always remember the one time I really was. You kind of told me off that time, eh?

Gilford Pierce (front row left) and crew of the flying fortress Vermont Lady.

Guess I'll hurry to try to get some rest. Did want to drop you a note, however, even tho I don't receive mail! Ya little vixen!

Heaps of Love to Smitty,   Your Gil.

On January 5, 1944, the Vermont Lady was "on a bombardment mission to Bordeaux when it was so severely damaged by enemy fire that the entire crew was forced to abandon it over the Bay of Biscay just before it exploded and crashed into the bay," according to a War Department letter. Only one crew member was rescued from a rubber raft in the water (by the French and then he was taken by the Germans before being liberated) and survived. He reported that the entire crew had bailed out, but that he never saw any of them again.

Gilford was declared missing in action, causing regular updates to be sent to his widow and family. On October 2, 1944, while still reported missing, First Lieutenant Pierce was awarded the Air Medal with Oak Leaf Cluster (by direction of the President) for exemplary service and having completed thirteen missions over enemy territory. A November (1944) letter followed with a presumed dead notification. A final letter gave a "presumptive finding of death" in September 1945. His body was never recovered. "This caused my mother to believe he would return some day, and when he never did, it broke her heart and ours, too. My mother never sang or whistled again," Marjorie said sadly.

A gravestone for Gilford was placed in the Northam Cemetery, where he is remembered with other family members. In later years, as part of Memorial Day observances, Marjorie would take local school children to the cem-

Always missed—never forgotten.

etery so they could place flags at the graves of men who served our country. She always included Gilford's story and how the crew was forced to eject over the water.

Florence took Gilford's death hard, almost suffering a nervous breakdown. It was particularly difficult for her because Gertrude believed he would return, a sister recalled. Devoted to his memory, Florence treasured Gilford's letters and planted red geraniums at his grave each Memorial Day. She never remarried. "She dated but never fell in love again," another sister said. Florence continued to teach in Shrewsbury, eventually retiring and living in Rutland, where she died in February 1997. A child born to her sister Damaris Dashner on November 2, 1946 (Florence's birthday) was named Gilford in honor of the uncle whom the family always cherished in memory. Gilford Dashner also planned to go into forestry, but he was killed in 1968 in Vietnam and is buried in the Laurel Glen Cemetery in Cuttingsville.

Historic "Memory" Place

When WW II began, the Northam Picnic Area was closed. It was never reopened as an official state park, probably due to the lack of water for swimming and boating and its hidden location in the mountains. However, the area and pavilion building continued to be used for many years. The park was used as a trailhead for the hike to Shrewsbury

Peak and was a popular picnic and bonfire site. Unfortunately, the ravages of animals who chewed on the log pavilion building and use of its timbers for firewood undermined the structure's safety and caused the Vermont Forest and Parks Department to tear it down in the 1980s.

Locals responded with concern since they had not been forewarned. Had they known, they said, they would have worked to preserve the structure through repairs. However, the deed was done, and today only the tall stone chimney and remnants of the stone walkway remain to recall a time when thousands once visited this area.

While the Northam Picnic Area was still operating as a state park, there was a short period when it saw many winter visitors and made skiing history. At the time the CCC Road and Picnic Area were built, the first rope tow in the United States had begun operating (February 1934) in nearby Woodstock. Perry Merrill, the commissioner of forests and parks, was in favor of utilizing mountains in good snowbelt locations for ski areas as a way to help the economy and to provide wholesome recreation. He employed CCC crews to build ski trails at Mount Mansfield (Stowe), so when Rutland skiers suggested cutting trails and installing a rope tow at Shrewsbury Peak, Merrill was agreeable.

Thus the Salt Ash State Forest CCC Camp #61 built the ski and bridle trails, the longest of which was over two miles and went to the top of 3,737-foot Shrewsbury Peak for a 1,585-foot vertical drop. Skiers had to hike up this and several other trails as the tow was located down below by an open practice slope. The CCC crew installed the rope tow for the Rutland Ski Club, which supplied the Packard Motor and then operated the ski area. One CCC leader later wrote to Marjorie that it was "the second tow in the United States," but research shows that its November 1935 installation most probably made it one of several rope tows installed in the Northeast during 1935.

A maintenance barn and a large Stone House, which served as a two-room park ranger's quarters in summer (and doubled as a lodge "for the comfort of visitors" in winter) were also built at the base of the ski area, just a few hundred yards from the Picnic Pavilion. A full-time caretaker was assigned to the area, and a "canteen" where skiers could buy snacks and hot lunches was erected behind the barn. Today, only the gutted Stone House remains. [In 1982, Glendon told a local forester that the CCC also built the first mile of the "Black Swamp Road" which goes part way to Shrewsbury Peak. Merrill's intention was to build the road all the way to the peak and then on to Killington Peak which at that time was still unreachable. Work on that project stopped when the CCC Camp closed, Glendon said.]

Marjorie said that her brothers learned to ski quite well, so it is likely they skied at the Shrewbury Ski Area, which operated the winters of 1935-36 and 1936-37. She added that the area was quite popular and was the location of the Williams College Winter Carnival in 1936 and its meet with Amherst and Weslyan in 1937. The area was advertised by the Rutland Ski Club, which touted its great "snowbelt location."

Ironically, the CCC Road proved difficult to keep open due to those deep snows. The town's rudimentary snow removal equipment simply could not keep up with the job and the three-mile road was often impassable. At other times the steep section of the road was too slick for cars to get up. The Rutland Ski Club consequently abandoned the area in favor of the new area at Pico which Brad and Janet Mead opened in nearby Mendon on Thanksgiving Day in 1937. They also contributed parts from the Shrewsbury tow to the Pico effort.

Also near the Picnic Area is the historic Meeting House Rock, the glacial boulder first used as a site for religious services in 1818. Marjorie related that the Rock had been long forgotten until local residents George Whitney and Harry Russell went walking one day and came upon it. With its rediscovery (circa 1936), a path was cut across the road from the Picnic Area to the Rock. A commemorative summer wor-

ship service was then held at Meeting House Rock, and thus began an annual pilgrimage that continues to this day.

Community and history were always important to the Pierces, but the significance of the Northam Picnic Area became greater to them because of their personal ties to this area. Willie had worked in this vicinity for two years at the former Russell Mill (located between the pavilion and

Stone House), and Gilford spent two years here through his CCC and caretaker work. Their grandparents and parents worshipped at Northam Church and now also at Meeting House Rock. The histories of the mills, the CCC, and the church were integrally connected to the community and to the beautiful recreation area that Gilford had helped to build at the foot of Shrewsbury Peak. With Gilford's death, the area became even more significant to the Pierce family. Additionally, the area was only two miles from where Ephraim Pierce had settled and raised his family and where Willie now owned 235 acres.

Rock Service, circa 1995.

It was this confluence of personal events and history that imbued Marjorie and her brothers with a desire to help commemorate the area each summer. It was one of their many ways to show honor and respect for God, country, community, and family that Gordon and Glendon carefully groomed the site and that Marjorie saw to invitations and publicity for the annual worship service for some fifty years. Often a glorious picnic would follow at the nearby pavilion, making it a social event reminiscent of the early settlers' daylong celebrations there.

Some years later, Glendon made his own tribute to Gilford. It is a handsome grandfather clock which he built after buying some old clockworks. Decorated with the AAF insignia from Gilford's dress-uniform cap, the stately clock still stands in the sitting room, gently striking the time and ringing out a poignant reminder of the price of freedom.

Although they say "time heals all wounds," Marjorie said that, "My mother never really recovered from Gilford's disappearance. In 1950 her health began to fail. She suffered from a bad heart and died in 1952." Marjorie had been looking after her mother summers but returned to Attleboro for the school year. She continued to do so until Willie began to get older; then she returned to Vermont permanently. That was 1958. Willie was eighty-six and Marjorie was fifty-five when she took "early retirement" and embarked on another adventure and a second career.

Chapter Eight

Vermont in Transition

L eaving the world of teaching near the cosmopolitan city of Boston to return to rural Northam was a major shift in lifestyle for Marjorie. She had been away for many years, and while she visited her home and family frequently—spending entire summers at home since 1950—the town to which she was returning in 1958 was vastly different from the one she had left in the 1920s.

When Willie and Gertrude had taken over the store at Northam in 1918, times were already beginning to change. The family would not only experience a passage from one era to another, but would live to see an almost entirely different world. The automobile, Great Depression, electric power, World War II, paved roads, and the interstate highway system were just some of the factors that over forty years conspired to change rural Vermont and the lives of Vermonters. It was a transformation that greatly affected what had once been a thriving business at the store.

As New England's only state with no ocean access or resource, Vermont was well off the main transportation routes and largely missed the post-World War I and II economic prosperity that occurred in southern New England. There were exceptions—fertile valleys like the Champlain lowlands for productive farming; railroad towns like Rutland; tourist towns like Manchester and Woodstock; and cities like Barre with its thriving granite industry, Burlington with the state university, and Spring-field with its machine-tool trade. But, as noted in Chapter One, such economic successes largely eluded rural hill towns which continued to lose their textile, lumber, cheese and farming industries and therefore their many smaller trades and their people.

As Vermont's young people continued to leave in the 1920s and 1930s, it became clear to the state's leaders that the rural towns were in trouble. The Depression exacerbated the problem, although New Deal federal work programs helped to a degree. Still, job opportunities continued to decline as more mills and farms shut down, and young adults and fami-lies continued to leave in the 1930s and 1940s (often for manufacturing jobs in Massachusetts and Connecticut). Then, World War II claimed yet more young men, leaving towns like Shrewsbury with historically low populations by 1950.

However, Vermont had already become known for its cool mountain air, glorious lakes, and flaming autumns by the 1900s. Summer and au-tumn tourism were an economic factor for a number of towns, espe-cially those that had capitalized on their mineral springs, lakes, or moun-tains to offer therapeutic rest and recreation. Summer tourism had be-gun in the early 1800s with the attraction of the mineral springs and lakes and by the late 1800s tourism had spread to the mountain areas as well.

Recognizing this potential for a statewide industry and seeking to capitalize on those natural resources, the state of Vermont began to tout its lakes and mountains in the 1880s and set up a publicity service in 1891, the first state in the nation to do so. The inaugural publication was unabashedly entitled "Vermont, Designed by the Creator for the Playground of the Continent." In 1913, the secretary of state published "Land of the Green Mountains," another publicity effort to attract tour-ists. Many camps for children sprang up in this era along with lake cot-tages and some fancier hotels.

The Vermont Commission on Country Life, a group of two-hundred Vermonters who wanted to revitalize the state, was formed in 1930 and spent considerable time studying every aspect of Vermont life. Con-cerned that only "forty towns had prospered in the last fifty years" while two hundred had experienced "backward movement," the Commission recommended steps to "halt emigration and ensure progress." It published its findings in 1931 in the book *Rural Vermont, A Program for the Future.*

In it, the Commission urged the promotion of summer tourism and state ownership of Vermont's highest peaks for forestry and park uses so as to help these two-hundred towns. Noting that "industrial growth was slow and agricultural problems difficult of solution," the Commission concluded that the state's future lay in its development for recreation, vacation homes, and a travel and tourism industry. It further suggested that leasing mountain summits for vacation homes and camps be explored as a way to capitalize on the views and use of "nonproductive land." Better highways, state police, and more information bureaus were recommended as a means to improve and increase tourism. Based on its findings that taking in tourists was beneficial to Vermonters— "people fix up their houses and their villages, meet new people and generally live in nicer homes"—the Commission concluded that:

> Vermont's development as a recreational region affords the most promising opportunity for business growth in the state at the present time, and so far as can be foreseen, for a considerable period in the future. The beauty and variety of our scenery, our proximity to great urban centers of population, our situation in the midst of America's principal vacation region, constitute advantages of great potential value. If industrial growth is retarded, if agricultural problems are difficult of solution, the recreational field offers a wonderful opportunity if we are wise enough to establish and maintain high standards of genuine hospitality and wise and consistent policies of protection for our scenic assets.

Coincidentally, the Depression-era federal government programs to get people back to work brought the Civilian Conservation Corps (CCC) to Vermont in 1933. As we have seen, this program was a boon to many rural areas and gave rise to Vermont's State Forests and Parks system as the young men built picnic and beach pavilions, shelters, camp sites, trails, roads, and other facilities. The forests and parks eventually proved an important building block to the vitality of Vermont's summer tourism industry, and hence to the state's economy, just as the Commission had hoped. CCC work also helped to launch early Vermont skiing at Stowe,

116

The Northam Picnic Area was once a very popular state park.

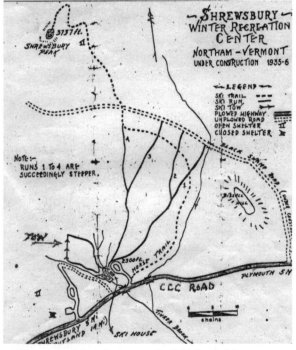

Skiing at Shrewsbury was highly touted but was short-lived due to impassable roads.

North Shrewsbury, and elsewhere in the state. As a result, the sport spread to many small towns in the 1930s and 1940s and caught on in the 1950s, eventually becoming a sustainable winter industry.

The promotion of summer and autumn tourism continued throughout the 1930s and 1940s as the state increased its efforts to develop its travel potential (as recommended by the Commission). *Vermont Life,* the official state magazine, was begun in 1946 as a way to attract people by promoting Vermont's scenic beauty. The magazine even established a Referral Bureau to help those who were thinking of moving to Vermont or investing in vacation property. Over the next twenty years, hundreds of books, guides, and promotions featured photos of the beautiful Vermont countryside. Many publications listed Shrewsbury farms as providing accommodations for visitors and vacationers.

The 1960s' state campaign "Vermont, the Beckoning Country" was developed as a way to attract tourists, investors in Vermont property, and new industries; thereby, creating more jobs in an effort to stem the tide of native emigration and initiate economic gains. With the proliferation of ski tows in the 1930s and 1940s, the advent of the interstate highways in the 1950s, and the growth of skiing in the late 1950s and 1960s, this campaign was also aimed at increasing winter visits. Although Vermont's winter tourism has never caught up with summer in terms of annual visitors, it does contribute greater revenues to year-round travel and tourism, which not only caught up with the state's declining manufacturing and farming industries but surpassed both by 1998.

During the 1950s and 1960s, Vermont was changing economically and socially, with more people taking up residence in larger towns and small cities and more giving up farming. But some Vermonters refused to give up a way of life that distinguishes this state from every other and stayed in the many small rural hill and valley towns. Despite the difficulty of the climate and making a living, they clung to tradition and a Vermont way of life that requires Yankee ingenuity and resourcefulness as well as hard work and perseverance to maintain a home and perhaps a few acres, or to operate a small farm or business. Some of these farm families had already begun to take in tourists to supplement their incomes, and this in turn contributed to the summer-visitor, second-home owner, and retiree movement in beautiful rural towns.

This movement began in Shrewsbury, as it did elsewhere in Vermont, in the 1920s and 1930s and picked up after 1950 with the greatest influx of new residents in Shrewsbury occurring in the 1970s and 1980s. Thus, joining a dwindling group of stalwart Shrewsbury natives were the many second-home owners, summer and winter people (due to the town's proximity to major ski areas), and newcomers who were part of a 1960s' and 1970s' back-to-the-land movement.

Some of these folks were retirees, but many were young, including educated professionals and Vietnam-era dropouts who were seeking a better way of life for themselves and their children. Looking to get away from the noise, crime, and congestion of the cities and suburbs or to escape the pressures of less-than-satisfactory jobs and lifestyles, they aspired to live more simply in natural surroundings with clean, fresh air. Many also held more lofty ideals like becoming part of a real community and practicing greater self-sufficiency—raising their own food, building their own homes, and heating with renewable energy sources. The earlier founding of Spring Lake Ranch in 1932, a therapeutic community located in the Cuttingsville section of town, was one example of such idealism that brought new people to Shrewsbury, thus becoming part of the town's renewal and growth in population.

Others who came to town were willing to drop out of a society that had lost meaning for them in the Vietnam era. They often favored a more bohemian lifestyle that focused on living-off-the-land and achieving as much self-sufficiency as possible. While Shrewsbury saw a mix of "long-haired and barefoot" types, and some who might have been regarded as "hippies" because they shared homes or experimented with drugs, there were no bona-fide communes in the town although there were some elsewhere in Vermont.

Natives like the Pierces "noticed the newcomers' differences and even thought some of them strange and talked about them," Marjorie acknowledged. Initially, such different styles and viewpoints were "suspect," but the Vermont tradition of tolerance was exhibited by folks like the Pierces who refused to judge by appearances alone. As they saw that the lifestyles of these "strange younger folks" were not incompatible with New England ways and values, but rather were respectful of the past and the land, they began "to accept them and appreciate their willingness to adopt country ways," she said.

Due to the perseverance of those who stayed and the influx of newcomers, Shrewsbury grew to 1,108 residents by 1990 (the latest official U.S. census), more than twice the population of forty years earlier. The willingness of farmers to sell some of their land for vacation homes and primary residences was a contributing factor as the greater availability of land spurred the building of new homes and also made it possible for some of the town's young to stay (by making cheaper land available). In the 1980s, the state's whole-herd buyout program (to reduce the milk surplus) similarly made more land available as farmers learned they could make more money by selling than by staying in farming. Despite these changes and this growth in population, the town retained its rural character. Ironically, this growth also helped make it possible for Pierce's Store to remain in business as long as it did.

The "flatlanders"—as out-of-staters are irreverently called by natives until they are adjudged assimilated by virtue of time spent in the community and their own good country behavior—soon outnumbered Shrewsbury's native-born residents. But with their keen appreciation for history, tradition, and the natural environment, most transplants chose to learn from the town's natives and to carry on their rural traditions. With most newcomers adopting country ways, change came more slowly and carefully, and the rural landscape was maintained as were many of the town's traditional institutions like the local church, grade school, and stores, as well as the community gatherings. Shrewsbury's institutions saw alterations—three congregations combined into one church family; the four district schools that were left consolidated into one large, modern elementary school; and the country stores dwindled in numbers—but they survived. Interestingly, greater unity was achieved as people who had once grouped around the various school districts and villages now shared a common school and church. "The local district-school system had been somewhat divisive so this change actually resulted in a greater feeling of townwide community," observed long-time resident and local historian Anne "Nancy" Spencer.

This successful "assimilation" of newcomers into the rural community not only fostered the more traditional "Vermont way of life" in Shrewsbury, but it also staved off the suburbanization striking more progressive areas of the state (particularly like those in Chittenden County where lifestyles began to reflect the new "citified" way of life). The growth and urbanization of larger cities and towns with populations over 10,000 (Rutland, Barre, Montpelier, Burlington, Brattleboro, Bennington, Springfield, St. Albans, and St. Johnsbury) and the modern development of a few ski towns began to more drastically change some areas of the state. But by resisting the modernization and commercialization trend to supermarkets, condominium complexes, strip development, shopping centers, mega malls, and industrial parks, Shrewsbury remained one of the many small towns that helped Vermont retain its image as a predominantly rural state of great natural beauty.

The vast majority of Vermont's 256 towns count populations of less than 2,000 souls, and in 1999 over half the towns in the state still have populations of less than 500 people. Although an agrarian economy no longer dominates these towns, which by and large have become bedroom communities, the Vermont way of life can still be seen in rural places like Shrewsbury where farms, forests, meadows, and plenty of undeveloped acreage comprise the landscape along with homes, small village centers, and a few businesses. What enabled Shrewsbury to adapt to changing times and a different economy without losing its rural character is a story of how the newcomers and natives mixed.

It was people like the Pierces (as well as several other of the town's older and some newer families) who helped make this possible. It was also practical natives like the Pierces who saw the summer and year-round flatlanders as desirable additions to the town. "We liked the fact that they fixed up and improved the often dilapidated properties they bought and thus contributed more tax money for the support of the roads and the schools," Marjorie said, echoing sentiments her father had expressed in the 1940s and 1950s. As more of these people moved in permanently, they reversed the declining population trend and ensured the town's very survival, a fact that was not lost on folks like the Pierces. In fact, many of these newcomers became customers at W. E. Pierce Groceries, where they received a warm welcome and learned what good neighbors and the joys of country life are all about.

With such major change elsewhere in Vermont, the story of the Pierce family—particularly their respect for preserving tradition, history, community, and the environment—takes on significance for the sustainability of small towns like Shrewsbury. Affected by the vast changes of the twentieth century, the Pierces managed to adapt in ways that allowed them to lead useful lives while also helping their town. Despite some personal setbacks (the loss of Gilford, two serious accidents, and the decline in store business), Willie steered that course with a calm acceptance of change as can be seen in excerpts from his 1960 interview with Boston Herald reporter Haydn Pearson:

In 1918, this was still a farming section, although the changes had begun. It was right after World War I that summer people began to come in hordes to Vermont. They bought up village places and farms, and we are all glad they did.

It was getting harder and harder to make a living on the farms, and places were running down. Schools and roads were increasing our taxes and we needed more revenue. When summer people came and folks began to retire on a year-round basis, they improved the properties and that gave us more tax money. If you are old enough to remember the country in 1900 to 1910, you know that roads and schools did not cost as much in those years compared to what we have to pay today.

I used to have a barrel of salt salmon in brine, and a barrel of salt pork. That whole side there, up high, had a row of horse-collar pads— yellow in color and all sizes. Horse collars didn't wear out very fast, but good farmers were careful about the pads under the collars.

When I saw the first Stanley Steamer come chugging up the road, I knew a new world was on the way.

Farming began to go down hill, due to economic causes that we could not control.

I liked the old way of life. It was slower, but seems to me people had more fun in living half a century ago.

Today all is speed and change. There's nothing we can do about it, so I guess we'll have to learn to live with the new way.

With those changes, W.E. Pierce Groceries slowly made a transition from a very busy general store that supplied footwear, clothing, farm tools, hardware, grain, kerosene, patent medicines, and groceries to an entire section of town to a country store that supplied candy, soda, convenience groceries, a few sundries, and gasoline to a much smaller population. (The entire population of Shrewsbury had declined to 464 by 1955.)

In 1958, the town was quite different from when Marjorie first left home. The number of dairy farms had decreased drastically. In 1931 there were sixty-five farms producing milk; in the 1960s, only a dozen:

Willie and Gertrude always enjoyed tending store.

the Chan Smith farm, Willard Smith farm, Korzuns, Sanderson Brothers, Woods, Kelleys, Mandigo, and Bersaw among others.[1] There were no lumber mills or cheese factories left. The host of small industries—Marjorie counted some thirty different occupations (small businesses) from dressmaker to cooper in the early 1900s—were now gone. Most people worked out of town now, a change made possible by the automobile and better roads and necessitated by the loss of an agrarian economy that had spawned hometown employment and self-sufficiency.

Augmenting this change were an array of "intriguing new stores in Rutland that were quite attractive to rural residents. It was exciting to go to Rutland to see the new goods now offered," Marjorie noted with enthusiasm. No longer a self-contained, self-sufficient farming community, the town of Shrewsbury was changing and the rural hamlet of Northam was transitioning into the twentieth century right along with it. But because Marjorie had already been part of the modern twentieth century, the transition process was not a difficult one for her. She rather enjoyed the return to her roots, where she viewed the changes as exciting and, like her father, chose to adapt and welcome the newcomers to town.

---

[1] *By 1999, only Julanne Sharrow's Pine Valley Farm (formerly Chan Smith farm) was producing milk. The law requiring bulk tanks had further reduced the number of dairy farms, along with some difficult droughts that encouraged remaining farmers to turn to raising beef cattle.*

Scene of a bygone era: Richard Mandigo haying on his farm at top of CCC Road.

Chapter Nine

Pierce's Store
1958-1990

With her decision to return to Northam, Marjorie's formal career as a school teacher ended and a new one as a storekeeper began. It was a fitting switch in occupation. A natural born storyteller, historian, and teacher, Marjorie simply changed the site and nature of her classroom from a school building to the country store. No longer were her pupils or lessons restricted to high school French; now they were all ages from all walks of life and history, the store, and the town were her beloved subjects.

Marjorie's return to the Pierce family home and store was a true homecoming. An educated woman, she had enjoyed her teaching career, had traveled widely, had met many interesting people, and had made many good friends. Contrary to what one might expect, coming home was not something she resented, but rather welcomed as a return to her roots. An independent woman, she chose to follow the call of duty. As she recounted why she left teaching, she said simply, "My mother had died and my father was elderly. Glendon was left to look after the house, my father, and the store in addition to his regular job. I felt that was too much responsibility for him, so I took early retirement and came home to help."

The 1960s were the years of the exploration of women's roles beyond that of a housewife or mother, teacher or nurse. Thousands of

Willie, Marjorie, Gordon, and Glendon circa late 1950s or early 1960s. Willie always dressed in a tie.

young women were beginning to get college educations and were entering the work force, thus spawning the "women's lib" era of speaking out for equal opportunity in the 1970s. Ironically, Marjorie, who had seen the world and done the things that these women were now fighting for, was returning home to care for her family.

Marjorie had studied, traveled, and taught, not out of any desire to be different or rebel, but rather from her own need to lead "a useful and upright life." Her parents' wish that their children become educated was the first step that propelled her along this path. Principal Abbott, who spotted her potential and encouraged her to go to UVM, was the second. Then, her own inquiring nature, love of learning, and determination took her in the direction of teaching and travel.

Teaching is often misperceived as a "woman's occupation," but that's not why Marjorie chose to teach. Rather, it was a vocation. She had gifts to share and as she "always enjoyed children," she found it natural to teach—as practical a choice for her as it was for the "dreamer" Marion to go into social work and counseling. With so many children to care for in the classroom and nice families to live with, Marjorie never felt alone. She often remarked on how she "felt at home with them" and even "like a member of the family" at the places where she roomed or boarded. At the same time, she had the freedom to travel and study. With the adventure of new places, her life was never dull, and she used those experiences to animate her classroom.

Now in her new role as a store proprietor, Marjorie would find herself tied to a six-day work week in one place year round. But she viewed this as allowing her to enjoy the beauty of Northam while beginning yet another adventure. She didn't mind giving up the routine of teaching because in part, it had become "old hat." Additionally, she had some flexibility and control over her day as it was not necessary to always be in the store since her father was still clerking and Glendon was helping out, too.

So when home beckoned in 1958, she went willingly, ending a total of thirty-two years in a classroom, twenty-eight in Massachusetts and four in Vermont. She entered another equally satisfying and fulfilling period of her life—thirty-five years of tending store. It was a second career that was longer than her first, and interestingly, each was longer than most Americans spend in any one occupation.

But Marjorie never really stopped teaching or learning. She used her time to operate the store, participate in community affairs, read periodicals and books, pursue her hobbies—collecting bottles, stamps, and autographs—and to do historical and genealogical research. Becoming an "unofficial" Northam historian was an offshoot of her interests and became yet another hobby that fit in with her love of history and the community. While she no longer had the time to travel extensively, she did continue to make short trips within the Northeast to see friends and relatives or to attend an historic event such as the dedication of Mount Independence.

Upon her return, Marjorie moved back into her old room and proceeded to take care of the Pierce household, which included: her father, who was still actively tending store; Glendon, who would retire from his job with Barrett in 1959; and Gordon, who remained employed at C.J. Stewart's Ford Service Station until his retirement in 1973. Marion came to visit at Christmas and summers. Ever the practical soul, Marjorie took on her new responsibility for meals and housework without complaint. However, she did recall that, "One time when Marion was visiting with a friend, I had to stay in the store until 5:30. But instead of putting supper on, Marion just waited for me to do it. I was the domestic one; cooking wasn't one of her talents."

This was a good natured, matter-of-fact observation with a realistic tinge of "it would have helped me out had she started supper, but it didn't really matter." Such responses were probably why the siblings never fought—they just took each other in stride, accepting strengths and ignoring flaws. It might well have been an ingrained trait that harkened back to Gertrude's "she's our guest" when the girls complained about "bossy Cousin Constance."

People who knew them well point out that there was an "inner goodness, graciousness and courtesy" in the Pierces that made them exceptional people. "We did have our differences of opinion and arguments; we disagreed on many issues," Marjorie noted. But as strong as these might be at times, there were no shouting matches, fights, or hurt feelings. Tolerance and respect prevailed.

Proud of their accomplishments and of their heritage, the Pierces found it easy to share the work of the store and to live harmoniously under one roof. Although there would be times when keeping the store going was trying, a deep sense of its historic value and importance to the community moved Willie and then Marjorie, with the help of her brothers, to continue operations for as long as they could.

When Marjorie returned in 1958, Willie was eighty-seven. He was a little stooped over and hard of hearing, but he continued to tend store, opening it up mornings at 7:30 and continuing this ritual into his nineties. He had a strong constitution and had survived two serious accidents. One occurred in 1935 while he was driving to Rutland with Gilford. "The truck was hit by a northbound train at the North Clarendon Railroad Crossing. He was treated at the hospital for head cuts and bruises, while Gilford had a slight concussion and a knee injury and stayed a few days. The truck was practically demolished," Marjorie said of their miraculous escape.

Gilford and Willie after accident 1935.

In the fall of 1945, Willie was severely burned by an explosion that occurred as he was making a fire in the store's woodstove. The store caught fire, but Glendon got there in time to save his father's life and the store. Willie was hospitalized for several months but recovered from second- and third-degree burns. He also survived the deaths of Gilford and Gertrude. Marjorie agrees that having the store to carry on helped to keep him going as did the support of his children.

Willie Pierce, 90, one of Vermont's oldest merchants, 1962.

Marjorie described her father as "a good man who was always civic minded and interested in the welfare of his Shrewsbury friends and neighbors." In his early years at the store, when the mills were still going strong, he had often extended credit, knowing that he might not be paid. There were many times when small debts were forgiven, and he simply allowed people to continue to do business at the store. But one year, when he instructed Gordon to write off a rather large debt of $4,000, Gordon had vigorously objected. "My father responded sadly but sternly, 'Just do it; I don't want to see my buildings burned down.' And he meant it," Marjorie noted. Willie could be the ultimate pragmatist as well as generous.

After being struck by illness in January 1965, Willie's days in the store ended and he passed away on July 6. "As Shrewsbury's oldest citizen at the time of his death, he was one of the few remaining members of his generation, a man who exemplified the traditional Vermont qualities of industry, thrift, wit, common sense, and integrity," Marjorie wrote for his obituary, which added:

> He was active in the community and served as a town auditor, an overseer of the poor, and a selectman. In 1912, he was elected Representative to the state legislature. He was a Mason, holding membership in the Mount Moriah Lodge, Number 6 of East Wallingford and was a life member of the Rutland County Agricultural Association. He was an incorporator of the Rutland Hospital and had been a member of the Shrewsbury Grange. He served as a trustee of the Northam Cemetery Association and also of the Laurel Glen Cemetery Association in Cuttingsville.

After returning home, Marjorie had written a short biography of each family member while they were still healthy so she could have accurate histories and so this information would be "ready when needed." Once when the three siblings were being interviewed at the store and were trying to recall some dates, Marjorie had exclaimed, "Wait a minute, I'll get you our obituaries!" Very much alive at that time, Glendon and Gordon enjoyed a hearty laugh as she quickly disappeared, leaving a speechless reporter in her wake.

Just two years after Willie had passed on, an article entitled, "The Changing Times Threaten to End Shrewsbury's Only Store's Operation" appeared in the *Rutland Daily Herald* on February 11, 1967. Reporter Howard Coffin wrote:

> Marjorie and Glendon Pierce, sitting by the store's only source of heat, a pot-bellied stove, both said Friday: "We just don't know what will happen."
>
> Marjorie Pierce explained: "A man with a truck delivers milk up here now. Another man delivers bread. The state wants to take away our meat license. Business has been going down and we don't know how much longer we can keep going. . . .
>
> The W.E. Pierce Grocery probably won't be open much longer.
>
> The state says that the Pierces must put hot and cold running water in the store, though their house, in the same building, has it.
>
> The state also wants the Pierces to install a new freezer.

Here was another change in Vermont. Government was becoming a major factor, and with it, more cumbersome regulations were being enacted—something that didn't always set well (and still doesn't) with rural folk who are used to independent and frugal ways. Fortunately, stubbornness and perseverance are also Vermont traits, and with the Pierces' respect for history and tradition, the rally of patrons and a few changes, duty and the store prevailed. One added practical factor was that since they were living in the home they had inherited and each had savings from employment, they were financially able to pursue store operations without needing to make a large profit (nor did they have pay off a cumbersome business loan or mortgage).

Still, Glendon was only forty-six when he retired from his full-time job with Barrett in 1959 in order to assist Marjorie, and being a frugal and industrious person, he hoped to make some income from his labors on behalf of the store. Marjorie felt the same way. Tending store was far from a hobby at this point—the ten-hour days and trips to Rutland to

Glendon tending store, 1960s.

get supplies were demanding of their time and energy. At the same time, a milkman who was now making the rounds to area homes offered serious competition to their small business.

But having each other to assist with operations made it a do-able, if not thriving, business. Where debt, mortgages, or families to feed were issues for other country-store owners, those stores began changing hands or closing down all over Vermont. Of those that survived, very few stayed in the same family. This made W.E. Pierce Groceries something of an icon and one of the oldest, continually operating country stores in Vermont. It also helped to draw tourists in its later years.

Interestingly, the store's ownership passed to Marjorie. Glendon and Gordon decided that "they did not want the responsibility of ownership," so upon completion of the probate process, the business was officially deeded to Marjorie on January 1, 1967. "My brothers reasoned that they had their own interests, but they promised to help so we could keep the store in the family," she said. As the new store owner, Marjorie became a vital part of the Shrewsbury community, and for the younger generation that was now moving to town in increasing numbers, she became synonymous with "Pierce's Store." [Although she never changed the registered name from her father's "W.E. Pierce Groceries," residents and visitors always referred to it as "Pierce's Store." In fact, many thought that all the siblings were the owners since they often saw the brothers or Marion there as well.]

Preserving the Store Tradition

The store retained its special charm despite the changing times. The official North Shrewsbury Post Office that actually functioned in the store from 1871-1907 was back on display, complete with real letters from the past which Marjorie stuck into the cubby-hole compartments. The old stereograph or stereopticon viewer was there, too, and still working. By inserting a penny, one could see ten or so three-dimensional pictures before time ran out. Found throughout the store were the souvenirs and mementos of history: metal ice skates, wooden skates, surveyor chains, a chewing tobacco cutter, hay knife, buggy-whip holder, Betsy Ross flag with thirteen stars, a ticking wooden-works clock, a

North Shrewsbury "Post Office"

In 1956, Willie loaned the old North Shrewsbury Post Office to the Vermont Heart Association for its campaign. It became the model for "Heartwell, the only post office of its kind in the world" and was used for many years. Replicas of the hundred-year-old "post office" were later used in future campaigns around the state. The picture of the Green Mountain Postmaster seated at the Heartwell Post Office was painted by Saturday Evening Post cover artist George Hughes and was used on the cover of the Heartwell Almanack and Heart Association letterhead and put to many other uses as well.

brass cash register circa 1900, and the real wooden boxes that crackers, biscuits, and other products once came in. A lending library was still tucked into a small, back alcove, and toward the back of the room stood the big iron stove that supplied heat as long as Glendon, Gordon, or Marjorie fed it the wood chunks it so readily devoured.

Wooden benches, a wooden folding chair, and a rocker invited the stranger or neighbor to "set a spell." The walls were neatly lined with canned goods, boxes of cereals, and other staples. There were two glass-enclosed candy counters—on the left side of the store, one case contained boxes of candy bars; and on the right side, the penny candy.

Here was the well-worn, turned-over box that toddlers climbed up on to better see the candy in the case below. The child on tip-toes, arms outstretched to give a penny and receive its sweet reward—a kindly smile lighting the well-worn face as the ever-patient gnarled hands carefully counted out candy and pennies with the child. This was the image of caring that indelibly burned into the hearts and minds of all who ever saw it. The significance of these informal counting lessons was that

Eighteen-month old Jim Lorentz has to figure out how to get his lollipop, which is clutched tight in Marjorie's hand. Marjorie could be as mischievous as Glendon—note her intent look and Gordon's knowing smile.

children were learning about caring and patience from another generation, as were their parents who witnessed such scenes over and over.

However, with regular travel out of town, most people were doing major weekly shopping at large supermarkets in Rutland, so purchases at Pierce's Store were smaller now. By 1968, the main roads had been paved and the automobile was no longer a novelty but a household staple that made travel much easier than when Marjorie and her siblings were growing up. Yet, for people living in the Northam area, Rutland was still close to an hour round trip, so many continued to go to Pierce's for necessities and gasoline. In addition, Shrewsbury's population was growing once again, thanks to the out-of-staters who invested in property and to those who continued to move in to retire or raise families.

Thus, in the 1970s and 1980s, children continued to buy candy and soda, and local residents continued to stop in for milk or cheese, soup or bread, or whatever else they happened to run out of. For the cooks in a family, it was true convenience to know the store was open six days a week with regular hours 7:30 a.m. to noon and 12:30 p.m. to 6 p.m. weekdays and Saturday. (The store was closed from 12 noon to 12:30 p.m. so the family could eat and on Sundays so they could have a day off.)

With the change to a utilitarian "convenience store," Pierce's had not lost its social function, however. The store was still a gathering spot. For adults, there was still the latest news or gossip to catch up on; or politics, hunting stories, fires, tragedies, and community events to discuss. For children, still the connections to be made with kindly people of an older generation, still a tradition of penny candy to enjoy—and fun to be had with Glendon. Humor, a Pierce stock-in-trade, especially of jokester Glendon, was always dispensed with enthusiasm and subtlety. So was advice.

Henry Fee, Gordon, and Glendon. Henry's cows once dotted the landscape across from Pierce's Store. Henry's father rented the old Tom Stewart place from Willie in the early 1900s and Henry and his sister Belle grew up there. Henry later bought the place below the store where N.J. Aldrich had once owned a large parcel and had a lumber and grist mill. Henry and his wife Myrtle lived there for many years.

Although Shrewsbury had become a "commuting community," unlike some "bedroom towns," people still saw their neighbors at church or school; cows, horses, and sheep still dotted the landscape; and the country store was still a meeting place that provided vital connections along with the latest news.

For those who were visiting the area, the store was also a special place. They could meet genuine Vermonters who would regale them with funny stories or priceless history. Here, they could step back in time as they opened the glass paneled door and entered another era, a quieter Vermont. There was a sense of untouched history—a bare light bulb by the register, a refusal to carry beer or wine, and the decor of the old natural country store complete with old photographs and posters of politicians and presidents, of the Republican persuasion, naturally.

During the height of foliage or "leaf-peeping" season, the store was a particularly busy and a frequently photographed place. Another time when Pierce's became inundated was when the Shrewsbury moose paid a visit to Larry Carrara's farm a mile up the road toward Shrewsbury Center. There, a moose nicknamed Bullwinkle had become infatuated with a Hereford cow named Jessica during the fall and early winter of 1986. The lovesick moose made national television and *Time* magazine as he steadfastly wooed the brown-eyed Jessica.

As a result, Shrewsbury was suddenly on the map and everyone's foliage tour. The increase in visitors to the Northam area was astounding, and a good number of them stopped in at Pierce's on the way to see the moose. Although it could be tiring meeting so many people, Marjorie loved it all. So did her brothers. They saw increased business levels and even sold some moose memorabilia (sweatshirts with a moose and cow) in support of a local cause to stop expansion of the Killington Ski Area into neighboring Parker's Gore. "We would look out down the road and see cars bumper to bumper," Marjorie recalled of the only time this had ever happened and their "most active season ever."

The excitement generated by the lovesick moose was captured by a series of poems and articles in the local *Times of Shrewsbury*. Marjorie contributed this poem, which she modeled after Joyce Kilmer's "Trees."

FRIENDS OF PARKER'S GORE

The Shrewsbury Moose

I think that I shall never see
A moose as beautiful as he
Who lingers long at Larry's farm,
Intent a soft-eyed heifer to charm.

The tourists come from near and far
In beat-up truck or fancy car.
Their cameras click, they hem and haw
For such a beast they never saw.

Will he return to wood's protection,
Renounce the object of his affection?
Who knows the journey he may take,
Resigned his loved one to forsake?

O, let us hope that he may find
A handsome cow-moose of his kind,
Forget his Shrewsbury blunder
And all the stress that he was under,
Delight in woodland's lush array,
Roam far and happy many a day!

Good luck, farewell, no longer on the loose,
You must go back to forests of your youth;
No humans there so heedless and uncouth;
God made you free to wander wild — a moose!

As the years wore on, the many school-aged children who made Pierce's their habitual stop for snacks on the way home from school, or for a Saturday treat, became an increasingly big part of the store business. As a drop-off point for both school-bus children and "walkers," the store became a bustle of activity as "bus time" approached. Parents, who met their children at Pierce's often arrived early for conversation, food purchases, or gasoline. When the buses arrived, Marjorie and her brothers would "man all stations" as hungry youngsters rushed in to buy candy bars, soda, or ice cream. Only one Pierce sibling would usually be on duty in the store during a normal week day, but you could set your watch by the faithful rush of the others to assist at bus time. (At other busy times, whoever was tending store could call to the house for help by using the store-to-house phone which Glendon had rigged up. Likewise, when Marjorie was in the kitchen and had their meal ready, if they failed to show exactly on time, she would use this intercom to "buzz" them in the store. Patience was a virtue, but promptness was expected.)

The penny-candy purchases were minor in terms of business revenues, but how dear the experience of waiting on the very young. All the Pierces enjoyed children. Marion delighted in hearing about their activities and interests; Gordon liked to wait on them with kindly patience while Glendon took pleasure in gently teasing them. Marjorie relished the opportunity to hear about their schoolwork or to tell them stories about her childhood. It was a simple joy of country living to stay in touch with the young and enriched oldster and youngster alike.

The Pierces had a small television in the store, which kept them company on a slow day or informed on a big news day. Other than that, the store was relatively untouched by the modern era. No electric cash register or computers, no fancy scanning devices. Most country storekeepers were modernizing, often carrying beer and wine, newspapers, videos, and the kinds of goods that would sell well enough to support them. Those who were new owners had often paid dearly for the opportunity to move to Vermont and run a country store; they needed to make a good profit to pay their mortgages and to live.

By the 1970s, many general stores reflected the town they were located in. A store in a ski town could expand and carry a general and diverse winter line of goods that were sure to sell to skiers. Wine, gourmet foods, gifts, moccasins, pottery, sweaters, and gloves could be big sellers along with bread, cheese, bacon, and maple syrup. A merchant in a more remote town who catered to a mix of locals and seasonal visitors could carry a complete line of insulated boots or ski mitts, knowing these items would be in demand and would sell well because there was no nearby competitor and it was convenient to buy there.

North Shrewsbury was not one of those towns. It was neither Waitsfield nor Woodstock, Manchester nor Cavendish. What was unique, and still is, is the fact that Northam remains a rural hamlet that is somewhat isolated and not easy to access in winter when snows are deep. The Pierces liked it this way as do most of the residents who stay. So quiet and peaceful, a nice place to visit and see how things once were. So the Pierces chose to make few changes, intent on maintaining the history of both home and store.

W. E. Pierce Groceries, as the sign above the front door outside still reads, was a rare breed by the 1980s and rarer still in the early 1990s. As a result, the Pierces were often interviewed for television and radio programs as well as for the print media. A photograph of Marjorie as seen through the front store window adorned the cover of the Christmas issue of *Country Journal* magazine in 1986. Vermont magazines and newspapers featured articles on the store or the Pierces, while histori-

Glendon & Marjorie posed for this January 2, 1994, Boston Globe Magazine *ad.*

138

ans recorded them for oral histories, film, and radio. The Pierces were also occasionally featured in articles in big-city newspapers and even in a magazine advertisement which had been photographed at the store. (Photographs of the store continue to be used in advertisements in local newspapers, although not always with permission!)

Through this media attention, the Pierces became well-known and made the acquaintance of hundreds of people traveling through. Locals stopped in for the necessities and for the latest news, but visitors were increasingly coming to seek out this authentic store, run by some of the oldest and longest continuing storekeepers in Vermont. Some of these people were distant relatives or friends from Marjorie's school, teaching, or camp days. Others were perfect strangers who heard about the genuine country store in its idyllic setting and made it a point to visit. They would purchase a candy bar, soda, cheese and crackers, or an occasional trinket; the opportunity to do so was as significant a rite for them as the lively conversation was for the Pierces.

The guests and dignitaries who dropped in were a treat and a reward. John Coolidge, Calvin's son, stopped by once a year on his way to visit the grave of Aurora Pierce, who is buried with Eli's family in the Northam Cemetery. People running for office were welcome to make an appearance at the store, and local or state candidates' posters were

June Wilk, Governor Richard Snelling, Marjorie, Glendon, & Commodore Carlos Bailey, 1980.

hung regardless of party. The late Governor Richard Snelling, his wife Barbara, the new minister in town, Rutland Mayor Gil Godnick, candidates for the Vermont House or Senate, or U.S. Senator James Jeffords could be seen stopping in to meet and chat with the locals, or to get a Pierce opinion on some issue of the day.

Jeffords, a Shrewsbury resident who lives a mile down the road, was particularly taken with the store and the Pierces' knowledge of events and issues about which they cared deeply.

Marjorie so enjoyed meeting people that she rarely tired of clerking in the store. In fact, if a regular customer happened to be come in late and Marjorie had to be heading off to the kitchen, she would be duly "miffed" to miss out on the conversation and would quite clearly let the guilty party know they were late.

Asked about this, Marjorie freely admitted as to how this could irritate her. "I couldn't count on Glendon or Gordon to come in and tell me everything," she said with a straight face dissolving into a smile that admitted she liked to keep up on the latest town gossip!

With this admission and always willing to poke fun at herself as well as others, Marjorie took great delight in reminiscing about "the store days." She spent an afternoon laughing over memories as she helped re-create a store scene circa 1981. It took several drafts to get it right, but Marjorie was especially happy to offer readers a glance into what a visit to Pierce's Store was like when she was the owner. The following is a composite story developed from Marjorie's and others' recollections of episodes that actually took place over a period of time. They are indicative of the wonderful one-on-one encounters that became precious memories for all who experienced them.

Marjorie loading the stove on her 90th birthday.

The two Snelling boys, Richard & Nathan.   Hannah, Linnea, & Ingrid Wilson.

The neighborhood children were all regulars at Pierce's Store.

December 1981 hot dog and marshallow roast at the Northam Picnic Pavilion.
Grandpa & Grandma Duch, Aunt Carolyn, and Jason and Jonathan Lorentz.

Chapter Ten

Pierce's Store
Circa 1981

Gone were the cracker barrel, the game board, and the red coffee grinder. Gone, too, were the large sacks of grain and the barrels from which flour, sugar, and other staples had once been sold. No longer were the doors reopened after dinner for socializing till nine in the evening, when the men would make their way home by lantern light. But the old cast-iron stove was still working and had been warming the store nicely on this frigid winter day.

Gordon had been unusually busy pumping gas all morning. Saturdays were always busier now with so many new folks and snowmobiliers stopping by. Things had changed; there were no grain or salt-pork sales anymore. Now, it was gasoline, soda, and candy. The new people bought a lot of cheese, bread, milk, and eggs, too.

Suddenly, Marjorie's attention was drawn to the door. She chuckled as she thought to herself, *Oh, oh, Glendon sees the two Snelling boys coming in. Hope they don't get too mad.*

Glendon loved to tease the young brothers. For a whole week he'd been greeting them with, "Hi Girls!" Their faces had turned bright red, but they had held their tongues and politely replied, "Hi Glendon."

Yesterday, when he said "Hi Girls," Richard, no longer able to contain himself, had retorted, "Hi Marjorie!"

What a chuckle Glendon got out of that! He even commented at dinner how the younger one had finally spoken up. "Can't have boys be too meek and mild," he joked. Smiling despite herself, Marion had tried to give him a stern look.

Like other local children, the two came in almost every day for candy, soda, or ice cream. Sometimes, their mother Jan sent them for groceries. Most of the time, though, they bought penny candy, and Jan came in at the end of the day for whatever she needed. Marjorie looked forward to chatting with her about quilts and what was going on in the family or in town.

Out of the corner of her eye, Marjorie could see that Glendon was going easy on them. Just then Marion walked in and over to them. Marjorie knew all would be well—no fireworks, just a nice conversation today.

As she finished waiting on the new couple from up on the mountain, Marjorie commented on the young crowd they had been seeing lately. "You folks eat a lot of cheese," she added, as she put a pound of Crowley Colby and two loaves of bread into a bag.

The two new boys from up on the mountain were coming in the door. They were shivering but went right to the candy counters. As the older boy approached the candy-bar counter, the smaller one climbed up on the box to peer at the penny candy. He could barely see over the top of the glass shelf. He reached his chubby little hand up and gave Marjorie his ten pennies.

"My, Jonathan, that's some sweet tooth you have today. What would you like?"

"I'll have Tootsie Rolls and Swedish Fish, please."

"Okay, one, two, three, four, five fish. And here's five Tootsie Rolls. Now, let's count the pennies. One, two . . . that's right, ten pennies. Why don't you come sit by the fire while you eat your candy? You look cold."

Across the room, Glendon waited on Jason, and then, they joined Marjorie, who sat down in her favorite rocker by the woodstove. The boys sat on the long wood bench next to Gordon and Marion and opened their candy.

"Where have you been swimming, boys?" Glendon asked.

Five-year-old Jonathan gave Glendon a funny look. "It's too cold; we've been skiing."

Seven-year-old Jason piped up with a detailed description of their long cross-country ski up to the CCC log shelter and told of their hot dog roast with their grandfather. "He came to visit us for Christmas and to ski. He skied back up the hill to get the car because we were too tired and hungry."

"Did you tell your grandpa what I told you about the road and the shelter?" Marjorie queried.

"We told him our road was built by the CCC boys and that they made the Northam Picnic Shelter and the big fireplace where we roasted our hot dogs."

"Do you know that my brother Gilford helped build the CCC Road you live on and that he helped build the shelter, too?"

"Is that the one you told us died in the war, Marjorie?"

"That's right, Jason, you have a good memory. So where did you go next?"

"We skied down to a place where there is this huge boulder. Up on the road there is a sign that says Meeting House Rock, 1818. Was there a house there?"

Gordon and Marion smiled as Glendon let out a loud guffaw. Marjorie gently explained, "No, that's an historic site. It's where the settlers held church services before they built a church. The church building was called a Meeting House back then, so they called it Meeting House Rock and held services there in the good weather. Sometimes, they would have picnics afterwards and stay and rest and sing songs. The minister stood on top of the Rock. I tried to climb up there once, but it is very steep and tricky and I never made it. So where did you go next?"

"We showed grandpa the old cellar hole where you said there was a sawmill. It was the one where Mary Russell grew up and heard the bears hollering in the woods at night, right?"

"Yes, and did I tell you the rest of the story? She married Orey Wright who had a sawmill on the old Bennington Camp Road. When the mill broke down one day, it took time to get it going again. So she worked all night, and they sawed the logs by lantern light and had them ready for building the new Northam church the next morning."

"You didn't tell us that story, Marjorie, but yesterday we skied down to the Bennington Camp to see the icicle. It's over the roof of the house, but we didn't see any camp or sawmill," Jonathan chimed in.

The Pierces chuckled as Glendon explained that the Bennington Camp was the name of the house next to the Ice Mound. "Some men from Bennington, Vermont, lease the land there, and they built that house to use in hunting season. It's a rough place to stay without electricity so they call it a camp, only we call it the Bennington Camp after the men who use it," he said kindly. Then he added, "Each winter they aim the

The ice mound next to the "Bennington Camp" December 1981. This is the former site of the old Tom Stewart farm on old Road 14. Ephraim lived on the right side of this road. Lands along road were bought by Willie in 1908.

pipe that is inside the spring straight up so the water shoots up into the air and freezes into an ice mound that grows all winter long."

Not to be outdone, Marjorie added, "There used to be a farm there. Our Great-great-grandfather Ephraim Pierce was one of the first town settlers; he lived near there. The Orey Wright Sawmill was at the end of that road, too, but it's gone now. Hedgehog Sam used to live nearby." She beamed as everyone chuckled at her joke.

Intrigued, Jason told how they had skied out that road and after going up a hill had turned left by the red gate. "Grandpa saw a stone that we never saw before. He said, 'What's this doing out in the middle of the woods?!' The writing on it said, Etta J. Pierce, Died 1881. Grandpa said to ask you about it, Marjorie."

"Well, she was a daughter of Ephraim's grandson Edwin. Edwin was my grandfather, so Etta J. was my father's sister. She died from scarlet fever when she was only ten-years old so I never knew her. Her family moved to Nevada when she very young, but they came back to Vermont and lived on the farm where the Orlich place is now.

"When Etta J. died, she was buried in the Northam Cemetery and her gravestone was placed there, too. But one day my father looked at the big monument for Edwin Pierce and decided he should simplify the family plot. So he took Etta J.'s little stone and put it out behind our red barn. When someone bought the barn, my father moved Etta's marker to a stone wall behind our house. After my father died, Glendon and Gordon didn't think it looked right there, so they reset it under an apple tree on their property near where her great-grandfather Ephraim once lived.

"There was a little silver plate on top of the stone that fell off; it's in a box with a lock of her hair and a sample of her handwriting. Wait a minute, I'll be right back."

Marjorie returned with an old box and showed them its contents. The boys' eyes grew big as she placed the paper and hair in their hands. They had never seen a piece of paper or a lock of hair that was one-hundred-years old before.

"Wasn't she a pretty girl?" Marjorie asked, as she produced Etta J.'s photograph. "Isn't it so sad that she died so young? Poor Etta's stone traveled from the cemetery to the barn and to our house, and now it's up on the mountain under an apple tree, where Glendon and Gordon mow the meadows to keep them nice."

"Wow, wait till grandpa hears this!" Jonathan exclaimed.

Curious, Jason asked, "Is the Orlich place that big white house where we stop to get mail at our box?"

"Yes, that's the Orlich place now, but it's where Etta J. and my father lived with their family, and where my sister and brothers and I grew up before we came to live in the house here at the store. It was a real farm then. When we were little, Marion and I played outside under an old apple tree there.

"We came to the store in 1918, when I was almost fifteen years old. Isn't that a long time ago?"

"Is that why this stove looks so old?" Jonathan piped up.

"Yes, it was here before we were. So was the cash register and the post office over there. Want to see me load the stove?" Glendon asked. At their nod, he opened the door and moved toward the woodbox. "Just a few

Etta J.

chunks will keep us toasty and keep Jack Frost away. Wouldn't want that naughty boy to come here."

"Is he a bully? Is he going to come after us on our way home from school?" Jonathan asked.

Marion gave Glendon one of her looks and reassured the kindergartner that Jack Frost was just a storybook character who made people cold. "Remember, Glendon has a big sense of humor," she added kindly.

Unable to resist, Glendon added, "But he might nip your toes." Even Gordon laughed.

Jonathan was looking more worried than ever, so to distract him Marion asked if he had seen a flag like the one on the wall.

As he shook his head, Jason said, "We saw a flag like that in our history book in school. It's a Betsy Ross flag with thirteen stars, isn't it? You sure have a lot of old stuff in here. Can we see the pictures now?"

The Pierces nodded, and the boys made their way over to the stereopticon viewer, eagerly inserting a penny. They loved the three-dimensional pictures of the wonders of the world. The viewer got stuck, so Marjorie picked up the heavy machine and gave it a shake. The boys put in two more pennies. They had already seen thirty different cards of photographs, but Marjorie said there were dozens more. It was going to take a lot of visits to see them all they figured.

"Well, Marjorie, there's Grandpa to give us a ride home. We had fun talking with you. Thanks for the candy and the history lesson. Bye Glendon. Bye Gordon. Bye Marion."

"Well, thank you for your business and come again, boys. Hold the door for Hannah and Mandy, Jason. That's a good boy," Glendon responded.

"Say hello to your mother and father for us," Gordon added softly.

As the door closed, Glendon stepped up behind the penny-candy counter and asked the girls what they would have. "That's ten fish and one Tootsie Roll, Miss Hannah Wilson?"

"No, I said one fish and ten Red Hots."

Mandy Heitzke & Marjorie

"Oh, okay. Let's see, here's one fish, five Tootsie Tolls, and five Red Hots. Right?"

"No, I didn't order Tootsie Rolls! You know I don't like them."

"Oh, Mandy, you want the ten Tootsie Rolls?"

"No, I wanted five Tootsie Rolls."

"Okay, girls. Let's see, Mandy Heitzke wants . . ."

Marjorie smiled as she rocked by the fire. Glendon sure had them going now. Finally, they came over to the stove, and Hannah told her and Marion all about her new kitten.

As they chatted, little Amanda Mitchell came in quietly and climbed up onto the box with help from Gordon.

From behind the counter, Glendon greeted her. "Hello, Amanda. Boy, that sure is a pretty name. I wish my name was Amanda!"

"You're a boy Glendon; you can't have a girl's name!"

"Oh, that so? I see. I guess that's why my mother named me Glendon, then. So what will it be, Amanda Panda?"

"Mitchell, I'm Amanda Mitchell, Mr. Glendon Pierce!"

Gordon smiled as he went outside to fill Tom Mitchell's car with gasoline. He knew Amanda would still be counting candy and pennies for Glendon when he went back in and that Marjorie would be standing next to her, helping the toddler with her numbers.

Mr. Glendon Pierce

Amanda Mitchell

The Old Pump Organ

The old pump organ is silent now,
But there in the corner it stands
Where it answered with heavenly voices,
The touch of my mother's hands.

We would gather there at the long day's end —
I'll remember those hours forever,
For cares were never so far away
As when we sang together.

How sweet were its notes for the weddings,
How tender its tones for prayer,
How much a part of our family life
And the memories we share!

And even now, if I close my eyes,
I can hear it swell and sigh —
Nudging and tugging my heartstrings,
A voice from days-gone-by.

Barbara Burrow

The parlor in the Pierce Home with Damaris's Estey Organ in the corner.

Chapter Eleven

A Memory House of Yesteryear

The Pierce home is yet another special place that provides a unique tie with the past. The house has been largely kept the way it was when Marjorie was growing up, with the exception of some modernizing of the kitchen. Willie had added an electric hot water heater in the 1950s, so the water reservoir attached to the woodburning kitchen range was no longer necessary for heating water and was replaced with two propane-gas burners. Sometime later, he converted the Home Comfort Range to propane gas and replaced the old cast iron kitchen sink with a stainless steel double sink with Formica countertop. Marjorie also did some "updating" in the 1980s when she substituted a modern washer and dryer for the wringer washer and had both kitchen and pantry floors recovered with linoleum. Otherwise, the water still came in by gravity feed from springs on the mountain behind the house and the furnishings remained much the same as when Gertrude kept house—except for the televisions, which were acquired in the late 1950s.

Visitors to the Pierces are often given a house tour and the opportunity to delight in another era. The kitchen is the first area guests see because the front door used by the Pierces leads directly into this room. Setting a welcome tone is the vintage Home Comfort range, a stove that still warms the entire area (with no other heat source in the kitchen

except for the hot water pipe that runs across the ceiling to the nearby bathroom). Two heavy kettles full of water and three antique cast irons can be found on the top of the range, regardless of the season.

In the center of the kitchen is a large wood table where the family ate and where Marjorie still takes her meals. Above the table is a fifties-era, pull-down light fixture that Marjorie adjusts for mealtime light and late night reading or typing. A vintage rocking chair that Edwin once enjoyed, a pendulum clock, and an antique barometer with powder horn hanging from it are among the family heirlooms found in this cozy room. A framed print of the Morse Monument, which had hung in Damaris's home, and which keepsake led Marjorie to believe that they are related (through Caty Morse, her great-great grandmother) to Samuel F. B. Morse, hangs on a wall. Glendon's

The "front door" to the cozy kitchen with Edwin's rocker on right.

small blackout lamp, which he used in the war, sits on top of the large, modern refrigerator. A small television on a table and a rotary-style phone complete the room, which is an eclectic blend of past and present. There is no microwave or toaster oven, no breadmaker or blender, and no automatic dishwasher.

Off to one side of the kitchen is an old-fashioned pantry, a large unheated room lined with shelves on two walls. Upon those shelves are meticulously arranged canned goods, other foodstuffs, and supplies. Marjorie had kept the wringer-washer in this room until it expired; only then did she give in to modern appliances. She was, after all, in her eighties and doing laundry for three or four people, she reasoned. So now there are the washer and dryer along with a small electric stove lining the third wall.

Another back door off the kitchen opens out onto the long glass-enclosed, unheated porch that Willie built. Here a long table is surrounded by the eight chairs which Marjorie salvaged from the old blacksmith shop. Glendon had fixed a rung or two, and she painted them black or red and then alternated them around the table. Some of the furnishings on the porch (and in the home) had been brought down from the farm, among them a child's rocker and an unusual settee de-

The sunny back porch which overlooks the stream.

signed to accommodate a sitting person and a sleeping baby. It had belonged to her Great-grandmother Catherine Colburn Aldrich. Marjorie has filled this room with some of the three hundred bottles that she collected, a myriad of antiques, and several of her many plants.

When family groups, the cemetery association, or the Shrewsbury Ladies Club meet at her home, they are ushered onto the back porch or into the sitting room (living room) depending upon the season. Chairs and several rockers line the sitting room along with a mission table, a roll-top desk, and the grandfather clock which Glendon built. The clock strikes the quarter hour and plays a tune on the half-hour and hour, keeping memories alive in what can best be described as a memory house of yesteryear. Plants, books, and photograph albums are found in this room, which is made pleasant by a large bay window that lets in light and warmth.

To the right back of the sitting room is the bathroom with old-fashioned claw-foot tub, sink, toilet, medicine cabinet, and towel racks and stand along with a 1950 calendar from W. E. Pierce Groceries. In 1999, reproductions of those fixtures were the fashion in new home construc-

The Pierce sitting room with the grandfather clock which Glendon made in 1962.

Willie and Gertrude's Room

tion and remodeling—in the Pierce home, they are the "real thing" and still working.

A second rear door off the sitting room leads to Willie's and Gertrude's meticulous bedroom, and from there another door leads to Gilford's room. Both rooms remain as they were, with photos and keepsakes that belonged to their former occupants. In each of these and the others' bedrooms, there is also a watercolor painted by Marion.

Off the front end of the sitting room is a small hall, which has a seldom-used "front door" as well as a door to the formal parlor. Here are found family portraits, a fifty-year-old plant, and many heirlooms, including Damaris's Estey organ which Gertrude had so lovingly played.

A set of narrow, steep steps leads to the upstairs hall and four bedrooms. These are tidy rooms with vintage beds, dressers, and washstands; two have very small windows. Still fully furnished, each room reflects its former occupant with their photographs, keepsakes, and diplomas on display. Marjorie's is the smallest room. There is a single bed, chest, bookcase, and a lady's dresser graced by a converted kerosene lamp with frosted chimney globe. Artfully arranged throughout the

Gilford's room.

Marjorie's room with some of her bottle collection in cabinet at right.

room are special gifts, knickknacks, a curio collection, and photographs—all treasured reminders of friends, trips, and events.

Gordon's room is larger with a big carved bed that came down from the farm, a small washstand, and a neat dresser. There are few wall hangings, mostly certificates. Marion's smaller, back room features a lovely "spool" bed from the farm—it may have been her grandmother's or great-grandmother's—braided rugs which Marion made by hand, and a curio collection of animals and figures.

Like Gordon's room, Glendon's is bigger. "They didn't move away from home so they had larger rooms," Marjorie explained. Army keepsakes and Republican Party certificates are prominently displayed. A large desk, a file cabinet, dressers, and a large rope bed (ropes in place of a box spring to support a mattress) make up the furniture. An explanation as to the origin of the saying, "Sleep tight, don't let the bedbugs bite" can be found on a piece of paper on the desk. It explains that by pulling on the ropes to "tighten" them, one could prevent the bed from collapsing under the weight of its occupant.

Gordon's room with the large carved bed.

Glendon's room with desk and memorabilia.

Marion's room with spool bed and some of her drawings on wall.

The house is heated via a large floor register in the sitting room. It allows heat to rise from the basement below (where an oil furnace replaced the original wood furnace) and spread to rooms on the main level via the doorways. Ceiling registers allow heat to rise to the second floor and heat the bedrooms above.

The antique furnishings of the Pierce homestead consist of both upholstered and wood furniture, oriental and braided rugs. Carefully maintained, these furnishings remain comfortable and functional, creating a throwback to another era, when, honoring frugality, one did not redecorate with the times. Books, magazines, and Marjorie's many plants attest to a homey atmosphere where daily reading is still important. Perhaps the only real concession to modern life is the television. The news and sports shows were enjoyed by her brothers, but except for the news, Marjorie doesn't spend much time by the television. Her reading, visitors, and correspondence still take up most of her leisure hours.

Surrounding this home is a neatly kept yard that gently slopes to Sargent Brook out back, where a wooden bridge built by Gordon crosses to a small lawn area. Beyond, the wooded hillside provides a sturdy mountain backdrop to the charming scene below. The remains of Marjorie's vegetable and flower garden—kept up by her and Glendon until recent years and now blooming with perennials in season—lies below the store where the tennis court once stood. Across from the store, there are perennial flower patches that Marjorie planted and a flag pole. The old red barn (now a residence), which her father had owned, and a large triangular green on which stands an ancient pine tree (that she reckons to be ninety-feet or more tall) lie opposite the parlor side of the house. Marjorie recalled that one year a resident tree surgeon brought up a cherry picker and put lights on the pine at Christmas.

The Northam Church, fire station, Town Office and a nursery school (former Northam School), and a few homes and gardens complete the crossroads scene where the Pierce home still stands proud and pretty. It is a place that Marjorie finds both peaceful and relaxing, one that she notes "has been spared by floods and other natural disasters."

With so much history and tradition in the home, store, and village, it is little wonder that folks like U.S. Senator James Jeffords have expressed the wish that the entire homestead could be put "into the

Smithsonian." By taking us back into Vermont history, the Pierce home and store show us a simpler time when connections, tradition, and community were a treasured part of daily life.

Aerial View of Pierce Home and Store.

Adults liked to meet at Pierce's Store for talk and penny candy, too. Sitting with the Pierces are Edward Rondina (top left) and Willard Smith, right.

Chapter Twelve

Good Citizens

Marjorie, Glendon, and Gordon each had their own social lives and special friends whom they saw regularly. Each also participated in various town organizations and events, and this played an equally important part in the social fabric of their lives. Whether filling an elected position or simply volunteering to do something (often without being asked), their deeds sprang from a genuine spirit of helpfulness and caring. Working to help make Shrewsbury a better place was something that they did quietly, but often and well. Their efforts were recognized by the community with a celebration in their honor, several Town Report dedications, and awards of various kinds. But through it all, they remained modest about their accomplishments—though pleased with, and grateful for, the recognition given.

In discussing the early era of neighbor helping neighbor and how that engendered a greater sense of community, Marjorie remarked, "I think we were taught to be helpful. Not everyone was that way. It's something you were taught." Willie and Gertrude had set good examples with their own industry and willingness to help others. Like them, Glendon, Gordon, and Marjorie served on various boards and took on the types of small jobs that are depended upon to keep a small town functioning. Marion displayed this trait where she lived in Philadelphia and willingly helped with charitable events when visiting Shrewsbury.

160

Marion tending a flea market booth in Cuttingsville, 1983.

Following her retirement in 1967, Marion did volunteer work for the American Friends Service Committee, Material Aids Department. She was a trustee of the White-Williams Foundation, which provides scholarships for promising high school students from economically deprived circumstances, serving on this board for many years (she was previously a counselor there from 1926-1942). Marion was also an active life member of the Philadelphia Public School Employees Association and later the Pennsylvania Retired Teachers Association. During the summers when she was in Northam, she made stuffed animals for the annual Ladies Aid Bazaars and helped out in other ways as well.

In her private life, Marion socialized with friends, enjoyed drawing, painting, and various crafts, and took courses in oil painting and ceramics. Marjorie recalled Marion as being quite talented but also very modest. One of Marion's hobbies was to collect brass and copper goods that were sold on the streets of Philadelphia. "She enjoyed helping the immigrants who were selling their wares," noted Marjorie, who still has several pieces on display, including her favorite, a copper ritual washing cup.

Marion returned to her Vermont home in 1982 and helped out with town activities and at the store where she was especially attentive to young people. A quiet person by nature, she always drew out children, engaging them in conversation where they did the talking despite any shyness they might have, and she, the careful listening. Marion was also attentive with adults and had a lasting effect on those who knew her.

Like Marion, Gordon was modest and retiring, but he also had a competitive streak and especially enjoyed sports. Several townspeople recalled Gordon as being quite serious about golf, tennis, and horseshoes, noting he took real pleasure in friendly competition. While growing up, he and Glendon had regularly played baseball on a meadow at the family farm and joined in family croquet games. After the move to the store in 1918, they built a grass tennis court and later converted it to clay.

"Gordon was quite a player. He played tennis at Spring Lake Ranch and golf at Freddie Oresman's (where a couple of holes were set up on the back lawn). Later in life, he enjoyed watching football, baseball, and basketball on television," Marjorie commented in an 1989 interview.

"But he really loved horseshoes," Glendon had added, pointing out that Gordon once "played in a state horseshoe tournament."

He was also an avid amateur actor, occasionally performing in summer plays with Dr. Martyn, Shrewsbury's resident physician. "Not many people knew it, but he played the violin. He would retreat to his room where he

Glendon, Gordon, unidentified, and Gilford playing horseshoes, 1941.

played behind a closed door for his own enjoyment. He could be a very private person," Marjorie said, adding:

He was exceptionally good in math and tutored a friend who later became a surgeon. Dr. Layden used to tell him, "I've got to do a good job taking care of you because you helped me with my math."

Gordon was a meticulous bookkeeper. He would sharpen his pencils and keep neat, accurate records. He was very conscientious.

Often there would be a light bulb burning in the store at night. It would be Gordon going over the books. "I'm just checking prices," he would tell us. If he found mistakes with the orders, he would always let the wholesalers know if the store was under or overcharged.

From 1942 to 1960, Gordon applied those considerable math skills to his job as Town Auditor, and he audited the books of the Shrewsbury Community Church for many years as well. He took special care in whatever he did, working at Stewart's Service Station, stocking shelves, and maintaining his truck, their home, or the land "up on the mountain."

Although slight of build, Gordon was extremely strong. He tackled difficult projects that often involved heavy lifting or backbreaking hard labor. He put in a new foundation under the garage by himself, and when the roof needed work, it would be Gordon fixing the slates or scraping off the moss as Glendon had a bad back. During a fierce storm in the mid-1980s, a large tree blew down near the Pierce home. Instead of accepting an offer of help from the local Boy Scouts, Gordon and Glendon cut the tree up, and then Gordon hand dug the root ball until it was uncovered and he could pull it away with his truck.

But it was the "mountain lands" he enjoyed most, whether improving the acreage Willie had purchased on the Bennington Camp Road, which he and Glendon now owned, or preparing the site at Meeting House Rock for the annual pilgrimage and worship service. Gordon also loved to build and repair

Gordon building a bridge across the stream behind the Pierce home, 1978.

rock walls. Like neatly stocking the shelves, he found this work immensely satisfying. He had an aesthetic sense that utilized the skill of his hands, the mental acuity of his mathematical mind, and the facility of a big heart to tackle the lowliest or loftiest task and then took simple pleasure in his accomplishments. As Marjorie and others noted, "Gordon was a very smart man, but he was a country boy at heart."

In appreciation for his help in looking after the property at the Northam Fire Station and keeping up the Northam Flag Pole, Gordon was made an Honorary Member of the Shrewsbury Volunteer Fire Department (SVFD) in 1982. In 1989 the SVFD named a newly acquired pumper truck after Gordon in recognition of the generous donations made to the fire department in his memory. (Later, in 1993, five Remembrance Trees were planted at the Northam Fire Station in honor of each Pierce sibling—further recognition of their dedication to the town.)

Like Marjorie, Glendon was outgoing and sociable and had done some traveling. He saw other parts of the state in his job with Barrett, as well as something of his country and the world due to his years of military service. He was particularly proud of having served in the Army Air Force and used many of the skills he gained during war time both in his job back in the states and as he tackled any kind of repair work throughout his life. He could analyze a problem, then use his experience and pure inventiveness to figure out a solution. This was also seen in his ability to repair and build clocks, a hobby he took up after buying a collection of clock works in the early 1960s. As for fixing things, there was no task he wouldn't attempt to help a neighbor or prolong the life of something useful. He had a large, well equipped and neat workshop off the back shed between the house and store.

Glendon also took special pride in grooming the "land on the mountain." As previously noted, he and Gordon carefully maintained the meadows and stone walls on the 235 acres they owned on the Bennington Camp Road. He also took care of the lawns and garden at the Pierce home and maintained the grounds at the Northam Cemetery, Community Church, and Firehouse for many years. He not only mowed the lawns but noticed if things needing restoring. If the church paint needed touching up or a fence began to fall into disrepair, Glendon would fix and paint it so that respect might be shown. He always admired beauty

164

Glendon enjoyed using hand tools to scythe the meadows on the mountain.

and nature; the conservation of resources was an integral part of that respect.

His service to the community included making out the Shrewsbury Grand List book for many years, serving as a Justice of the Peace, and sitting on the Board of Civil Authority for sixteen years, five of them as chairman. Glendon was a trustee and president of the Laurel Glen Cemetery Association, which took care of the cemetery in Cuttingsville, and served as a juror in Rutland Superior Court and in U.S. District Court. He was a member of the American Legion, the Disabled American Veterans, the American Defense Preparedness Association, and the Rutland County Agricultural Society. In appreciation for his volunteer lawn and snow removal services at Northam, he, too, was made an Honorary Member of the SVFD in 1982.

Marjorie was no less active in Shrewsbury than she had been in Attleboro. Here, her "outside" activities included being a Deacon in the Shrewsbury Community Church, secretary of the Ladies Aid, and treasurer of the Northam Cemetery Association (thirty-one years). She reported social news to the Times of Shrewsbury (eighteen years), was an active member of Amnesty International, and served as a trustee of the Shrewsbury Historical Society, taking on many research projects and typing up reports on long-forgotten cemeteries and old schoolhouses. Marjorie was an auditor and member of the Rutland Ann Story Chapter of the Daughters of the American Revolution and belonged to a number of other groups, including the Calvin Coolidge Memorial Foundation, the Sierra Club, the Nature Conservancy, and the Heritage Foundation.

Her interests and contributions were many and varied. She corresponded with pen pals in Switzerland and France as well as with many former students, with some of those correspondences continuing for fifty years! Long before the local Amnesty International Group was organized in town, Marjorie had written letters on behalf of prisoners of conscience to government leaders and dictators all over the world. Through her extensive reading and attendance at Amnesty International meetings, she was well informed on political issues and wrote meaningful letters seeking release of persons detained for their beliefs.

Preparing the Northam Church for summer services was one of Marjorie's annual tasks. Since the Northam congregation joined with the Center Shrewsbury and Cuttingsville Churches to form the Shrewsbury Community Church in 1950, the Northam Church was used for summer services only. Marjorie would unlock the heavy wood doors each spring, air the building out, sweep the floor, clean and fill the oil lamps, and dust the sanctuary. Before each Sunday service, she arranged fresh flowers from her garden on the altar table. She also researched the history of this church and organized a 150th anniversary celebration that was held in 1973 with about one-hundred people attending. Throughout the various changes of ministers and church leadership, Marjorie encouraged the continuation of the commemorative Meeting House Rock Service, sending personal invitations to "old-timers" and former residents to attend and placing notices in local newspapers. Following the Pierces' example, others now groom the site and see to the invitations and publicity, thus carrying on this unique and long tradition.

"Miss Pierce" also brought history to life and became known to every school child in Shrewsbury over the many years during which she led a Memorial Day tour of the Northam Cemetery. When children were in first or second grade, their teacher would line them up with little American flags and march them down a country lane to the burial lot, which sits high on a hill, about a quarter mile from Pierce's Store.

Here, Miss Pierce would meet them, be introduced by the teacher, listen to them sing a patriotic song, and proceed to show them the final resting place of Shrewsbury's soldiers who fought in various wars. "Now here's a Page," she would say. "Do we have a Page this year?" If a Page child were in the group, they would be designated to place a flag at that grave while Marjorie told about the ancestor buried there and how they served or died for their country. Her dramatic tales entranced the youngsters who long remembered the story of Edwin being afraid, the tragedy

Marjorie leading a class in Memorial Day observances, 1980.

of Gilford's plane being shot down, and the murder of Johnny Gilman (a Civil War veteran who was shot by some feuding types at Cold River after he had returned from the war).

Another way in which she helped people relive or learn about history was to take part in a variety of functions of an historical nature in town. There were historical society, church, and town events like the ice cream socials, national, state, and town Bicentennials, or a Ladies Aid Bazaar where she would dress in vintage apparel and delight guests with stories from the past.

In 1993, Jan Snelling, a former resident and close friend, nominated Marjorie as one of Rutland County's "Women Who Make a Difference." In March, she received this award from Castleton State College in recognition of her lifetime of academic, professional, and community achievements. In summing up her attributes, former neighbor Mark Hamelin wrote, "Marjorie Pierce is one of those rare individuals who are literally a Vermont and a national treasure. The depth of her knowledge and thirst for life's experience is a reflection of what is best in America."

In 1985, Betty Heitzke, another neighbor, organized a big party in honor of all the Pierces' dedication to Shrewsbury. It rained the day before and the day after, but on Pierce Sunday, September 1, 1985, it was absolutely beautiful! Some three-hundred townspeople and invited guests from Rutland and beyond celebrated the many Pierce contributions to the community. In good country tradition, there was an abundance of fine food, lively music, and a big card which everyone in town could sign. A pastel portrait of Marjorie, Glendon, and Gordon was presented to them and hung at Town Hall in honor of their continuous help to the community. Local resident Edward Cook read a poem he wrote about the Pierces, including Marion and Gilford who, though not there that day, were not forgotten.

Caught on tape at the occasion, State Representative (the late) Pete Sarty recalled campaigning in town and stopping at the store. "It really

From L to R, are five honorees: Susan Farrow, Audrey Butler, Marjorie Pierce, Jane Shortsleeves, and Jacki Lappen. Lt. Governor Barbara Snelling, who presented the awards, is on the right.

Gordon, Glendon and Marjorie display the pastel portrait painted by Doris Erb. It now hangs in Town Hall as a reminder of their service to the community.

tickled me to talk to whomever was at the store; and you couldn't find an ice cream sandwich anywhere else for thirty cents anymore," he said.

(The late) Commodore Carlos Bailey was also recorded. He recalled "knowing the Pierces, Willie and all the children. Over all my years in Shrewsbury, whenever I went into the store, I looked left and right and the goods were still the same as they were years ago," he said to gales of laughter.

Freddie Oresman, told of knowing the Pierces since 1945 when she bought the Bellany place.

I was in the Ladies Aid with Marjorie. In the early years that we held the bazaars, we made $40 and gradually got up to a $1,000. I thought it would be a good idea to do something for the nursing home residents and talked it over with Marjorie. . . . That's how we started the visits to my house on a bus we rented to bring the residents out here to the country.

Marjorie rode the bus and picked them up and brought them to my place. We served them homemade cookies and ice cream, and Marjorie Plumley led the singing.

Hull Maynard, who cooked the hamburgers for the party, observed that, "The Pierces did much for the town without any expectation of return, from painting the church and mowing the lawn, to keeping the flagpole up."

Charlie Wise, who was from Sherburne, commented that as an outsider campaigning in town, he was "warmly welcomed by the Pierce Family, who made me know what small town Vermont is, and that it is a thing we all need to treasure."

Former Representative and resident (the late) Don Moore and his wife Jean summed up the occasion, saying "no one is more deserving of a day like this than the Pierces," a sentiment echoed many times during the day and in the many messages on the community card, a few of which follow.

Congratulations on your years of unselfish service to Shrewsbury. Your friendship is highly valued by us.

Many thanks for all you have done to keep our town Shrewsbury as it is today, rural and a town we are all proud of.

The Four Pierces, the four chambers of the heart, each separate, but working together to make Shrewsbury the place we all love.

You are the best. Like the zucchini, abundant and bountiful in your love for this town and all of us. We love you, too.

David Rice was an artful master of ceremonies for the "roast," but as an ever-candid Heidi Mitchell noted, "People were mostly paying serious tribute and sharing their appreciation rather than poking fun as you're supposed to at a roast." With that, she told a story about Willie (that Glendon had told her) selling fresh chickens at the store. "A woman asked for a chicken, and when Willie presented one, she asked for something bigger. Willie went out back and flattened the chicken a bit more to make it appear bigger, and then the lady said she'd take it. "But," she added, "I'll take the other one, too."

Another story was told about normally mild-mannered Gordon. One day while on a car ride with Marjorie and some ladies, Marjorie told a rather long story about some people who had stopped in the store and told about all the places they had been to, including Paris. Gordon showed his irritation with, "I bet they haven't been to Chippenhook."

With the crowd warming up to the "roast" concept, resident story-teller George Erb recounted the tale of an infamous, former neighbor.

> The FBI had approached Gordon and asked if they could use the store for a stakeout of the house across the way. Gordon acquiesced, and unbeknownst to Marjorie, agents began their watch. After witnessing the after-dark arrival of cars for a period of time, the FBI swooped down and arrested the drug dealer, who went to jail.

As Erb continued, he embellished his tale with a little fiction.

> The FBI took great quantities of angel dust (PCP) and put it in storage in the backroom at Pierce's Store. One day when I asked Glendon what had happened to the stuff, he said it was for sale at $100 a bag. Pierce's Store became a very popular place, a kind of modern-day mecca.
>
> Then one day, I decided to check things out and went in and said, "I'll take a bag."
>
> "Sorry," came the reply, "Marjorie used the last one in the biscuits last night."

An appreciative crowd howled with delight.

In more recent times, the Pierces were feted with the naming of the new playground at the Mountain Elementary School, the Pierce Play-ground. Since so many parents and their children had their lives touched in some way by the Pierces, the playground committee found this a natural way to celebrate their connection and contribution to the com-munity. The event was commemorated with a formal dedication on August 27, 1994, at which time, Glendon gave this wonderful tongue-in-cheek "acceptance speech."

> Dear Friends and Neighbors,
> On behalf of the Pierce family, I would like to thank all of you for coming here today, and the Playground Committee for naming this facility in our honor.

Glendon reading "acceptance speech" at dedication of the new Pierce Playground. The building to the right is a "Pierce's Store Playhouse."

The Mill River Newsletter, in referring to this project, said it was, "A sign of the close of one era and the start of another."

Both Marjorie and I attended Northam School through all eight grades where a prayer or salute to the flag was not prohibited. There were no lights, no running water, and the only heat we had was a large flat-top stove located between the teacher's desk and her class. On the coldest winter days, we were allowed to go to the woodshed to secure a chunk of wood to sit by the stove and study. Perrin Whitney, our local blacksmith, was paid $5.00 per winter for starting the fire each morning. I recall Marjorie telling of my mother wrapping her in newspapers before putting on her coat, then giving her two hot potatoes to put in her mittens to keep her warm during the half-mile walk (to school).

Outside, and of course unheated, was a very small building housing the boys' and girls' toilets. Signs were unnecessary for one didn't have to be too smart to learn which was which.

School would be from 9:00 a.m. to 12 noon, then 1:00 p.m. to 4 p.m., with fifteen minutes recess in both the morning and afternoon classes. There was no custodian. A lady was hired to clean the school before each session began—after which the teacher would sweep, if necessary, at the end of the day.

We had no busses, hence all students had to walk to school—some of them for over a mile, often on unplowed roads. I do not recall being provided with any recreational equipment. In some respects this was unnecessary expenditures as we received our exercise during recess, and in addition, most students had work to do at home. My job was to water, clean out the stables, and pitch down the hay for six to eight head of cattle and a pair of horses.

I relate to you our experience in attending an old-fashioned Vermont, one-room school with pride and wonderful memories of the simple lifestyle, uncomplicated by today's problems of drugs, sex, crime, and volumes of rules and regulations. Basically, success is in large measure, a problem for the student as exemplified by one Northam graduate, who, it is said, in later years became a millionaire.

Thank you, and in the years to come, may God bless each one of you real good!

Always the wry jokester, Glendon enjoyed having the last word on the "end of an era!"

In a most unusual honor, Marjorie was recognized for her frugality and conservation of resources on Dumpling Day 1998. This is an annual recycling celebration where Dump Master George "Chester" Brigham throws a party in honor of conservation and recycling at the spruced-up-for-the-occasion transfer station, better known as "the dump." In addition to bountiful food and a gala air of music and socializing, there was a small parade with a band and Marjorie, as the Honoree Dumpling, was carried Cleopatra-style by the dump master and his helpers. Marjorie, who was born in a time so simple that little was left to recycle—"everything was used up or fed to the pigs"—was still out and about at ninety-five and having fun while being honored as a thrifty soul.

Looking at the photographs of that day, Marjorie observed, "I never throw anything away." The emphasis on the never connotes sinful waste, but the wide-eyed face she made indicated that she is aware of just how big her collections are!

There is an old story about the contents found in Vermonters' attics: "Found in Miss So and So's attic was a bag labeled String too short to use." In Marjorie's small but neat attic, there is a little bag labeled, "Short pieces of string."

Marjorie was and continues to be sparing in her use of water, electricity, and just about anything else one can think of. It was her heritage to be frugal, and she remains unapologetically proud of it.

The Pierces were solid citizens and wonderful people. Friendly,

Dumpling Day 1998.

but not too friendly, helpful but not intrusive. They could be serious, but it was more their style to exercise wit and humor. There was definitely a playful side, whether Marjorie's play on words, Gordon's understated hamming it up, or Glendon's teasing. All were equally capable of the deadpan delivery of a joke, and even Marion could play along with an innocent air or by feeding a good line to one of her brothers.

Brought up on traditional Yankee values, they were independent, thrifty, industrious, resourceful, respectful, and self-reliant. But they also were raised in such a way that each possessed an innate sense of duty to try to make the world a little better place. Through a love of children, the land, the past, and tradition, they were helpful to others and to the community in which they lived.

So why, given these extraordinary gifts and their own sociable natures, had they never married?

Responsibility and Duty

Marjorie chuckled as she explained her single status but became more pensive as she described Marion's and her brothers' reasons.

I had lots of invitations and liked to dance and go to parties when I was young. I liked boys, but the right one just didn't come along, I guess. I didn't choose them, or they didn't choose me. We didn't click. There was one fellow I liked pretty well, but he moved to California. I was not a woman's libber, but I was pretty picky!

Marion was less a party person. She was more serious and reserved. She was devoted to her work and felt a lot of responsibility toward ministering to those who didn't have advantages. She felt a need to be of service. It was a quiet, reserved concern for the welfare of other people— social responsibility.

She was very smart, keen, bright, capable and extremely modest about it all, but she wasn't domestic. I was more domestic. I was more practical. She was more of a dreamer; social work was right up her alley.

Marion was more mild mannered and self-effacing, more like Mother. I'm a little more fiery, more aggressive. I'm like my father.

Gordon was a homebody. He fought a lack of energy all his life. I think it was a result of his illness as a baby. He nearly died. He would sit on the porch curled up and watch others play. I think he was burdened by frailty and didn't feel as strong as others and that affected him.

He had a girlfriend Vera Jenkins, who was a nurse—a nice, old-fashioned type girl that he liked. He met Vera through our sister-in-law Florence Pierce; her sister Helen Smith was Vera's roommate in Massachusetts. They shared an apartment there, and when Helen came home to visit, Vera often accompanied

Glendon, Vera Jenkins, and Gordon, 1963.

her. They met on one of those visits. He was more comfortable with a home-style person and enjoyed her company.

But he was a homebody. He tried working in the city, but he missed the country. He loved the land and taking care of it. I think that made him happy.

Glendon went to a family reunion and that's how he met Minnie Shaw. Her mother was a distant relative of my mother. She graduated from Rutland High School in 1930.

But she lived with her mother and sister in Rutland and felt a duty to them. Minnie's mother was along in years. There was a sense of duty for Minnie to take care of her mother, and Glendon wouldn't leave the store to go live with three women. He felt a strong sense of responsibility to the store and to Minnie. After Minnie's sister Susie died, Minnie was needed to look after her mother more than ever.

Glendon and Minnie were engaged, but I think it was a sense of duty to their responsibilities that they didn't marry. She was a city person, and he was a country boy, like Gordon.

Minnie and Glendon, who made Captain in the service.

Those who knew Glendon agreed that he felt strongly about the family tradition of the store and that "preserving it the way it was" was as important to him as having served his country in World War II. His connections to his ancestors and the land that they had farmed was also important to him. For Glendon, as for the Pierce family in general, loyalty, duty, and patriotism ran deep. So, just as leaving the store or the land was impossible for him, asking Minnie to leave the mother who needed her was something Glendon couldn't do. But knowing that the place where Minnie lived was to be sold, Glendon purchased a beautiful home in Rutland in 1990 and she moved into it. He also maintained it, and Minnie continues to reside there today.

While Minnie believes Glendon had hoped to join her there, she noted that it was important for him to help at the store as Marjorie could not operate it alone. "He got up at 5:30 in the morning to open the store. I couldn't ask him to live in Rutland and then commute to Shrewsbury because it would have meant that he would have had to get up even earlier," Minnie explained.

176

Minnie and Glendon, 1990s.

After the store closed in 1993, Minnie said she felt that Glendon was needed to help Marjorie, who was getting on in years (age ninety then). Minnie said she fully understood and accepted this type of responsibility because she had seen her mother take care of her grandmother, and then she herself had taken care of her own elderly mother. In discussing this, Minnie was accepting of the fact that a sense of duty and responsibility kept them from marrying, saying "We lived in different times and had different expectations."

But it didn't keep them from enjoying each other's company. From their first date in 1939 when he took her to the Weston Playhouse for her birthday until Glendon's sudden death in 1995, their relationship and time together were a source of joy and fun. Anyone who ever saw them on their dinner dates at a local restaurant or elsewhere always commented on their "lovey dovey" courtship that lasted throughout the years.

Marjorie often referred to Minnie and (the late) Florence Pierce as "sisters." Along with write-ups on each of her family members, Marjorie did one on Minnie. She was as much family as if she and Glendon had actually married and was included in family occasions over the years. Glendon's interest in Minnie probably played a role in his not wanting the responsibility of ownership in the store when that opportunity presented itself. As Marjorie had explained, "they had other interests," too.

Gordon was never engaged, but he had dated others before he established a relationship with Vera, who was very important to him. He went to see her at least one weekend a month except in winter. Occasionally, Vera visited him, sometimes bringing a sister or her parents with her. He spent holidays with her, and she visited him in the hospital during his last illness.

Minnie observed that while Gordon and Vera were very fond of each other, he didn't seem interested in marriage. Vera was taking care of her parents in her later life, so that duty might also have kept her from marriage. Marjorie thought that a deep attachment to Shrewsbury and an unwillingness to leave home for very long—he only spent five years away from Shrewsbury in his entire lifetime—contributed to Gordon's lack of interest in marriage. Marjorie also allowed that Gordon's working outdoors might have been his way of making himself strong (to overcome what she perceived to be his feeling of frailty).

In describing Marion, Marjorie was eloquent and admiring, but as she spoke of Glendon and Gordon she became pensive and wistful, observing: "I didn't know my brothers as well. I knew what made Marion tick. But although I lived with my brothers longer, I don't think I know what made them tick." It was as if somehow she was doing them an injustice by not being able to put her finger on what was so admirable about them in the way she had with Marion.

Being closer in age and benefiting from the "older sister influence" probably engendered some of that understanding. But Marjorie also had more in common with Marion. Like her, she had found her vocation in working with people. She could understand and appreciate Marion's "higher calling" to work with the less fortunate. She could openly admire the "dreamer" who wanted to make the world a better place. That was ambitious of Marion, and Marjorie understood that type of ambition that comes from being "useful."

With Glendon and Gordon, there was a different side. They had chosen to stay in Vermont, yet had declined to share in the store's ownership, preferring to help her and have the store in her name only. They respected the store tradition but had other interests, too. They were loyal but seemingly not "ambitious."

While she was aware of their stewardship of the land, Marjorie tended to see that as a practical thing, something she admired but didn't view as particularly ambitious. But within this stewardship, there was a different side that may have escaped her. Because they grew up doing more outdoors—helping Willie with farm chores, playing baseball in

Gordon

the meadow, building a tennis court, and clearing acre upon acre—they had a hands-on type of experience that was more old-fashioned and "pioneering" in nature.

They liked being outdoors and working with their hands. They had a keen aesthetic sense of how the land should look that complemented their own meticulous natures. But they had been practicing this stewardship of the land well before threats to the environment were in the forefront of the news and before it had to be "saved." So sensing that they derived enjoyment but not an income or livelihood from the land, Marjorie may not have seen it as important or ambitious of them. It was just something they had done for a long time.

Yet, the physical hard labor of clearing and maintaining one's land restores a kind of order and perspective that engenders great satisfaction and pleasure for those who engage in this work. It enhances the environment for wildlife as well. As trees also provide firewood, pride is derived from the independence that comes from heating with the wood one has cut (or given away or used in some project as Gordon often did). There is much "usefulness" in working with the land.

Marjorie knew about a different type of independence, one that sprang from her personal ambition. Her independence meant going off to see the world and experiencing it on its modern terms. Her spirit was that of travel adventures and leaving Shrewsbury, not staying. That was different from the pioneering spirit of her brothers who held fast to their Shrewsbury roots—theirs was an old-fashioned lifestyle that came from carrying on a pioneering tradition.

While Marjorie learned about land protection from her father and brothers who bought up parcels around the store and house and on the Bennington Camp Road, she herself never experienced the more basic connection of physical labor, or the satisfaction that comes from clearing meadows, building rock walls, or cutting firewood. She knew they

Hannah Wilson and Gordon early 1980s

enjoyed this work, but perhaps lacked the understanding of their "pioneering" usefulness and the deep contentment that it brought them. Hence, perhaps that feeling that she didn't quite know "what made them tick" as she called it.

But a fortuitous, later occurrence did illustrate that she knew them well. Looking through a stack of papers, she spied a photograph of Gordon with a young child and a kitten. Marjorie beamed as she exclaimed, "That is a good one. That is the side of Gordon that I don't think people saw."

Perhaps, in some way, she thought that people might not see a person's gentle and loving spirit as important, or that like her, they occasionally forget just how significant these simple things can be. But on another level, she instantly recognized that rural life is about the celebration of simple things and especially connections. Connections to one another, to the young, and to the land. That is what her brothers were about.

Responsibility, connections, and respect for tradition made Glendon and Gordon "tick," just as they did for her and just as wanting to leave the world a little better place did for Marion. This was another of the best traditions of a generation rooted in the past.

In the Pierce family, bonds were felt to the land, the store, one's neighbors and the community. Independence and maintaining traditions entered into this picture—the Pierces never lived by the expectations of others. Nor did they have to for fiscal reasons. With an inherited home and store, each sibling's financial position was enhanced by their own earnings and frugal lifestyles. Thus, they were all free from the financial pressures that can sometimes adversely influence life's decisions. In this respect, all were able to be truly independent and live according to their own sense of duty and responsibility. Each was true to a personal calling, and within that context, led an upright and useful life.

Interior of the Northam Church, which Marjorie kept up for many years.

Marjorie has never stopped teaching. Here she is seen giving a lesson in 1998 to second grade students of the Mountain School.

Friends attend annual birthday parties for Marjorie, returning the affection she has shown others for so long. L to R: Howard Coffin, Senator James Jeffords, Jan Snelling (organizer of the parties), and Minnie Shaw.

A vintage year for the "Ice Mound." The Pierces all enjoyed the humor of this sculpture at the Bennington Camp and our reactions to it.

In recognition of their service to community and country, Senator Jim Jeffords formally presented the Pierces with several Congressional Record plaques at Marjorie's 90th birthday party at Town Hall.

Gilford (on May) & Glendon, 1925.

L to R top row: Angie Guild, Damaris Aldrich Pierce, Celestia Lord. Below: Ella Headle Works, Ella Lord Aldrich, Minnie Sanderson Whitney, circa 1900.

Bathing suits at camp (Marjorie right).

Willie cutting a "wheel" of cheese.

Gilford circa mid-to-late 1920s.

Chapter Thirteen

Time and Change: Marjorie's Perspective

When Marjorie Pierce was in high school from 1917 to 1921, penicillin, polio vaccine, and antibiotics didn't exist. This was a time before radio and television, talking movies, and electric service in rural Vermont homes, to say nothing of modern conveniences like central heat, washers, dryers, refrigerators, dishwashers, and microwave ovens. Radar, florescent lights, credit cards, ball-point pens, frozen food, nylon, permanent press clothing, and Velcro had not been invented. Hawaii and Alaska were not yet states, and no one had flown solo across the Atlantic Ocean. Time sharing referred to being with your family, a chip had to do with a piece of wood, hardware meant goods bought in a general store, and no one had even heard of "software."

When Marjorie went to college in the twenties, women wore skirts or dresses below the knee and bathing suits that came to just above the knee. Ladies dressed up in ruffled, high-button-collar dresses and left cleavage to butchers. Men did not wear long hair or earrings. Clothes were kept in closets, bunnies were small rabbits, and rabbits were animals, not cars. Among "flappers," short hair was the rage and so was smoking and the illegal use of alcohol. A pot was something to cook in, not smoke. The grass was mowed with hand tools, not power machines. Angel dust was something spread in fairy tales, not PCP. You used a net

Marjorie, 1925.

to go fishing, not to "surf." This was before yogurt, the forty-hour work week, and minimum wage. The electric typewriter, word processor, FM radio, cassette recorder, electronic music, and disco dancing weren't around and neither were Ms, NATO, UFOs, SATs, BMW, ERA, HUD, IRAs, the CIA or the Web.

In the 1930s, you could actually buy things that cost five or ten cents at a Five-and-Ten-Cent Store. One could ride a bus or make a phone call for a nickel. Gas was eleven cents a gallon and a car could be purchased for $659, although that was hard to afford since the Great Depression was on.

Imagine life without dry cereals, instant coffee, fast food, television, or E-mail. For that matter, before "conspicuous consumption." It was a time when things were "used up" and people were grateful for what they had.

But also imagine the excitement of seeing so much change! Many Vermonters led hard lives in the upland towns, and they often suffered from loneliness and isolation, especially during winter months. Imagine the thrill of indoor plumbing, the pleasure of hot showers, and the enjoyment of central heat. As electricity came to rural homes, consider how it improved family lives as cheerful light brightened homes on dark dreary days and long winter evenings. Or how the auto meant getting out more often, and how a radio could bring fun to otherwise quiet lives and connect families and entire communities with the rest of the world!

Marjorie remembered their first radio—how everyone had gathered "round my father who was bent over the voice coming from the box on the table." It was pure excitement to hear the faraway voice of Edward R. Murrow in their home. "We welcomed such changes that made our lives better and more interesting," she said.

She also recalled her father expressing his "wish to live to see the dirt road from Rutland to Northam paved." The approach from Cuttingsville had been tarred in the 1950s, but it was 1958 before local crews began paving the Cold River Road to North Shrewsbury (the most direct route to Rutland for residents of Northam). Each year some progress was

Gilford and Florence below the pine tree in 1942. Whitney house and barn in background are no longer there and the road is paved now.

made on the ten-mile stretch, but there were still about two miles to go when Willie died in 1965.

Labor-saving devices—indeed, anything that improved the lot of one's life—were welcomed. Most advances which we take for granted today made rural life more pleasant. With the new tractor, farmers could suddenly mow an entire field in a few hours, a chore that previously took days by hand. Domestic duties also took less time with advances like refrigeration and the automatic washing machine. As modern science improved general sanitation and medical practices, human health improved and longevity increased. Women no longer had to bear large families just to insure the survival of a few offspring. Children's lives improved, too, as a high-school education became possible for everyone. Central heating systems and electricity not only improved the living conditions of rural Vermonters, they also improved the safety of their homes. Kerosene lamps, candles, and woodburning stoves may evoke images of romantic warmth, but the fact was that thousands of Vermont homes had been lost to fires started by these sources.

The mountain town of Shrewsbury never saw a McDonald's, an avenue of spiffy shops, or a large supermarket. But it did see a reversal of its declining population as more summer folk, retirees, and vacationers began to discover its delights and move into the area. A few set up small businesses and even created some employment opportunities for locals, but as the town's population grew, it was largely as a commuting community. As noted previously, the newcomers appreciated the traditions that old-timers like the Pierces stood for and passed on. Times changed, but, as a beautiful rural town, Shrewsbury remained well-preserved. Residents, both native and non-native, worked to keep it that way. They

186

also often did with less, preferring the quality of rural life to the abundance and wealth found in places where the living was, and still is, easier.

Having lived through the twentieth century, Marjorie Pierce has seen and experienced these and many other changes during her lifetime. The following stand out in her memory.

When I started teaching, we were more prim and proper. Not extremely proper like the ladies I had as teachers, but not like the more friendly teachers today, either. We were friendly, but not "of them." Students were not my pals. I kept my distance; I was on a different level. I demanded respect; they wouldn't make sly remarks or jokes. I was "Miss Pierce." I gave homework. Most did it. There were always exceptions, the lazy ones.

As teachers, we didn't wear slacks. We wore skirts and blouses or dresses, jewelry, sweaters. We wore heels, but they weren't high heels. I was quite proud of my pretty shoes. I wore medium heels.

As young girls, ages five to ten or so, we wore black cotton stockings; no silk except maybe later in high school. We had high-button shoes and later came lace [tie] shoes. Our dresses were made by our aunts or mother and were below the knee. I never saw dresses above the knee until recent years. [In Marjorie's framework, recent can—and usually does—mean the last thirty or forty years.]

We never wore slacks or pants!

We had white cotton drawers with wide legs and lace. They were

Gordon, Glendon, and Gilford wore knickers from 1908-1920s.

longer and had a band with buttons on the side. No zippers; you'd button your drawers. Our petticoats had a fancy crocheted edge around the bottom. I wore a flannel, off-white petticoat in winter with a crocheted or knitted edging.

We had woolen materials, maybe heavy serge, for dresses in cold weather. I had a blue winter dress that mother had embroidered in the front. Our coats might have a fur piece. I

Cousin Olin Hill, Marion, and Marjorie with their fur muffs.

had a fur muff with a purse in it. Willie D. would put a penny in my purse when I went to church.

In summer or up at camp around 1922, people our age wore navy blue serge bloomers and white middy blouses with a black or navy tie. Now the styles have changed tremendously.

When the boys were young, they wore pants bloused at the knees called knickers. There were suits for best wear. On the farm, father wore blue overalls. He had a suit, white shirt, and a necktie for dress. I remember he always wore a necktie, even in the store. I never saw him with an open shirt. The boys didn't wear neckties, though.

Around 1940 I got my first fur coat. It was muskrat. It was a pretty one. I still have it stored in the attic. It was perfectly straight; I paid $100 for it.

We dressed formally in our Sunday clothes to go to church. Lots of people don't anymore. My grandmother dressed in black to go to church. We wore hats and gloves to church until recent years.

Today, we wear slacks. Now, young girls wear low-cut blouses to school or short tops that show the midriff. Today, it shocks me to see TV at night. To see the cleavage—I think that's going too far, don't you?

After discoursing on the morality of dress today, Marjorie had a sudden recollection that caused her to giggle like a school girl. Laughing, and expressing her own disbelief that she could have thought such a thing when she was very young, she proceeded to tell this story.

Delia Mandigo, Royce's mother, was a very charming and pretty woman. I thought she was so beautiful. But I thought to myself, "I wonder if she has legs!"

I knew I had legs, but I had never seen my mother's legs because I had never seen her in anything but long petticoats or dresses—so I wondered if Mrs. Mandigo had legs attached to her feet!

That is so silly, but it shows you how fashion and the times have changed. I never saw ladies in anything except long dresses to the ground. Women never showed an ankle, let alone their legs or knees when I was growing up.

Asked about their social life in early Shrewsbury, Marjorie grew thoughtful and pensive. Then her face brightened as she recalled the role of music and singing both at home and at community functions.

My parents worked hard. They had to tend to business. There wasn't much social life except with neighbors in Northam. Maybe I went to Cuttingsville once a year. We had visits from cousins. We had to be nice to them. Our values then were to be polite and proper. Our mother made us play with Cousin Constance and be nice to her, even when she was so bossy!

Everyone in Northam was a farmer except the storekeeper and blacksmith so you stayed home more. There were five lumber mills and cheese factories and more stores and post offices in town.

George Whitney and his wife Minne out for a ride in the buggy. This photo was taken from the home of his brother Perrin J. Whitney, the Northam blacksmith. The barn of Henry Fee is in background. This pasture was opposite the store and Pierce home and was dotted with cows and horses in the first third of the twentieth century.

Social life was the church, Christmas services, a ballgame on the Fourth of July, or a grange supper. There was no historical society or library group.

Mother and father belonged to the grange at Shrewsbury Center. They attended Oyster Suppers and Harvest Suppers there twice a year. I saw Willard Smith and Mary dance there. Marion and I would sing a duet that mother would teach us.

We did recitations too. We called it "speak a piece." We did that at graduations at Shrewsbury Center for school programs or at Christmas in Northam. (There were about five grammar schools left when I attended school, and they held their eighth-grade graduations together at Town Hall.)

When we were growing up, my grandfather Joseph Spaulding would sing to us. His was a very musical family, with some like his brother Hosea playing the fiddle. Music was one of the entertainments for "socials" at a Grange Hall event, at home in the evening, or sometimes when neighbors and friends got together.

My father played the guitar some and sang a little; my grandfather Edwin also sang a few war songs. My mother taught Marion and me songs to sing for church, school, grange, or Modern Woodmen programs.

My mother was interviewed by Helen Hartness Flanders for her collection of traditional New England music at Middlebury College. She was recorded in the 1930s singing some of the old songs. (I was interviewed by the curator of this collection in the 1980s and also sang some songs for her and once for Vermont Public Radio.)

When Marion and I lived with Aunt Jennie and Uncle Clyde in Rutland, there was a routine on Sundays. In the afternoons we would have to walk up the railroad tracks to go bird hunting. When we came back from the bird walk, we would sit down in the living room and my uncle would open up the big Victrola and play classical music. He would explain, "Now this is from Aida." He would tell us the stories of the operas, and we would have to listen.

One time he took me to the Paramount Theater in Rutland to see the great European actress Sarah Bernhardt in *Anthony and Cleopatra*. She was playing Cleopatra and I remember her dramatically reclined on the couch as Anthony strode in.

Later, there was a Thimble Club in town. We were living at the store then. The ladies would get together to tie a quilt or make something like an afghan. This was really a social occasion for them. It was important

Ladies of the Thimble Club tying a quilt, circa 1942. L to R: Ella Works, Gertie Barber, Marion Pierce, Dorothy Brown, Winnie Haley, May Poore, May Johnson, Gertrude Pierce, Mrs. Frank Baker, and Myrtle Fee.

for women to have the opportunity to talk. They would discuss the weather, their gardens and children, and gossip. They would tell who had gone to visit someone, a relative in Burlington or something, or share a postcard from some other place. They would exchange recipes and in war time, the latest news.

In recalling major events that occurred during her lifetime, Marjorie cited World Wars I and II, the Korean, Vietnam, and Gulf Wars, Lindbergh's crossing of the ocean, Amelia Earhart's flight, and man's exploration of space. She described her excitement at seeing Halley's Comet in 1910: "I saw it quite clearly from my grandmother's porch at the farm. I remember it was surprisingly big." Another event which made a keen impression occurred while she was teaching.

Amelia Earhart came to Attleboro and addressed the student body at an assembly. I remember she stood straight and tall with her hands at her side. They were the biggest and longest hands I ever saw. I guess she talked about flying, but what I remember were her hands.

The loss of Earhart's plane, kidnapping of the Lindbergh baby, explosion of the Hindenburg, sinking of the Titanic, and the Flood of 1927 are among the tragedies that are still vivid in Marjorie's mind. She still expresses shock at the memory of "seeing a newspaper photograph of heads bobbing in the water" when the Titanic sank. Witnessing entire houses floating down a raging river in the 1927 Flood and experiencing earthquake tremors while at a party in a Burlington (Vermont) hotel are likewise recalled as "unforgettable and scary" encounters.

While Marjorie has seen a succession of presidents during her lifetime, the one she remembers best is Calvin Coolidge.

He was the first president I voted for after registering to vote when I was in college. I think I remember him best because he was a Vermonter, and we took a more personal interest in his election. I never met him, but I often saw his son John on our visits to Plymouth to see Aurora or when he stopped in at the store.

As for politics in general, Marjorie offered the following:

We were Republicans, but other than following the elections and voting, we weren't very active. We were not political. My Uncle Ernest Aldrich and my father served in the legislature and Glendon was a page, but that was about all.

There is a funny story that I heard, though. When my father's sister Kate would walk down from the farm to go to school or get the mail or something, the people in Northam would say, "There goes Katie Pierce, Edwin Purse's daughter." Then shortly thereafter, Edwin changed from a Democrat to a Republican and his name from Purse to Pierce. He never spelled it P-u-r-s-e — that's just how they pronounced it. It was the old generation that said Purse, but the new generation pronounced it Pierce. He was the new generation, now.

On changes in behavior and traditional values, Marjorie observed:

Another major difference is that we used to be more reserved, polite and less spontaneous. There was more decorum in children than we have today. Etiquette was—you were just told— "This is what you should do.

Say hello Mr. or Mrs. or Aunt Minnie or Uncle Ernest. Speak when spoken to."

Today, we say "Hi, John." Everyone calls me Marjorie now, except Lynette Over; she still calls me Miss Pierce! Even my former pupils call me Marjorie now. This is a definite change.

Discipline was much more strict and more by word of mouth. If we did something bad, there would be a sharp reprimand. We were not physically abused. There was no corporal punishment in our family. But we were told, "This is the way things should be done."

If I did something bad, I would have to sit on a chair for awhile. I would ask, "Can I get up?"

Mother would ask if I thought I could behave. One time I said, "I don't know," and she answered, "Well, sit until you do know." When I said, yes, then I could get up.

Once, when I was only three or four years old, Cousin Kenneth came. I remember he had been to the barn and gathered the eggs. He stood out there in the middle of the lawn and broke an egg and held it up. He tried to make me swallow it. He started to swear, and of course I started to swear. My mother heard me and felt obligated to discipline me. She grabbed me under her arm, took me to the kitchen sink, and washed my mouth out with soap and water. I remember that vividly.

Mother didn't let us do certain things on Sunday. Sunday was for quieter activities. But times changed. My brothers could do things that

Willie watches Reno and the boys play tennis on their court below the store.

we couldn't—they could play tennis on Sunday. They were allowed more privileges. When we were older, Marion and I would complain to Mother, "You never let us do things like that."

Thrift and frugality were major values when we were growing up. When my father bought the blacksmith shop, we went to the second floor and were excited to see all the things that were there. It was a big, two-story building. His wife never threw anything away. She just put all her discards upstairs there over the shop, so it was full of things. I found ten chairs and Glendon fixed them. I painted them, and now they're on our back porch. They're antiques now. I saved many useful things.

I have an Oxalis plant that belonged to my Grandmother. I brought it here when she died and we sold her house in Rutland. The asparagus fern in the window was my mother's. It is over fifty years old. We were taught to take care of things.

Generally there was a lack of money. It was a simple existence of being self-sufficient. There were horses, gardens, farms, and some were prosperous farms. We were taught saving and thrift. People were taught to save, not to splurge or keep up with the Joneses. We didn't know any Joneses.

Regarding poverty and charity towards one's neighbors, Marjorie had these comments:

We were taught to help others. I think that some weren't taught that, but many were. You know in the early days, the community cared for its own people. Shrewsbury had the Poor Farm and an Overseer of the Poor.

Today there is welfare to help the poor, and the government taxes us to support these programs. But then each town took care of its own or pretended to. Some towns didn't do a good job, I guess.

My father was an Overseer of the Poor. There were some very poor people. One woman, Mrs. Farmer, received $4.50 a week from the town. She would come into the store and choose things from the shelves and place them on the counter. My mother was expected to keep track of the total and help her make sure she had everything she needed. They were extremely poor and made do with very little.

One day when Mother was helping her, she noticed that she hadn't purchased any soap that week and asked if she needed some. "Why, Meese Peerse, that's something we use very little of," Mrs. Farmer replied. That was real poverty which is not seen today.

For Marjorie, the increase in the cost of living is one of the most startling changes she has witnessed:

> The cost of things is a tremendous change. It is hard to get used to the prices today. Of course, wages are higher. If they weren't, you couldn't live and you'd have to go to the Poor Farm; only, it isn't in existence now. Glendon worked for $1.50 a day, but back then an egg cost two cents, so we weren't so deprived as it sounds. I can't get used to people making $10 an hour. One summer when I was a waitress, I made $70 for the entire season.

Thinking back to earlier prices, Marjorie went out to the store, returned with a large card on which she had copied some items from an 1880 store ledger, and dusted it off with a tissue she removed from the trash. She laughed as she read them, noting that the "morphine was stocked for a woman who was addicted."

6 lb codfish	.49	1 dozen eggs	.16
5 lb salmon	.60	3 dozen crackers	.15
40 lb Ham	6.40	1 tub butter 51 lbs	10.20
1 lb coffee	.45	10 lb sugar	1.20
2 lemons	.04	1 cake soap	.05
1 pair boots	3.50	1 bottle morphine	.65
1 plug tobacco	.15	1 twist tobacco	.10
10 postal cards	.10	1 box (men's) collars	.28
1 gal kerosene	.30	1 bushel grass seed	3.25

Of all the many changes Marjorie experienced, she commented that advances in communication and transportation have most permanently and significantly impacted the community and the rural way of life.

> There is more communication and more people know about more things. Today, we know what's going on all over the world, but years ago Rutland and Proctor seemed like China and Tibet today. We were confined to our area. Things were regionalized. The world was a smaller place for us.
>
> Transportation was on narrow dirt roads. It was very difficult to travel over them, so we didn't go places very often as we do nowadays.

I didn't go to Cuttingsville but maybe once a year. We didn't get out except to visit relatives. I had never been to New Hampshire although my mother's people were from there and some from Woodstock. We only visited our aunts summers in Bridgewater and our relatives in Rutland.

Maybe we would go to Rutland two or three times a year. I remember the Rutland Fair. That was exciting, sitting on my father's shoulders to watch the races or riding on the merry-go-round. Great Uncle Will Aldrich and his family lived on Madison Street in Rutland. We visited them one cold winter. My father took us with the sleigh and horses and got stuck in a snowdrift.

We didn't know too much about Rutland until we went to high school. Even then, we didn't come home every weekend. My father went to Rutland more often to get groceries but that was for business, not personal pleasure.

Before the automobile and paved roads, the rural areas were more stable. With a lack of transportation, families intermarried more—not blood relatives but within the area or town more. I imagine that's where Vermonters got their common characteristics; they were apt to marry someone from their region and so clung to their temperaments—thrifty, opinionated, and independent. Our world was home, school, church, grandparents, aunts, uncles, and visits in summer. There was more stability in that environment, I think.

Life was much more quiet without the automobile. Today civilization is far from quiet.

Richard Mandigo bought the first auto in Northam. My first ride was when I was about twelve or thirteen years old. Uncle Ernest, who lived where the parsonage is now, had an auto and maybe the Smiths. The auto required better roads. It took a long time to widen them, get the rocks out, and pave them.

Improved roads, the auto, and modern transportation caused people to move around more because it enabled them to go where there were better jobs. When the mills and other businesses closed down in Shrewsbury, that was a big change which caused people to move. Today, more people live here, but they have to work somewhere else. There aren't too many businesses in town anymore. In the 1800s Shrewsbury had probably thirty different industries, but they were small.

Some left because they didn't like the cold or felt hemmed in by the mountains. Marion and I left because there was nothing to attract us here. With the preparation we had and our qualifications, we had to go elsewhere—there was no high school or social services in town to employ

On Killington Peak, circa 1921. Ella Works (age 65) center next to Gordon in cap. Marjorie is third to her left in hat. The group hiked up to the Porky Shelter (behind them), had a picnic and then went to the summit (4241-feet high).

us. The lack of opportunities was one of the reasons so many left Vermont; salaries were another. People would go to work in the factories in Rutland or Connecticut or where opportunities were better. Then the war took some, too. That changed a lot of lives.

Change and the Future: Vermont's Dilemma

Having witnessed so much change during the twentieth century, what does Marjorie foresee for the future of Shrewsbury, or of Vermont? Does she think the geographically large town will ever change from a rural community? Will Vermont lose its rural character?

"No—well, not in my lifetime, anyway," she said with a laugh.

Then on a more serious note, Marjorie expounded on the dilemma of rural areas being both "beautiful and troublesome" and the complicated issues that make a successful rural existence in Vermont a precarious struggle.

Vermont is a small state and a difficult place in which to live or do business due to the cold climate, rugged geography, poor transportation systems, and the high cost of living. The economy and the environment are tricky issues. Today, Vermonters worry about things like sprawl, big-box stores, and the loss of family farms.

I know that rural life is hard; hill farming was difficult in this town. The loss of the mills, farms, and all those small industries was a big change. People like my parents wanted more for their children, and so they gave up farming. They were resourceful and worked long hours to see us become educated. But then Marion and I wanted to use our education so we left.

I know that we need to have challenging jobs for young people in Vermont today, or that they will move away as we did. But we don't want to turn the state into places like Burlington and the surrounding towns that have rows and rows of houses where farms once stood. It is hard to balance the needs of the environment with the need for better jobs.

The old Vermonter, who was born here, is concerned about poverty and wants to develop better work opportunities. The new Vermonter, who wasn't born here, wants to keep Vermont rural. They favor business centers and sometimes work against development in order to protect the environment.

I think the challenge is to develop business centers in a careful way so that the whole state doesn't become a Chittenden County. Burlington has a better climate, opportunities, and transportation. But as Burlington has grown, the surrounding towns have changed. They have lost their rural character. They are like suburbs in states to our south.

We have to watch the kinds of businesses that come in or the rest of Vermont might change as Chittenden County is doing. There are business entrepreneurs eyeing Vermont, thinking it is a new market. They seem to be targeting Vermont. Unless we strengthen laws like Act 250, we could lose the old Vermont identity of being a rural state. That would hurt our tourism.

Tourism is good. You can't do away with tourism or jobs. I think the answer lies in seeking a happy medium. We need a balance. I would like to see more small industries in rural areas. We have a few businesses in Shrewsbury such as bed and breakfast places, small stores, and Spring Lake Ranch. I would like to see our store used again—maybe to sell Vermont products to local people and tourists. But there are regulations so I don't know what will happen.

It would be nice to have more businesses in town, but the problem is people go to Rutland to shop—or the business center near where they live. The city has a multitude of attractions that hurt rural areas, and the auto enables us to go and seek these things. So it is hard to compete, and that is part of the dilemma of small places.

There are business centers in Vermont and there are rural places. Rutland is a business hub, but it is too difficult for small communities like ours to compete. We're like two-year-old children competing with sixty-five year olds. Shrewsbury doesn't have the resources or the right type of population. We're more or less a conglomeration of working and non-working, retirement and vacation people, and a bedroom community.

I don't think any major businesses or big-box stores are going to come to Shrewsbury. There aren't enough people here, and it is too out of the way—they have to go to the business centers. So, I don't see any immediate threat to small rural areas. They are in less danger of over development than business centers, which are more attractive targets. I don't see this changing any time soon.

But there is a danger and problem of sprawl in some areas. That is what has happened to Chittenden County so other business centers and surrounding towns must guard against it.

Because there are so many small towns like ours, Vermont hasn't become a suburban or urbanized state like those to the south. I don't think Vermont will ever become a New York City. We don't have the possibilities to attract so many people, nor do we have the appropriate space.

There are Vermonters who moved here who are doing good things. They bring energy and ideas to projects and help organizations like the library, fire department, church, school, newspaper, and town's governing boards while some work for preservation of the environment. Many retirees are useful to the community. There are newcomers in the historical society—look how much good they have done with the museum and preserving our history and traditions. That is a very good thing that is special about rural places. People care about and feel a responsibility to the community. We have common goals and work together on projects.

Some come but don't stay too long. That might be due to the climate or jobs. If they leave, they don't become part of a community. That is a problem of our modern, transient society.

I used to know all my neighbors but not any more. Some newcomers never came into the store. There were some neighbors I never met. Some new people are aloof. That is a change in people and ways. If people change their ways and forget about our traditions, the community will change. I think that is a danger.

Most of the people in Shrewsbury like our town; they want to preserve it and keep it rural. But if that ever changes, then who knows what the town will look like in fifty years—I don't think I'll be here, though.

I am trying to help maintain the rural nature of Shrewsbury by deeding the store and our home to preservation. I am doing something to help the environment, but I haven't done anything for jobs. I know our young people can't find good jobs and many of them leave our town and state.

Clearly, Marjorie has seen some major changes, but she has also witnessed Vermont's most persistent problem—creating a strong economy that makes it possible for all people to make a decent living while at the same time maintaining the cohesion and character of rural communities. Recognizing the dilemma of rural towns and the easy mobility that the auto and paved roads have brought, Marjorie sees the potential for progress to be detrimental if it leads to a loss of population or to the loss of neighborliness and traditional values.

Mentioning the changes occurring elsewhere in Vermont, she stops short of predicting that her home town will stay forever rural or will never see condominiums or suburban sprawl. Because she finds "Shrewsbury a nice, peaceful place to retire to," Marjorie believes it will continue to attract vacationers as well as retirees and new young families with rural values. She also sees travel and tourism as helping to sustain rural areas and serving as an impetus to preserve the beauty of Vermont. And although she notes "the problems that a difficult climate and geography bring," she stresses that they conspire to "keep Vermont rural, too."

Fran Patten, Marjorie, and Delores Ryffel dressed in vintage clothing for the town of Shrewsbury's bicentennial parade and celebration.

The new playground at the Mountain School was named Pierce Playground to honor the ties that bind young and old, school children and community members.

Museum Committee with Marjorie, now a SHS Honorary Trustee, on August 7, 1999, prior to debut of new Shrewsbury Historical Society Museum in Cuttingsville. L to R: Fran Patten, Lois Butler, Ruth Winkler, Marjorie, Anne Spencer. Items from Pierce collection, including Florence Pierce's scrapbook were on display.

Chapter Fourteen

The Pierce Legacy:
Useful & Upright Lives

The years were generally good to the Pierce family. One could tell the time or the season or that all was well by their dependable habits—opening and closing the store; Glendon's trips to Rutland to see Minnie; Gordon's run up the mountain to tend the meadows; Marjorie's late night presence at the kitchen table to read or catch up on correspondence; and Marion's visits.

Marion formally retired in 1967 but remained active in Philadelphia until she returned to Vermont for good in 1982, spending summers in Northam and winters at Hilltop House, a Brattleboro retirement home. Then, with health failing, she entered Eden Park Nursing Home in Rutland in September 1984. She passed away there on January 22, 1987, at age eighty-five. A letter Marjorie received from Jennie Scheller, one of Marion's dearest friends who lived in New York, paid fitting tribute to this gentle soul, who as a young woman had aimed to leave the world "a little better" for having been here.

Dear Marjorie and Brothers,

I have your letter telling me of Marion's death and [have been] a long time reflecting on her life and my relationship to her. Marion was my

Marion and Jennie when they were visiting Northam, circa 1920s. Their friendship lasted for over 65 years, starting with washing dishes together in the college dorm.

oldest friend. We worked together in the kitchen at Grasse Mount for three years. She was very conscientious at the job of washing the dishes (I wiped), and she was the cook's favorite because she never left the job until everything was in order!

She was the most selfless person I have known, and she influenced me in my choice or profession, social work. She was too unselfish, and I felt that it was at a cost to herself, but she always was so willing to be of help.

I know many of her friends in Philadelphia were much older than she was. She was a wonderful listener, genuinely interested in all aspects of your life, and I could tell her almost anything and be sure she would understand. I remember meeting her Christmas 1951, a few days after we had lost our little girl Rosie. Marion's comments were, "She was everything you wanted in a child." I have never forgotten her words; they summed up all my feelings.

Marion never lost her child-like sense of wonder and delight. That was one of the most endearing aspects of her personality. I remember our visits together around Christmas time when she was on her way to Vermont. She was very sensitive to beauty—loved old things and soft colors. She had very good taste. I still have a beautiful scarf (she gave me), paisley, gray and soft rose that I treasure and will no longer use for fear of losing it. It is old and warm and still beautiful.

Marion had a delightful sense of humor. Some of her letters, years ago, used to have little cartoons that were precious. I remember clearly her laugh; it was beautiful and contagious. We had some wonderful times together.

A thing about Marion that impressed me very much—she did not complain. I know the osteoporosis that caused her back curvature must have been a source of great discomfort and unhappiness, but she never complained except to say that finding proper blouses was difficult. I know that she had other physical ailments that caused her discomfort, but beyond mentioning them briefly, she never dwelt on them. She had great fortitude. I see that more clearly now.

Marion was a delightful letter writer; her letters were full of homey news, activities, descriptions of scenes she loved. I kept all of her letters and I plan to get them all together. They will be something like an autobiography.

Marion and co-workers in Philadelphia.

She loved her home, as I don't need to tell you, and all the activities and happenings. I have never known anybody so attached to a place as Marion was to the home—others would have been dissatisfied with their lives, but she apparently never missed traveling—she was a real homing pigeon, and home was the source of her greatest satisfaction. She shared your pride in the family's history and the respect given it by the community. She was also very proud of the activities of the family members, your wide range of activities, Marjorie, and of your brothers, and the historical prominence of the "store."

It is good that Marion spent her last years in Vermont near the family. That must have been a source of great comfort to her.

I loved and respected Marion and wondered at her zeal and self-denial. I would have wished that she be less self-denying, more able to take something for herself— but the attitude was deeply in grained. Maybe what to me appeared extreme self-denial did not seem that to her—she perhaps saw it as duty and took satisfaction from fulfilling her duty. All in all, she was a rare person, rarely met.

Thank you for sending me a copy of the services. I can picture how lovely it was, something Marion would have appreciated. I shall keep your letter as long as I live. It is very beautiful, especially the picture of the house Marion loved.

Thank you again. My love and Herman's to you and your brothers,

Jennie.

As time marched on, Marjorie made some small changes to the home. One was the aforementioned updating of the kitchen with new flooring and a refitting of the pantry with a modern washer and dryer. If these simple improvements were long in coming in the 1980s, it wasn't that the Pierces were against modern conveniences, it was simply a matter that they used things until they wore out or could no longer be fixed.

But some changes they could do nothing about. Their old Esso gasoline pump had long since become an Exxon pump. Then there was the switch to unleaded, although they continued to pump leaded until they could no longer obtain it. Subsequently, environmental regulations mandated replacement of underground storage tanks. Deciding that they didn't sell enough gas to merit the expense of a new tank, they closed down the pump and by 1990 had removed both the old kerosene and gasoline tanks. "We were forced to dig them up," Marjorie said, annoyed at not being able to use something until it wore out.

Their customers were upset, too. It wasn't just the inconvenience of having to drive to Rutland for gasoline, or worrying one would run out; it was the loss of meeting Gordon or Glendon at the pump. The conversation alone was worth the purchase price, and now that opportunity—along with the convenience—was gone. (Marjorie noted that she also pumped gasoline.)

In 1989, Gordon became ill. He passed away in June while in the hospital and was laid to rest in the Pierce plot in Northam Cemetery near his sister and parents. An eloquent eulogy given by his neighbor, Lee Wilson, concluded with these words:

> Are there giants who have walked the earth to clear the way and make it smooth for us? No, there are just people like Gordon Pierce, who believe in things being done decently and in order. He was a man who was just as content to count out pieces of candy one by one, and place them in the soft small hands of his youngest customers, as he was to wrestle and overcome a huge gnarled root ball, or to help a neighbor in need. To each task was appointed its own time and place, and for each task there was quiet patience and a strong will to see it done right.
>
> A few words cannot encompass a life. One poet wrote, "Not people die but worlds die in them." Who can describe an entire world? We could all say more about Gordon, and in these hours of remembering we should

Tending their "mountain lands" was always a source of pleasure for Gordon and Glendon, who enjoyed the simple things in life and being active in the outdoors. These lands are now part of the Coolidge State Forest. Photo 1978.

say more. We are here today, because in ways large and small, we have each shared a part of the world of Gordon Pierce and found it was a place of surprising strength, enduring patience, and much gentle good will. We will remember Gordon when walking through his meadows, buying candy in the store, or seeing the stream flow by the rock wall and the forget-me-nots.

Now there were just Glendon and Marjorie to take care of the family home and keep the store going. Pierce's Store had retained its special charm, but as business volume was declining in the early 1990s, liability insurance and paperwork were growing—due in large part to increasing regulations. Children continued to visit for candy and soda, so there was always a steady supply of change crossing the glass countertops, and "big folk" still came in for a quart of milk or whatever else they needed in a pinch. But these were not large purchases. In the bigger scheme of things, reality was beginning to set in. There was a newer store about a mile-and-a-half away and the competition from the larger store, which carried beer and wine as well as videos and other modern conveniences, was being felt. After Gordon died, tending store meant longer hours and more work for Marjorie and Glendon, who were now in their late eighties and seventies, respectively. They had managed because they so "enjoyed meeting people," but with their own advancing years, they "began to consider that one of us might get sick and the other would not be able to manage alone," Marjorie said.

And then the IRS sent Marjorie a notice, claiming she had failed to report a small earning, which she said she had reported. They threatened a hefty fine. She sent them a letter to clarify the issue, half expecting to get back an apology but knowing she wouldn't. "It was just getting to be too much," she said, explaining that the thought of another year of more regulations and paperwork, tobacco, meat and dairy licenses, sales and income tax records, bookkeeping and wondering what the economy was going to do just wasn't appealing anymore. So practical as ever, Marjorie decided the time had come to close the store. Glendon concurred. Minnie recalled that he had long viewed the store as a "losing proposition" but had felt a sense of duty and responsibility to this tradition and to Marjorie.

The closing of the store was planned to coincide with the end of the 1993 tax year. It was a landmark day in Shrewsbury. Vermont Governor Howard Dean declared December 31, 1993, "Pierce's Store Day," and the media duly noted the significance of the occasion. Many people turned out to pay homage to the passing of this rural institution, and the steady stream of well-wishers pleased Marjorie and Glendon immensely.

Still they had mixed feelings. The responsibility and work with little financial return made it a relief to close, but the friendships and long history were hard to lose. Glendon acknowledged how difficult it was to break that long tradition, telling people they were "very sad to do it."

No Shrewsbury resident could remember there not being a Pierce's Store, and now they were losing that venerable country institution—a place where so many of their own connections with their neighbors were forged and soldered. With sadness and more than a little nostalgia, friends and neighbors celebrated the life of Pierce's Store; then at 6 p.m., Glendon locked the door one more time, saying simply, "Thanks for the memories."

If the store closing was difficult, Marjorie didn't dwell on it. Always practical and constantly busy with visitors and an abundance of activities, she continued to "tool around town" and make trips to Rutland in her black VW, attend meetings and church, cultivate her garden, and bask in the attention of those who continued to seek her out.

As the study of genealogy had become popular, more and more local residents and out-of-staters were coming to Marjorie to fill-in historical loose-ends relating to their families. Marjorie also continued to travel—more in the company of others and closer to home now—visiting historic sites and attending special events. Each birthday brought visitors and more attention and life continued to be good, if a little less full with Gordon, Marion, and the store no longer part of it.

Then, in January 1995, Glendon died suddenly but peacefully. He had been sick with the flu a few weeks earlier but had recovered enough to be out shoveling the walk. He was just watching the evening news one night after supper when he dozed off in his chair, not to reawaken. His funeral service in Rutland was overflowing with friends and neighbors paying their last respects and lending moral support to Marjorie and Minnie. A eulogy offered by Glendon's good friend Howard Coffin movingly captured the essence of this good Vermonter.

> When I lived in Northam, each summer a church service was held (guess it still is) at Meeting House Rock on the CCC Road. It was a wonderfully historic event commemorating that early time before a meeting house was built. There to greet the attendees were Marjorie Pierce and her sister Marion. Glendon and his brother Gordon were nowhere to be seen. But the area of worship around the ancient rock was always scythed and picked up, carefully groomed. It was, of course, the work of Gordon and Glendon. There are many ways of giving thanks and praise.
>
> Glendon's life was one of quiet and good deeds, a good neighbor always helping others. It was the way Vermont got up and going and has survived. His was a deceptively simple way, a reminder that in this era of me-first and megaplexes and internets, there IS another way. He was as fine a human being as I've ever known, and I count it as one of the great privileges of my life to have known the Pierces and Minnie Shaw. Would that I had known Gilford.

View of Shrewsbury Peak from the former Headle Farm, which Glendon and Gordon groomed over the years. This meadow is surrounded by stone walls and some refer to it as "Pierces' Park." Locals enjoy summer picnics, skiing, sliding and just visiting this beautiful place in the mountains. The trees here are flaming red during foliage season. Located at the beginning of the Bennington Camp Road, this meadow is now part of the Coolidge State Forest.

Glendon, I will miss our explorations through the mountains seeking the cellar holes; bringing in the wood each fall; burning brush on days when the clouds lay low on Jockey Hill; talking things over on chilly mornings around the woodstove in Pierce's Store—that great good humor and wisdom, the long memory, always the twinkle in the eye. Last time I saw you last week, we planned to meet in Montpelier to visit the Legislature where you were a page the year of the 1927 flood.

It was, of course, that flood that brought Calvin Coolidge back to his home state to assess the damage and to close his sad tour with a speech at Bennington. Hear again his words:

"I love Vermont because of her hills and valleys, her scenery and invigorating climate, but most of all because of her indomitable people. They are a race of pioneers who have almost beggared themselves to serve others. If the spirit of liberty should vanish in other parts of the union and support of our institutions should languish, it could all be replenished from the generous store held by the people of this brave little state of Vermont."

Good and gentle shepherd, our hope in ages past, he is headed up the mountain now. Leave the light burning and open the door wide. You never sent among us any finer.

He was my dear, dear friend, and I suspect I will miss him most when autumn fairly blazes on the hillsides and when Vermont, this wondrous little state he so loved in this nation he so nobly served, is most Vermont.

The era of Pierce's Store had come to an end and now with her family gone, Marjorie was on her own. Still active, independent, and sound in mind, she remained in the family home, receiving her many guests and taking care of the Pierce property—hiring someone to cut the lawn, paint the house, take down a tree, fix the roof, and rebuild the front porch at the store. At night, she could be seen, and still can be, sitting at the kitchen table with the pull-down overhead lamp providing an eerie dim light. She was sometimes at her typewriter, her faithful Smith Corona manual, corresponding with her numerous friends or far-flung distant relatives. Most often, she is reading the newspaper or magazines that so delight her—she has never lost her love of learning and keen interest in the world. There is rarely a night that one drives by that the light isn't on until eleven in the evening, even twelve midnight. Hers is an insatiable thirst for knowledge, friendship, and staying in touch with a world that has vastly changed.

At any given time, there is a pile of photographs and notes from people around the world on her table, attesting to that all-important connectedness to friends and events. Invariably, a visit to Marjorie is interrupted by more visitors. Ever a gregarious soul, she still has much to offer the world. And as if paying homage to a fading century, the world is still seeking her out—eager to learn about the past, see how she is, and share the news of the day.

Chester Brigham, a frequent visitor, brings Marjorie a piece of his rhubarb pie, fixes something around the house for her, or can be found sitting at the table pouring over old photographs and learning about the history of the area. He has explained being late to open the dump occasionally, as due to Marjorie's saving the latest town gossip for last.

Contentment

And what of Marjorie's own life? Any complaints? What would she change?

"Well," she said in the fall of 1998, "I suppose I ought to have a computer and be on the Internet, but I don't think I have the time to learn that now. Claire (Bailey) Hooper was here, and she explained the difference between the Web and Internet . . . like a TV channel."

No complaining about the loss of her family or getting older or her inability to drive any longer. No bemoaning the weight she had lost or the digestive trouble that had sapped her strength on occasion. Only infrequently would she mention the frustration of not being able to write quickly due to the inherited tremor of her hands (hence her typing on the Smith Corona); mostly when she referred to it, she would joke about "not being able to read my own handwriting." Living at home at almost ninety-six, Marjorie was still deriving joy from her past and a life well lived.

However, she did express two regrets. One day, as she presented her five pages of "A Few Recollections of a Teacher," she confided that, "My biggest disappointment is I never wrote the special stories that I had in mind. I always intended to do that. I had the intention, but I didn't follow through. I was always too busy with other things." Her other regret is that she "always wanted and intended to go to Alaska but never did. These are things I wish I could have accomplished," she said with genuine sadness.

In December 1998 and again in January and February of 1999, Marjorie endured some serious illness that required hospitalization. She was left weak and tired. Refusing to go to a nursing home, she allowed friends and neighbors and then round-the-clock aides to give her the assistance that her frail condition required. During a long winter of convalescence, Marjorie was surrounded by the love of friends and neighbors. Not a day went by that someone didn't stop in with food or call to say, "We love you." As her neighbor Betty Heitzke tucked her in one night when she was just home from the hospital, Marjorie commented,

"It's like I'm a child again and being well cared for." Although she was the last of a family line, Marjorie was not alone.

Then, with a problem with some medication addressed, she miraculously began to get better. As she recovered, she insisted on reviewing hundreds of photographs. She enjoyed retelling the history of family members and relat-

Marjorie receives many cards and visits from Shrewsbury youngsters.

ing their various achievements. Ever the ambitious soul, she began to eat more and get about with a walker, which she carried more than relied upon. Her mission now was to make sure she identified photographs to be used with her family's story. She began to point out where certain photographs were. "Go to Gilford's room and in the second drawer of the washstand you will find . . . I want you to go to my parents' room . . . You'll have to go to the attic and look in the trunk, which is almost half empty. There you will find three black albums."

True to form, her ambition began to drive her spirit and will once again. Short one-hour interview sessions lengthened to two and three hours. "No, I am not tired. I want to get this done. What tires me is the worry that I won't live to show you all the pictures," she would reply to inquiries about continuing another time.

After the photographs were identified, she began to proofread chapters, correct punctuation, shorten lengthy sentences, and add more stories. To the suggestion of "Quintessential Vermonters" being used in the book's title, Marjorie queried the meaning of the word quintessential. "It isn't in my dictionary," she said in all earnestness. "What is the publication date of that dictionary?" she was asked. Shown modern articles with the word, she enjoyed the learning and the banter. As winter gave way to mud season, her typewriter came out, and she typed a little change to the story told by a former pupil, embellishing it with more dramatic details. The walker was discarded as she regained her muscle tone and tackled the steep stairs to the second floor once again.

One day in early April, she said, "Look at me. Don't I look better? Except for these wrinkles and my skinny arms," she joked, lifting her sleeves and adding in jest, "How poor I must be to look so thin."

Then she demonstrated her strength. As instructed, I put up my hands to resist her as she pushed against me. Surprised by her power—by then she was half my weight—I was propelled backwards in my chair, almost knocked to the floor. Next was arm wrestling. We engaged hands, and she tried to push my hand to the table while I tried to push hers down. Neither of us could budge the other's hand more than a half inch. "It's a tie," Dorothy, her assistant, announced—much to my relief and Marjorie's great and joyous amusement.

Next, Marjorie clasped my hand in hers and said, "I know you are rushing to get this done for my birthday, but I know now that I'm going to live at least a few more months so you don't have to hurry. Take your time and don't ignore your family or your health. I know there will be a birthday party so you don't have to have it done for May. Autumn will be good."

"Aha," I replied, "you want two parties."

We joked some and recalled that Willie's sister Kate lived to 101. I looked at Marjorie and told her that I thought she probably was going to live a lot longer than a few months. The wan look was gone and the sparkle was back. No longer worried that the project wouldn't be able to be completed, she was being considerate and practical once again. It was an amazing recovery to witness and awe inspiring to see just how sharp and strong she was. But even more impressive was to see and know that Marjorie Pierce is still resourceful, responsible, helpful, and connected to people and to history. Neither illness nor the frailties of age could conquer her indomitable spirit or change those traits.

Nor were the wit and sense of humor gone. To the suggestion that she might even live to be one of those "old ladies of 120," she retorted, "Then you will have to write a second book and call it The Decline and Fall of Miss Marjorie Pierce." Soon after, she dismissed her caregivers and with the exception of a person hired to occasionally clean house and another to do bookkeeping, she resumed her independent lifestyle.

On a bright and beautiful, warm May 1, 1999, Marjorie Anna Pierce celebrated her ninety-sixth birthday with two cakes and a room full of flowers and well-wishers. As she blew out her candles, she announced her wish for "four more years" and gamely challenged a guest to an arm-wrestling contest!

As friends and neighbors mingled and local musicians entertained on the back porch, Marjorie sat there enjoying the attention and the conviviality. In a century of change where women went from domestic, family roles to careers and even being elected governor, Marjorie had seen and experienced these changes in her own quiet, special way. At ninety-six, she wasn't missing a trick or the significance of a life well-lived. Still independent and proud, she was happy to be her sociable self once again and basking in the embrace of caring friends.

As we've seen, Marjorie and her siblings valued the bonds of friendship, not only with family members but with members of the Shrewsbury

Marjorie is seen "cheating" at arm wrestling with Dianne Barclay. Your elbow has to be "on the table" Marjorie! The occasion is her 96th birthday.

214

community. Marjorie's personal relationships with so many interesting individuals were a source of fulfillment, and, in a very real way, those individuals all became part of her extended family. Human connections and a sense of belonging have always been important to Marjorie, as this story that she so poignantly told illustrates.

Old John Quinlan, who was in the Battle of Gettysburg and at Little Round Top, drank and was ostracized by the Charlotte Quinlans [his relations who lived in Charlotte, Vermont].

He was a handy man who lived in Shrewsbury and went around working for people. He worked for my father and helped with the haying.

When Old John lived with Harry Russell, where Wilsons live now, we would pass by after school. He would wave to Marion and me and say, "Hi girls, wait a minute," and he'd come out and give us a delicious fresh pear or a peach that he had bought in Rutland. You have to understand that we didn't have a lot of fresh fruit—except for apples—in those days, so that was a very special treat. Each Christmas Marion and I received a $5 bill from John.

I remember seeing John sitting on the store porch or bringing in eggs to swap. He later moved to the Brown place below the store. When he died, he willed it to my father who, not needing it, sold it to Dorothy Brown for $200.

He was a good man, but he loved to go every while to Rutland and get his liquor, his only fault. He must have had a sad life disconnected

John Quinlan and friends at the Cheese Factory.

from his early home and family. He's buried in Northam, not in Charlotte with his family.

When Marjorie's health began to fail in late 1998 and early 1999, it brought the foreshadowing of a time when the Pierce family will fade from the Shrewsbury scene altogether, marking not only the end of a family line but a vital connection to Shrewsbury's past. But as we have seen, Marjorie recovered by spring 1999, and with her indomitable spirit was enjoying life and history, friends and community once again. Now, in the fall of 1999, she is the oldest person in Shrewsbury; the sister and brother duo of Florise and Cecil Sanderson are the only other nonagenarians (ages ninety-two and ninety) at this time.

As she was looking back and reviewing a century of changes, Marjorie observed:

> Much has changed as a result of the auto. Today, I no longer drive, and I'm once again in a quiet environment. Marion and I were content to play with our dolls in the sitting room. I am thinking of the many changes I have experienced and how much I have enjoyed. Now I am happy to be in my own home and this peaceful environment, enjoying visits with friends.

There are only a few native families in town with roots going back to the first settlers, a couple of large working farms, a few smaller ones, and a trio of historic inns to serve as active reminders of Shrewsbury's nineteenth-century heritage. But thanks to them and to the traditional Vermont values of people like the Pierces, the town itself is still rural, not just in landscape but in its ways. Their example has been a contribution and inspiration to others to preserve what is best about Shrewsbury.

There are no condominiums or suburban-style housing developments in the town, no shopping centers or strip developments, and no malls. The town plan and zoning ordinances promote conservation and careful development. There is a clear intention to retain Shrewsbury's rural character even though taxes keep going up. And to help promote this goal of keeping the area rural and in touch with its historic roots, there are two very special Pierce legacies to show that cherished Vermont values might endure and prevail.

Thinking about the future and bumping into a state forester while up on the mountain one day in 1994, Glendon had inquired about whether the state might be interested in buying his land. He then arranged to preserve the acreage which he and Gordon had tended on the Bennington Camp Road by selling it to the Vermont Land Trust (VLT) that same year. In turn, VLT sold it to the state to become part of the Calvin Coolidge State Forest (a sale funded though the Vermont Housing and Conservation Board and made possible in part because Glendon sold at a price well below fair market value). VLT imposed some conservation easements and restrictions in keeping with Glendon's intentions, including one which states that any management plan the forestry department develops for the parcel must be approved by VLT.

The 235 acres that line the Bennington Camp Road and continue up onto Jockey Hill are now being managed for wildlife habitat and non-commercial recreation by the Vermont Forest, Parks, and Recreation Department. Some restrictive covenants, stipulated by Glendon, see to it that the stone walls, apple trees, and two meadows are maintained. This is a shining but quiet example of how special places can be preserved and protected and thus appreciated by generations to come. (The state's purchase of similar and contiguous lands in the Balch Estate is another.) As part of the Coolidge State Forest (CSF), the Pierce lands are now linked with the (former) Northam Picnic Area, the old hiking and ski trails, and Meeting House Rock, which site was in the former Balch Estate but is now also part of CSF. This entire area "up on the mountain" was special to the Pierces, and now their meadows and stone walls will remain forever special to others as part of the state forest.[1]

In a similar vein, Marjorie took steps to see that the store and home will be preserved for future generations. Pondering how she might do this during a fortuitous discussion with a total stranger, Marjorie learned about the Preservation Trust of Vermont (PTV). Exhibiting the same practical foresight of her brother, Marjorie did a little homework and arranged for the house and store to be deeded to the Preservation Trust of Vermont in December 1997. Marjorie retains the right to reside here as long as she lives and is responsible for all repairs and upkeep, but she

---

[1] *The forester thought Etta's stone should be in a more appropriate place so Marjorie had it moved back to the cemetery, thus completing "a long journey for a little girl."*

no longer owns her home or the store. Through arrangements that they will make after her death, Marjorie's hope is that the home and store will continue to be visited for years to come. She did this to help preserve and pass on rural traditions and to engender appreciation for history and country ways.

When the day comes that PTV must take charge, they would like to be able to arrange to have an operating store that serves the community once again. However, there are regulatory restraints that might make this too costly or impractical. An alternative might be to have it serve the traveling public in some way, noted PTV's Executive Director Paul Bruhn. The Trust will actually serve as a landlord by leasing the store to an interested party—there is no intent for the Trust to operate it themselves. If this cannot happen, the possibility of use by the historical society or other similar use, perhaps as an outdoor interpretive center, would be explored. Marjorie has suggested that the store might become a shop for tourists with Vermont products like cheese, honey, syrup, crafts, and other specialties sold there.

Tentative plans also include having the Land Mark Trust, a group that manages Naulauka, the Rudyard Kipling Home in Dummerston, Vermont, offer a similar service at the Pierce home. They would rent out the Pierce home for short stays of a week or so, giving visitors an opportunity to experience firsthand the simple joys of rural Vermont life.

With endowment income from generous funds she is leaving to this preservation project and a simultaneous effort by future tenants to produce income, Marjorie's hope is that the Pierce Homestead will become a self-sustaining historic place. The other Pierce repository of history—the family albums, artifacts, and heirlooms along with Marjorie's extensive collection of articles—are intended to be preserved, either at the home or store, or through donations to local or state historical societies as an advisory group determines most appropriate. Whatever shape the final plans take, the clear intention is to maintain the store and home as an historic place.

For both Marjorie and Glendon, this planning to preserve mountainous rural land, an old country store, and a vintage Vermont home for posterity was a major source of satisfaction. As she discussed the importance of preservation, Marjorie noted that when the Poore cottage next to their home burned down, Gordon bought the parcel to both protect and enhance the Pierce home. Maintaining this property meant extra work for him (and now an extra expense for Marjorie), but he willingly made the effort, she said, noting that they all valued this beautiful addition to their property.

The Pierce family and their forebears have been a vital part of a rural community for over 200 years. They are part of its history and also what is best in human history. They have epitomized the Vermont traits of industry, integrity, honor, duty, frugality, and helpfulness, as well as that wry wit, dry humor, and Yankee wisdom. But most of all, they have epitomized "responsibility." From farm family to country-store keepers to friendly neighbors, the Pierce family have been part of the best Vermont traditions.

And now in good Vermonter fashion, the Pierces have become part of the late-twentieth-century grassroots tradition of environmental conservation and historic preservation. Always careful with their use of water and electricity, the Pierces have exemplified the conservation of natural resources; now they have extended that to sharing their heritage of land, home, and store with others. Like Glendon, Marjorie arranged this in a quiet way, without fanfare and with few knowing about this special gift to the preservation of Northam history.

Marjorie Pierce was never a famous person, a politician, or a civic leader of high stature. Except for Willie's brief stint in the state legislature and Glendon's year as a page in Montpelier, the Pierces were not involved in state government. And although they were recorded on film and written up in print numerous times, they never became famous. The Pierces were what one might call "regular folk," but they were uncommonly good people. They worked hard and became meaningful members of their community because they felt a responsibility to lead "useful and upright lives."

Like Gertrude, Willie, Marion, Gilford, Gordon, and Glendon, Marjorie is quietly making the world a better place. Following her own interests and passions, she continues to care for, and do for, her community. Marjorie at ninety-six remains committed and connected to history, tradition, and rural life. And that makes all the difference. It is what makes her, like her family before her, a good Vermonter.

Chapter Fifteen

The Gift of Memories

French Club at AHS, 1948-49

In good Vermonter fashion, Marjorie and her family have touched the lives of many. As can be seen in the remembrances which follow, their respect and caring for tradition, history, and community deeply impressed those who knew them. But so did their sense of humor and love of a good joke. Here are a few of the stories that attest to the ways so many were touched by the Pierces. As Marjorie has always been first and foremost a teacher, it seems fitting to begin with some reminiscences from former students.

When Betty Edson and I were at a meeting together on March 13, 1999, we began talking about her recent visit with Miss Pierce and reminiscing about our French classes at Attleboro High. I was class of 1949.

My dearest memory of those years was my last year there in French class. There was no textbook. We learned about Paris. She made it so real that even today I feel that if I went to Paris, I would not be lost.

She instilled in me a love of language. I was able to take an advanced French class my Freshman year at Colby and enjoyed reading the classics. Unfortunately, I was never able to master the spoken language. That love of languages continued into my three years in Seminary, where, preparing for ministry, I enjoyed three years of Greek. (Luckily, I didn't have to speak Greek!)   *Bettsy Harrison (formerly Mary Ellen Betts)*

It is our first day of French I. I expect we were Sophomores, for in 1945, one was not allowed to take French I until one had mastered Latin I. We knew who Miss Pierce was, of course; it was not a large school. We knew her to be the petite woman with brown wavy hair and sparkly brown eyes, who seemed to enjoy teaching and young people, but whose classes were taught with healthy good discipline which resulted from her poise and self-confidence, rather than from a raised voice or any unpleasantness.

But we were hardly prepared for that first class! She never spoke a word of English! (Not the norm in 1945!) With pantomime, and speaking French in her very precise manner, her eyebrows rising and falling in that characteristic little scowl, she let us know that she was leaving and would shortly reappear.

The door opened and in she came, beaming and saying as she entered and pointed to herself, "J'entre dans la salle de classe."

With great drama, she looked all around the room as she declared, "Je regarde autour de moi!"

Then, after a grand, sweeping glance from the pupils' desks to her own, she continued, "Je vois les eleves....et le professeur. Je dis 'Bonjour' au professeur, and she bowed ceremoniously in the direction of her desk before announcing with feigned finality, "Je prends ma place!" and sat down at one of the students' desks. As we waved hands in air, trying to ask her questions in English, she would just give us that beaming smile and shake her head. We watched with widening eyes as her mini-drama was repeated several times, after which it was our turn to give it a whirl!

Fifty years later, I visited Marjorie, and when she asked me to reminisce about Attleboro High, I said, "Well, I remember that first class, do you?"

"Do it with me," she responded. And together, we said, "J'entre dans la salle de classe! . . ."

That evening, I called my best friend from high school, who still lives in Attleboro. "What," I asked, "do you remember about Miss Pierce?"

"Well," she replied, "the main thing, of course, is that first day."

Suspicious, I said, "What about that first day?" And two hundred miles and fifty years melting away, we said in unison, "J'entre dans la salle de classe! . . ."

To say that Marjorie was a fine teacher who made a lasting impression on her pupils would clearly be an understatement!

Five years after that memorable class, as a Junior at Middlebury College, where I was a French major, I approached Miss Pierce to request that she allow me to do my student teaching under her supervision. I'm not sure whether she or I was the more pleased! Since I chose to do it in my home town, it had to be a solid dose, rather than a class or two a week for an extended period. My remembrance is that it was a two-week stretch; Marjorie doubts that, and she is probably right, as I don't know when I'd have been home for that long at a time when school was in session. It probably just seemed that long, for she had an amazing schedule! Back-to-back classes, with, I think, a twenty minute lunch break and one free period, during which she supervised a study hall!

Thus did I discover that I loved Miss Pierce and I loved French, but that I would never be one who easily was in command of a classroom. I did well; I don't mean to imply that I didn't, but the kind of inherent calm authority which Marjorie had was not one of my gifts.

My parents were friends of Marjorie's, and at least once in the course of my time at Middlebury, they brought her to her home for vacation en route to pick me up at college. Our friendship continued over the years, with periodic gatherings at my parents' home or mine, after they had moved to Vermont, where my husband and I had settled. These reunions were attended by Marjorie, and by her good friends and ours: Jessie Graves, of Walpole, NH who had taught Latin at AHS; Dot Simonds, now married and in VT, who had taught history at AHS; and former AHS Chemistry teacher Ken Goding and his wife.

Years later, after my parents had died, my husband Dave and I came to North Shrewsbury, bringing friends to see the Ice Mound. (I can still remember Marjorie's excited directions, the first time I came to her home. "You turn," she said several times, "at the hos-pi-tal, at the hos-pi-tal." Not having known her when she was very young, I don't know if this way of pronouncing words syllable-by-syllable was natural to her or if it was a result of her careful pronouncing of French, in teaching the language so effectively!

We enjoyed a tour of the country store, and then, we all walked to the Ice Mound and were properly impressed. It was a vintage year, I gather, for the Ice Mound.

I had figured we might be offered a cup of coffee to warm us up when we returned, but to our delighted amazement, Marjorie and her brothers insisted that we all sit around the table and out came delicious homemade apple pie! Marjorie and her brothers hovered about us, and we all held our breath, as she and her brother poured the steaming coffee with visibly shaking hands, but nary a drop missed the cup!

It was such a special day and visit. In many ways it was like a visit to the past to be so warmly welcomed by such down-to-earth people—people of such good heart and solid values and simple tastes; but it was no mere nostalgia trip, for Marjorie and her brothers were full of life and interested in so many different topics and knowledgeable about all kinds of interesting things.

This, though delighting our friends, was no surprise to me, for I had received Marjorie's Christmas cards, year after year, in which she would describe her active life and her many projects. Dear and amazing people! A privilege to have had my life touched by theirs, and, especially, by hers.   *Betty Edson*

Country Humor

One day Glendon wanted to show me some land clearing he had been doing on a remote, almost inaccessible mountain. It was a tortuous trip even in his four-wheel drive truck. We spent an hour or more inspecting brush piles and examining trees for signs of bear, deer, and other wildlife. The trip down the mountain was every bit as arduous as the trip up. As the truck crept along the deeply rutted and rock-strewn path that passed for a road, pitching and lurching up and down and side to side, we came upon Gary Arthur, who was inspecting nearby trails that would soon be used by members of the local snowmobile club. He looked up as we bounced to a stop close by, and Glendon rolled down his window. "Pardon me," shouted Glendon, "Is this the way to Burlington?"

John Heitzke

Marjorie is really a modern woman, who keeps current on just about everything. One winter an old-timer who had been away for some years returned. Stopping by the store, he expected to see a group of men lolling about, smoking pipes, and discussing the news of the day by the woodstove. Instead, he walked in and saw Marjorie and a group of women deep in conversation. He expressed surprise, and Marjorie piped up with, "This is what women do these days. This is the nineties."   *Jan Snelling*

Joyce, Marjorie, & Gordon

Gordon and Marjorie took us on a hike up on Jockey Hill to see the balancing rock. Gordon had a large paint can hitched to him with bailing twine Asked why the paint can, he said it was to mark the trees in case we got lost. Once we got up to the rock, he opened the can and offered us grape jelly sandwiches. His humor was subtle but the twinkle was always in his eye.   *Joyce Wilson*

Glendon was always joking in the store. One day their close neighbor Myrtle Fee was baking a cake and ran out of eggs. She sent little Edith up to the store for six eggs. Glendon handed her a bag and when she got home, her mother found six potatoes. Another time Edith went to the store barefoot, and Glendon painted one toenail black and one white. Her mother was horrified!

Minnie Shaw

Glendon always enjoyed a good joke.

To the Rescue

One winter day two men stopped at the store and asked for directions to my house. Gordon obliged. Then, after they'd left, he began to wonder about these burly men with heavy foreign accents. He got in his car, drove up the slippery hill to my house, and finding that the men were indeed family friends, he said with his infinite tact that he wanted to be sure they'd found the right road.

Suppose they'd been bad guys? What then? This was an act of kindness and courage to be cherished forever.   *(the late) Edith French*

224

We had just put in thousands of dollars worth of dirt and topsoil to create some lawn areas on our ledgy mountain property when a hurricane suddenly threatened. We had seeded and put hay down but ran out of the last of the nearest farmer's hay. So we stopped at the store and asked the Pierces who else might have some. Not only did they send us to Spring Lake Ranch some six miles away, but Gordon hopped in his pickup and went with us so as to bring back as much as we needed. Then, he and Glendon came up and helped us spread the hay on the steep banks. Thanks to their help our expensive dirt was saved!   *John Lorentz*

Once when we had a broken window at the church, Marjorie went home to see if she had a matching piece of glass. Sure enough, back she came, carrying the heavy, big pane of glass into the church. She wouldn't think of asking for help, she just did it herself.   *Donna Smith*

When I was ready to go for my driver's test in Rutland, I discovered that the emergency brake on our station wagon was not working. I stopped to see Glendon, who owned the same car in a sedan version. "Take my car," he said. So off we went to Rutland in "the cigar car." Glendon liked a good cigar! I was worried that the man who gave me my test might say something, but he didn't. I got my license that day thanks to Glendon. I can't tell you how much that meant to a sixteen-year-old living in a place "you can't get to from here."   *Jason Lorentz*

Old Ways

The patience and respect that the Pierces showed to little children picking out their penny candy was amazing. They would wait on them as if they were the most important customers in the world; it was as if they were making a hundred-dollar purchase, instead of just pennies.
                    Tom Mitchell

When we lived at "the barn," we would see Glendon go out to get his car after dinner every Tuesday, Thursday, and Saturday evening and also Sunday afternoons. He would drive it around and park it in front of the house. Then, he would go in, get dressed up, always wearing a nice tie, and leave for Rutland and his date with Minnie. It was like the old way of bringing the horse around before you went out, so you wouldn't get dirty!
                    Susan Ray and Mark Hamelin

We gave Gordon some new work gloves for Christmas one year, because his had holes in every finger. Two years later, he was still wearing the same old pair. He just believed that nothing was too bad to throw out and that there was no need to replace something that still could be used.

His contentment in life was as strong as his patience.

Betty and John Heitzke

When we had just moved into town and were in the process of building a home "up on the mountain," we sometimes got a call that there was a package for us at Pierce's Store. One day we entered the store to see the three Pierces gathered around a large box. "It's awfully heavy," Marjorie said. Taking a cue, I saw it was from Metos Sauna and told them it was the rocks for the sauna.

Shaking her head in disbelief, Marjorie exclaimed, "Why you didn't have to go buying rocks, we've got plenty of them around here that we'd have been happy to give you!"

Karen Lorentz

Gordon kept a book where he recorded every cent he spent. Glendon kept a record book, too, but he told us that he didn't record anything under a dollar!

Glendon enjoyed his cigars and an occasional brandy. His sense of humor was unbelievable and even randy at times. He was also capable of great feeling and sensitivity. On his eightieth birthday, he addressed a gathering of friends. First, he toasted Minnie and then he thanked his [departed] parents for a wonderful, happy childhood; and then he thanked Minnie, his siblings, and his friends for a wonderful life. There wasn't a dry eye in the house.

Marjorie tore around town like a teenage driver in her Volkswagen "Beetle." She had two, first a used 1957 version, and then a 1966 new one. She bought them in Rutland [from Larry Coo-

1962 Marjorie & bug.

per who still remembers her even though she didn't give him much business]. As a practical joke, Glendon made a red key out of wood and fitted it into the air slots at the rear of the car. It was reminiscent of wind-up toys, and everyone got a kick out of seeing Marjorie tooling around in her "VW windup bug." Marjorie still has the original paper pattern for the key! It was used in two instances when the key was broken and had to be replaced.

She didn't give up driving until 1998. It is due to Pierce frugality and ingenuity that this car was kept in such excellent shape for so many years.

Jan Snelling

There was a bumper sticker on Marjorie's VW that read, "A little courtesy won't kill you."

Susan Ray

As a child, Pierce's Store meant penny candy and every time my family drove by, my brother and I would sing out, "Can we stop?" Luckily, some of the time the adults decided we were deserving. We were each given a nickel and then let out to go into the dark, cozy store.

I was the youngest, so I always chose last. And the shortest, so I had to stand on the wooden box to see the candy. Mr. Pierce, Marjorie's father, would come over to stand behind the cases, patiently and quietly waiting for us to point to our choices. One by one, he would take out the pieces of candy and place them on the counter.

The first four were easy; it was the fifth that caused the dilemma. I could never decide between my two last favorites. Finally, I would tell him my choice with a sigh, knowing I had to leave the other behind. I paid Mr. Pierce my nickel and good-byes were said.

As soon as I was seated in the car, I looked in my bag to begin eating the prized candy. To my grateful surprise, there was always that sixth piece of candy secretly placed in the bag by Mr. Pierce.

Claire M. Hooper

A Day at Pierce's Store

I ran down the road to Pierce's General Store with my nickel jingling in my hand inside my mitten. I couldn't wait! This was the first time I had been allowed a whole nickel to buy penny candy. I rushed into the store and there, behind the counter, was my best friend Glendon Pierce.

He wasn't exceptionally tall. He always had a leather case for his glasses in the breast pocket of his sweater or shirt. He had plain colored pants and black shoes. His face was wrinkled and sagging with old age, and he was bald. He smiled at me as I came in and said, "Hello, Snowball." That was his nickname for me.

The black potbellied stove in the middle of the old store was keeping it warm. I took off my mittens, warmed my hands, and went over to the counter. I wasn't tall enough to see over the top so I climbed onto the overturned box to look through the glass case at all of the candy. I decided to get two red fish, one pink tootsie-roll, and "For my last two pennies," I said, "I'd like two windbreakers."

At this, Glendon started laughing for I had meant to say Jawbreakers. He took out all the candy, including the two "windbreakers" and put it on his scale. Then he took the scale tray off, and lifting it high in the air, dropped the candy into a paper bag waiting on the counter below. I started laughing and he smiled.

He moved over to the great old cash register. It was silver and had a leafy raised pattern on it. He pulled the buttons down and with a great "cha-king," the drawer opened and I gave him my five cents. I went to sit down by the fire to eat my candy and get warm before heading home.

I looked all around the store. Behind the counter were rows of soup cans and cereal boxes. There was a cooler that held soda and there was another glass case that held the candy bars. There were shelves that had old rubber boots and shoes for sale which people seldom bought. They just collected dust.

Glendon sat down and lit his cigar. It always smelled like cigar smoke in the store from his smoking. We played a game with each other. We tried to see who could step on the other person's feet without them knowing it. I always caught him off guard and stomped on his feet. We would burst into laughter and I would try again, but this time he was looking so I didn't get him.

I stayed longer and when a customer came in, he asked me if I wanted to help him behind the register and to open the glass case to get the candy out for the customer. I pressed the big buttons and the register went "cha-king!" I put the person's money into the correct place and gave them their bag and they left. While I was behind the counter, I noticed huge bags of candy that Glendon used to fill up the boxes in the glass case. "Yum," I thought, "all of that candy looks good!"

Just before leaving I asked him for a penny. He opened the register and gave me a shiny penny. I went over to the stereoscope, an old-fashioned picture machine. To use the machine, you placed a penny in a small slot and looked through a viewer to see a picture. Each time you pulled

228

Ingrid and Glendon at Thanksgiving Lunch at the Mountain School in November 1989.

the trigger, a new picture would flip up. One penny would allow you a certain amount of time to see the pictures. My favorite one was a dog with glasses reading a book. I always hoped it would come up before my time was over. Whenever I saw it, I would laugh because it was so funny.

A few days after my fifth birthday, I received a letter from Glendon. The envelope was addressed to: "Miss Ingrid 'Snowball Huxtable' Wilson." Inside was the picture of the dog with glasses. I was so excited! There was a letter with it. "Dear Snowball, Enclosed is your favorite card as a souvenir from Pierce's Store . . . May you remember coming here as a little girl, asking me for pennies for the machine as well as stepping on my toes when I was not looking. Love, Glendon."

The picture is very special to me and I keep it in a safe spot. Glendon died in January 1995 when he was eighty years old. I am glad to have the picture, the letter, and the memories. *Ingrid Wilson, written at age 12*

Of Accomplishments Big and Little

The Pierces were truly nice, good people; not mean-spirited. They were honest, possessed good manners and a graciousness known in only a few others like Mary Smith. Their care for the cemetery, church, store, and historical tradition stands out. *Nancy Spencer*

I learned much about the history of the Coolidge State Forest from both Marjorie and Glendon, in particular where the early farms and mills were located and what the CCC did in 1934 and 1935. They were helpful and cared very much about history and the land. Glendon made it possible for the Pierce lands on the Bennington Camp Road to become part of the Calvin Coolidge State Forest. It was a wonderful gift to the community and to Vermont to preserve this area for recreational uses and the enjoyment of others. *Gary Salmon*

I was struck by the things Glendon kept from the Republican party, how he displayed various memberships and certificates on the walls of his room. It showed a respect for politics and his pride to be an American and a Republican. You don't see that so much today — we've lost something. *Liz Jeffords*

I worked with Gordon for eight years; he taught me how to audit the Town Books. Gordon always kept a pen knife, and he never used an eraser. If there was a mistake, he took his pen knife out and scraped it carefully and neatly, eradicating the error without ever tearing the paper. He was very learned and capable with figures. He could do columns in his head; he was incredible. He was never wrong in his reports; he prided himself on doing things right to the penny—absolutely correct! He didn't complain, but I think it bothered him if people weren't accurate.

He was perfectly happy. He was close to the land. He was sinewy and very strong for his weight and frame. *Leonard Korzun*

Gordy was always good-humored, obliging, hurrying to wait on customers at Stewart's Garage. He was never too busy to slap a tire patch on a kid's leaky galoshes or bicycle inner tube. *George and Francis Brigham*

Gordon lived with us during the week for several years. Because of making his lunch every day—a sandwich, two doughnuts, and a piece of pie—I have lots of practice in making doughnuts and pies. Our kids were little and loved him as he loved them and the far-away ones always asked for him. He used to visit with them, remembered birthdays and Christmas, and was just part of our family. If the girls had a leaky boot, Gordy would take it back down to the garage after supper and put a vulcanized patch on it. They never had boot with a hole in it for very long because they knew Gordy would fix it. *Lucille and Clint Fiske*

Webster's Dictionary defines GENTLEMAN: 1) a man who combines gentle birth or rank with chivalrous qualities; 2) a man whose conduct conforms to a high standard of propriety or correct behavior. This is what Gordon Pierce was to us. *Joan and B.J. Stewart*

Marion made dozens of patchwork dogs for the bazaars when she visited in summer. She would also paint the big woodstove in the store black each year. That was her job. She went to activities with me and enjoyed being back in Vermont. *Jan Snelling*

I knew Marion to have eyes of kindness, especially for children. Young people were her life, and she had the quietness and gentleness of spirit to allow a child to feel at home in her presence. She had the interest to ask the child questions, and the patience to listen to childish answers and make sense out of them. She had the perception of inward sight to read a child's face and know something of the child's heart. And she had the gift of expressing wonder and taking delight in whatever the child described with wonder and delight. *Lee Wilson*

I am so impressed with my friend Marjorie's accomplishments. She tends her house plants, cares for the birds with feeders on her porch, puts flowers in the church, and keeps in touch with so many people, especially former students. She does so many things, but what impresses me most is that she is still accomplishing so much at her age! *Marjorie Plumley*

When we started the local Cuttingsville Group of Amnesty International, I was given a list of people who were already members in our area and Marjorie was on it. She had been writing letters on behalf of prisoners of conscience for some time.

What was superb about her letters was that she thought about whom she was writing to, took that into consideration, and had a delightful way of personalizing it. "I see your president is meeting with so and so in Washington," she might say, and then she would suggest what they might enjoy seeing. Then, she would mention the prisoner being held and the wrong that needed to be addressed. Her letters were good examples of how to write effective letters that would get noticed; so as a district coordinator, I took them to other groups to show them how a good letter should be written. They were always succinct and got the name of the prisoner into the first sentence.

I believe she ended up corresponding with a prisoner in Sri Lanka. She had been designated to write to him, and they corresponded for a long time. I think she half expected him to show up some day at Pierce's Store. *Phyllis Wells*

In Japan there is an honor whereby distinguished elders are designated as "national treasures" for perhaps an art form that is no longer practiced or their scholarliness. If America had such a tradition, Marjorie Pierce would be so designated. Marjorie is a living conduit, a liaison between the past and present. She has a gift for animating history.

Susan Ray

When first moving to Shrewsbury, I remember looking out from our porch towards Pierces' and seeing their lawn sweep down to Sargent's Brook. It was like a park in miniature, with the stream, the lawn on either side of it, a dark stand of spruces, a large apple tree, a beautiful old swamp maple, and forget-me-nots growing by the stream.

Containing the stream was a rock-wall embankment. It appeared to be old. Its smooth face easily deflected the current with every stone securely and tightly fitted into place. I assumed some sturdy Shrewsbury pioneer had built that rock wall embankment many years ago. It looked like the product of a by-gone era, when men and women were strong enough to push back the woods, clear the fields, and lay out miles of rock wall boundaries with no power other than what their own hands or animals could provide.

Gordon's embankment and the north lawn he maintained like a park.

One day in Pierce's Store, I told Gordon how much I admired the rock-wall embankment, and the way the lawn swept down cleanly to meet it. I wondered out loud what person had the strength, know-how, and persistence to build it. He gave me his characteristic laugh, with his head thrown slightly back and to one side, and let me discover he had done it. There in front of me, weighing in at no more than 120 pounds, stood my supposed pioneer giant.

Gordon had a way of surprising a person. He did not push himself forward, but walked his way through life with a quiet gentleness. He was a gentleman.   *Lee Wilson*

My aunt, Florence (Smith) Pierce was my mother's sister and the widow of Gilford Pierce. I was born in February 1944, just a month after Gilford was reported missing in action. If I had been a boy, I am sure I would have been named for him, but that honor went to my brother.

Many years ago, while going through a closet, I came across a box of old letters. I read just one. It was from Gilford telling Florence how much he missed her cold feet and waking up to the aroma of freshly brewed coffee. I never went near that box again—the thoughts of what could have been were overwhelming. In later years, my aunt destroyed the letters because they were so personal, but she saved the last one he ever wrote to her.

From my earliest memory I always thought of the Pierces as my extended family. We visited them often. My mother had been named Damaris for Marjorie's grandmother, and it became my middle name also.

I recall standing by Gertrude's bed when she was ill and thinking what beautiful white hair she had. And I remember Willie, always the quiet gentleman, tending the store. I got to see Gordon most often as living in Cuttingsville, we passed Stewart's Garage whenever going to the post office or the store. Once he bought me a St. Patrick's Day hat and a fold-out shamrock, which pleased me no end. I watched Glendon tar the road and was sometimes on the receiving end of his humor. It seemed that Marjorie was always in the kitchen cooking and doing what she does best—talking. Marion was always quiet and sweet, but I only saw her during the summer.

Of course I remember the penny candy and the stream out back, but my fondest memory is of the baby-tender on the back porch. It is similar to a deacon's bench, but has a spoked gate in front of one side of the seat to protect the infant from falling. A mother could put her baby on that side, while sitting on the other to peel apples or sew and sing her baby to sleep. As a child visiting, I would bring my doll and a book and settle in for a long read.

In later years, my daughters also visited the Pierce home and store. Now I have two granddaughters who always want to hear about the "old days." After visiting my special memory places in Cuttingsville and Northam, we would stop at the store for a cold drink and some penny candy.

One day after the store had closed, I took them to see Marjorie at the house and thus another generation, the third generation of my family, sat in the baby tender as Marjorie told them about its use and the bullet mold and other artifacts that she has on the porch.

Marjorie was always a fascinating teacher. Her uniqueness was in the way she accomplished it. She never talked down to us as children, but talked up to us as human beings worthy of what she was saying.

My grandchildren didn't want to leave and expressed hopes for a return visit for another conversation soon. What a wonderful tribute— children seeking and enjoying the company of a lady well into her nineties. Maybe there isn't a generation gap after all.   *Dawn Hance*

Preserving connections, human and historical, was an important Pierce legacy. For those fortunate to have experienced penny candy or a store conversation, those encounters have become the stuff of warm memories and of a link with our Vermont heritage.

Looking into the vacant store now, your mind plays tricks and you can almost see Marjorie sharing a story or Marion listening to a child. Or while walking down old Road 14 and enjoying its rustic beauty and tranquility, you can suddenly feel a stirring and in memory's eye meet Gordon and Glendon bouncing along in the old truck and calling out, "Excuse me, is this the way to Burlington?"

Photo collage next page: Willie & Gertrude on 50th anniversary; Gordon playing golf; Pierce family circa 1950; Florence and Gilford; Marion; Glendon's grandfather clock; and a visit to the store by (the late) Governor Snelling.

Chronology

1775-83   Revolutionary War.

1761   Gov. Benning Wentworth of NH granted 24,000-acre Shrewsbury tract to Samuel Ashley and 63 associates.

1770   New York granted 12,000 acres of Shrewsbury to James Abeel & Company.

1776   Lemuel White, first permanent settler in Shrewsbury, operated a tavern.

1777   Republic of Vermont framed a constitution much like that of Pennsylvania's but added prohibition of slavery and establishment of universal manhood suffrage.

1780   Significant settlement began with settlers arriving from Barre, MA; Richmond, NH; and RI.

Ziba Aldrich came to Shrewsbury as fourth settler.

1788   Ephraim Pierce located on Road 14.

1791   Vermont became the nation's 14th state, joining the original 13.

1800   Moses Colburn in residence on parcel below later store.

1811   William Jarvis of Weathersfield brought 200 Merino sheep to VT.

1812-15   War of 1812; Vermont enjoyed war-related prosperity with good harvests/grain sales, iron and textile business. Wool prices soar.

1813   Outbreak of lung fever killed 30 people in Shrewsbury.

1830   First U.S. steam locomotive the Tom Thumb built.

1837   John Deere developed the steel plow.

1844   Samuel F.B. Morse invented the telegraph.

1846   End of protective wool tariffs marked decline in VT sheep industry.

1849-55   Building of railroads in VT.

1861-65   Civil War; Vermont sent 34,238 volunteers, 5,224 killed; 600,000 deaths total.

1870   Edwin and Damaris (Aldrich) Pierce marriage.

1872   Willie E. Pierce born.

1875   Edwin Pierce family migrates to Nevada; returns to VT in 1877.

1877   Gertrude Spaulding (Pierce) born in West Bridgewater.

1893   Ford built his first auto.

1899   Willie and Gertrude (Spaulding) Pierce marriage.

1900	Average U.S. Life Expectancy is 49 years (plus 7 for women).
1901	Marion Pierce born in West Bridgewater at Spaulding home.
	Marconi sent transatlantic wireless message.
1903	Marjorie Pierce born May 1 in West Bridgewater at Spaulding home.
	Henry Ford started Ford Motor Company.
	First crossing of the American Continent by car took 65 days.
	Wilbur and Orville Wright flew homemade plane for 59 seconds.
1908	Gordon Pierce born at Pierce farm in Shrewsbury.
1908	Ford introduced the Model T.
1912	Titanic sank on maiden voyage.
1913	Glendon Pierce born at farm in Shrewsbury.
1914	World War I began; (Pierce Uncle) Clyde Spaulding served country.
1915	Ford developed a farm tractor.
1916	Gilford Pierce born at farm in Shrewsbury.
1918	April 24, Willie E. Pierce purchased Northam Store, house, 4 acres.
1920s	Era of "flappers" and carefree self-indulgence of 1920s; changing role of women as they cut hair and wear short dresses.
1921	First U.S. radio programs.
	Marjorie Pierce graduated Rutland High School.
	Marjorie and Marion Pierce enrolled at UVM for fall semester.
1925	Marjorie and Marion Pierce graduated from UVM; Marjorie teaches at Whitcomb High in Bethel, VT. Marion goes to Smith College.
1927	Great Flood of 1927, Vermont's worst disaster to date.
	The Jazz Singer with Al Jolson first talking motion picture.
	Lindbergh first to fly solo nonstop across Atlantic.
1928	Amelia Earhart flew across the Atlantic.
	Marjorie moved on to teach French at Montpelier High.
1929	Marjorie and Doris Hall went to France to study, travel for a year.
	Great Depression began.
1930	New Deal I & II Programs began (WPA, CCC, et cetera).
	Marjorie began teaching in Attleboro, MA.
1932	Lindbergh baby kidnapping and murder.
1933	Civilian Conservation Corps in Vermont; CCC employed young men in reforestation, flood control, and national parks projects in exchange for food, clothing, shelter and wages that were to be shared with their families.
1934	Electricity came to North Shrewsbury.
1935	Marjorie did summer study with Classroom on Wheels in Europe.
1936	Hindenburg landed at Lakehurst, NJ after transatlantic flight.

1937	Hindenburg disaster detailed in first transcontinental radio broadcast.
1939	Nylon stockings appeared; Pan-American Airways began regularly scheduled commercial flights between U.S. and Europe.
1939	World War II began.
1940	U.S. population 132 million; life expectancy 64 years; 30 million homes have radios.
	Marjorie awarded Master's Degree in French, Middlebury College.
1944	First Lt. Gilford Pierce killed in WW II on January 5.
1945	WW II ended on May 8.
	Women make up more than 1/3 of nation's labor force; first atomic bomb test; U.S. drops atomic bomb on Hiroshima.
1949	Marjorie's summer trip to CA, Pacific Northwest, Canadian Rockies, Great Lakes.
1950	Korean War began.
1952	Gertrude Pierce died.
1955	Consuelo Northrup Bailey, elected first woman Lt. Governor (VT).
1958	Marjorie took early retirement, returned home to assist family and at store.
1965	Willie Pierce died; Glendon, Marjorie, Gordon took over store operations.
1965	Vietnam War began.
1967	Marjorie officially became sole owner of store on January 1.
1969	Neil Armstrong walked on the moon.
1984	Madeleine Kunin elected first woman Governor of VT.
1985	Pierces' Party recognizes Pierce family contributions to community.
1987	Marion Pierce died.
1989	Gordon Pierce died.
1990	562,758 people living in VT according to census; 80 percent have high school education; 25 percent college education.
1993	December 31, Marjorie and Glendon closed Pierce's Store.
1994	Glendon sold mountain lands on Bennington Camp Road to VT Land Trust, and VT Land Trust sold land to Coolidge State Forest.
1995	Glendon Pierce died.
1997	Marjorie deeded Pierce homestead to Preservation Trust of Vermont, retaining right to live in home and responsibility for upkeep.
1999	Marjorie living at home, busy proofreading her story, receiving guests, and enjoying lifetime of memories as she looks forward to "four more years" and publication of the Pierce story.

About the Author

Karen D. Lorentz grew up in West Hartford, Connecticut and graduated from the University of Connecticut in 1968. She taught English at Scotch Plains-Fanwood High School in New Jersey before moving with her husband John to a remote mountaintop in Shrewsbury, Vermont, in 1978.

There, they learned to heat with wood, plow four-foot snowdrifts, and survive long cold winters as John developed a law practice and taught college courses, and Karen ran a bed and breakfast (Lorenwood) in their home and raised their three sons. Living on the CCC Road, they also enjoyed skiing and sliding on the nearby Pierce Meadows on Bennington Camp Road and visiting Pierce's Store. Today, the store is closed and like Marjorie and Marion, their two grown sons have moved away to pursue further study and work. However, they still visit the "Ice Mound."

Karen has been a freelance writer since 1978 and has written more than 2,000 articles for various publications, including a column "Country Roads" for seven years for the *Rutland Herald Express*. She has also written for the *Rutland Business Journal* since its debut in 1984. Her interest in writing books began with copy editing the history of Shrewsbury. She has since edited and produced an anthology of works by Vermont writers and has written three books, including histories of the Killington and Okemo ski areas.

Finding Vermont conducive to the small press business, Karen formed Mountain Publishing, Inc. in 1990. Currently, she is following up with more interviews of Marjorie so as to help preserve twentieth-century North Shrewsbury history for whomever undertakes the updating of the town history. Plans for her next book are to write a history of Vermont skiing and ski areas.

Besides being an active volunteer with the Boy Scouts, Karen serves as treasurer of the League of Vermont Writers and vice president of the Southern Vermont Branch of the National League of American Pen Women. She is a member of several ski-writer and ski-history organizations and enjoys learning about Vermont and New Hampshire mountain history. She welcomes feedback from readers and hopes you enjoy this story of the Pierce Family.

Order Form

To order books, fill out legibly and mail to:
Mountain Publishing, 1300 CCC Road, Shrewsbury, VT 05738.

Name_____

Street Address _____

Town, State, Zip_____

Phone (   )_____

Number of copies of Pierce book: *Good Vermonters*
     @$22 (includes UPS Shipping)   _____
West of Mississippi @$25 per book   _____

Total enclosed $ _____

Check here if you wish to have book signed by author_____
Name of person(s) to receive inscribed book _____

Killington, A Story of Mountains and Men
  hardcover, 320 pages, 8.5 by 11 coffee table book with over 200 color &
  b/w photographs @$39.95 + $5 UPS=$44.95
  Number ordered_____Total enclosed $_____

Check here if you wish to have book signed by author_____
Name of person(s) to receive inscribed book _____

Okemo, All Come Home
  hardcover, 288 pages, 8.5 by 11 coffee table book with over 200 color &
  b/w photographs @$39.95 + $5 UPS+$44.95
  Number ordered_____Total enclosed $_____

Check here if you wish to have book signed by author_____
Name of person(s) to receive inscribed book _____

Please make check or money order payable to:
Mountain Publishing, Inc.

All books shipped insured UPS within 3 days of order being received.

Marjorie delighted guests with her wish for "four more years" at her 96th birthday party.

These I've Loved

These I've loved since I was little:
Wood to build with or to whittle,
Wind in the grass and falling rain,
First leaves along an April lane,
Yellow flowers, cloudy weather,
River-bottom smell, old leather,
Fields newly plowed, young corn in rows,
Back-country roads and cawing crows,
Stone walls with stiles going over,
Daisies, Queen Anne's lace, and clover,
Night tunes of crickets, frog songs, too,
Starched cotton cloth, the color blue,
Bells that ring from white church steeple,
Friendly dogs and friendly people.

by Elizabeth Ellen Lang